Video Modelling and Behaviour Analysis

of related interest

Applied Behaviour Analysis and Autism
Building A Future Together
Edited by Mickey Keenan, Mary Henderson, Ken P. Kerr and
Karola Dillenburger
Foreword by Professor Gina Green
ISBN 1 84310 310 9

Parents' Education as Autism Therapists
Applied Behaviour Analysis in Context
Edited by Mickey Keenan, Ken P. Kerr and Karola Dillenburger
Foreword by Bobby Newman
ISBN 1 85302 778 2

Raising a Child with Autism
A Guide to Applied Behavior Analysis for Parents
Shira Richman
ISBN 1 85302 910 6

Assessing and Developing Communication and Thinking Skills in
People with Autism and Communication Difficulties
A Toolkit for Parents and Professionals
Kate Silver, Autism Initiatives
ISBN 1 84310 352 4

Communication Issues in Autism and Asperger Syndrome
Do we speak the same language?
Olga Bogdashina
ISBN 1 84310 267 6

Achieving Best Behavior for Children
with Developmental Disabilities
Step-By-Step Workbook for Parents and Carers
Pamela Lewis
ISBN 1 84310 809 7

Succeeding with Interventions for Asperger Syndrome Adolescents
A Guide to Communication and Socialisation in Interaction Therapy
John Harpur, Maria Lawlor and Michael Fitzgerald
ISBN 184310 322 2

Video Modelling
and
Behaviour Analysis

A Guide for Teaching Social Skills
to Children with Autism

Christos Nikopoulos and Mickey Keenan

Foreword by Sandy Hobbs

Jessica Kingsley Publishers
London and Philadelphia

First published in 2006
by Jessica Kingsley Publishers
116 Pentonville Road
London N1 9JB, UK
and
400 Market Street, Suite 400
Philadelphia, PA 19106, USA

www.jkp.com

Library of Congress Cataloging in Publication Data
Nikopoulos, Christos, 1973-
Video modelling and behaviour analysis : a guide for teaching social skills to children with autism / Christos Nikopoulos and Mickey Keenan ; foreword by Sandy Hobbs.
p. cm.
Includes bibliographical references and indexes.
ISBN-13: 978-1-84310-338-7 (pbk. : alk. paper)
ISBN-10: 1-84310-338-9 (pbk. : alk. paper) 1. Autistic children--Language. 2. Social skills in children. 3. Communicative disorders in children. 4. Video tapes in education. I. Keenan, Michael. II. Title.
RJ506.A9N55 2006
649'.154--dc22

2006008440

British Library Cataloguing in Publication Data
A CIP catalogue record for this book is available from the British Library

ISBN 13: 978 1 84310 338 7
ISBN 10: 1 84310 338 9

Printed and bound in Great Britain by
Athenaeum Press, Gateshead, Tyne and Wear

*To the many families all over the world
who bring so much love
to their children with autism*

Acknowledgements

This journey began in October 1999 and since then many people have provided invaluable support and help to make this book possible. It is our great pleasure to acknowledge each of them. In particular, we are grateful to John Davidson, principal of the Linn Moor Residential School in Aberdeen, Scotland; Ruth Buchan, Head Teacher of the Freemantles School in Surrey, England; and Colm Davis, principal of the Tor Bank Special School in Dundonald, Northern Ireland. A special thanks to all staff at these schools for their co-operation and assistance. We are deeply indebted to all of the children who participated in the studies and their families. We are grateful to them for all they have taught us and for the confidence they have placed in us. Also we would like to acknowledge the support provided by the British Academy that enabled us to present parts of this book at the Second Conference of the European Association for Behaviour Analysis, Gdansk, Poland, 2005. Finally, we would like to express our gratitude for the unerring emotional support, limitless patience, flexibility and humour of Panagiota Nikopoulou-Smyrni and Karola Dillenburger. Children are our most important teachers. It is an honour for us to share our lives with Konstantinos, Orpheas, Kalinka, Tara, Kai and Jan.

Contents

List of figures and tables

Foreword
The slow and difficult advance
of behaviour analysis

The monthly *Appointments Memorandum* published by the British Psychological Society nowadays regularly carries advertisements seeking psychology graduates to work on educational programmes typically described as 'Lovaas' or 'ABA'. They arouse in me mixed reactions. On the one hand, it saddens me to think that they have been placed by families struggling to deal with the problems associated with Autistic Spectrum Disorder. On the other hand, I feel pleased that they are making use of methods which provide the best hope of helping the autistic child achieve as normal a life as possible. 'Lovaas' refers to the American psychologist whose pioneering work employing the methods of 'ABA', Applied Behaviour Analysis, has done so much to improve the prospects for those diagnosed as autistic. Bernard Rimland, who is both a psychologist and the father of an autistic child, has described Lovaas's methods as the 'treatment of choice' for autism (see his Foreword to Maurice, 1993).

A long and complex history lies behind *Video Modelling and Behaviour Analysis*, a history which is worthy of a book in its own right. Here I shall try to sketch some of it in broad outline. It is a history which has great personal significance for me, as it covers the half century during which I have been associated with psychology. As an undergraduate student of psychology in the 1950s I was struck by the diversity of different approaches which psychologists adopted. Some psychologists at the time tried to reconcile superficially divergent conceptual frameworks, such as psychoanalysis and behaviourism. Others seemed to accept that they were irreconcilable. One writer at the time seemed to me to provide the best hope of building a satisfactory scientific psychology. This was B.F. Skinner. He had made his reputation as a laboratory-based experimental psychologist in the 1930s. As was the fashion for some American psychologists at the time, he sought to establish basic psychological principles through research with animals. However, in the 1940s and 1950s he began to consider the application of those principles to human beings. In books such as *Science and Human Behavior* (1953), he envisaged the development of a deeper understanding of human behaviour by the application of basic principles of scientific enquiry. Skinner placed great emphasis on the value of careful observation and sought to avoid speculative theorising.

The appeal of Skinner's approach to me was twofold. First, he saw psychology as a branch of natural science. Second, he sought to use psychological knowledge to help solve human problems. Rather naively, I envisaged the gradual success of 'Skinnerian' psychology. By a process of natural selection, it would eventually show it had greater survival value than other approaches. It has turned out that progress has been much more gradual than I had anticipated.

That Skinner's approach to human problems was not more widely accepted when he initially published is not difficult to understand. *Science and Human Behavior* and his other early writing on social problems were not based on empirical evidence drawn from studies of human behaviour. His proposals involved extrapolation from research on animals. I saw this as a problem at the time, but was so confident of the value of his basic principles that I anticipated the accumulation of persuasive evidence from the study of humans. Such evidence did indeed begin to emerge, but it did not gain the acceptance I believed it was worth. Skinner created a stir when he demonstrated the possibility of teaching by machine. However, most of those who were attracted to what came to be called 'programmed instruction' did not adopt his carefully worked out proposals and the movement died out after a few years. Many psychologists saw the value of applying a Skinnerian approach in clinical settings. They founded the *Journal of Applied Behavior Analysis*, which has grown from strength to strength, and there are other journals now which specialize in the publication of research in applied behaviour analysis. Unfortunately, this has had less impact than it might have had, in part because psychology generally has grown so vast that many psychologists become specialists, familiar with little outside their own narrow field. Thus many who might benefit from knowledge of advances in behaviour analysis simply are unaware of its existence. That is one reason why I hope that a book such as this may reach a wider readership.

Lack of familiarity with actual research in behaviour analysis has allowed the development of misleading notions of what the Skinnerian tradition involves. Along with some colleagues, I have written about the relationship between behaviourists and others, most recently in the paper 'Beyond rumor and legend' (Hobbs 2005). Skinner is widely enough known amongst the general public for him to become the subject of legend. He seems to be the most eminent figure of the twentieth century in the eyes of fellow psychologists, despite the fact that most of them do not adopt his approach to psychological issues. However, when one considers how much misinformation circulates about the behaviourists' work, it is hardly surprising that they prefer the friendly audiences found in the readership of their own journals than the hostility they may expect to find in the wider psychological market place of ideas. Nevertheless attempts to familiarise a wider audience with the achievement of applied behaviour analysis must be made. This is one reason to welcome this book.

Many psychologists today consider themselves to be 'cognitive' in approach. I find it very difficult to see what common factors unite them, other than a willingness to engage in the sort of fanciful theory building that Skinner rejected. However, for good or ill, there are many who see themselves as 'cognitive psychologists'. It is common for those adopting this position to offer a rather fanciful account of the history of psychology in which, for a time, behaviourism supposedly dominated psychology. Behaviourism supposedly squeezed out alternative approaches and suspended investigation into various important questions, such as attention and animal cognition. According to this view, a cognitive revolution overthrew this outmoded behaviourism around the middle of the twentieth century. Although a multifaceted behaviourism was strong for a time in the second quarter of that century, it explored many of the supposedly neglected issues and coexisted with other thriving approaches such as psychoanalysis and gestalt psychology.

Although it is possible to treat these disputes as aspects of the history of psychology as an academic discipline, it is important to recognise that they have a significance beyond the academic world. If a scientific approach to psychological issues can help deal with real human problems, it is important that people get an opportunity to make use of that scientific knowledge. Anything that impedes the spread of that knowledge is harmful to those who might benefit from it. Catherine Maurice's *Let Me Hear Your Voice* (1993) is an autobiographical account of a mother's attempt to find effective ways of dealing with a child's autism. She had many unhelpful experiences with supposed experts who provided no substantial help and who, in some cases, had misleading and damaging theories, of the nature of autism and its possible treatment. When Catherine Maurice first heard of Lovaas's methods she was suspicious of them and, significantly, was encouraged in her suspicions by people hostile to a behaviouristic approach. In the end, she broke through these doubts and found that Lovaas provides solutions to many of the problems which other supposed experts had failed to tackle. However, more than a decade after the publication of her book, there remains a great deal to be done to achieve general acceptance of the potential that applied behaviour analysis has to tackle the problems posed by autism. Happily, it is also the case that many parents are making common cause with behaviour analysts, to the benefit of their children. This can be seen, for example, in the book, *Parents Education as Autism Therapists* (Keenan, Kerr and Dillenburger 2000).

Behaviour analysis is a scientific approach and, as such, does not stand still. Understanding of autism continues to grow and needs to do so. One slightly misleading aspect of Catherine Maurice's book is the emphasis it places on the individual contribution made by Lovaas. The value of his work is great, but many other researchers have made important contributions to the understanding of autism, including Gina Green and Bobby Newman. Thanks to the efforts of many researchers, there are now a variety of ways in which behaviour analytic techniques may be applied to autism. For that reason, it is much more appropriate that the advertisements which I mentioned at the outset should refer to 'ABA' therapy rather than restrict themselves to 'Lovaas' therapy.

Video Modelling and Behaviour Analysis has two basic contributions to make to applied behaviour analysis. First, it enhances our knowledge of effective principles which may be applied in the teaching of autistic children. Second, it provides ways in which more efficient and economical use may be made of our resources. Since I have met Christos Nikopoulos and Mickey Keenan, I know that they share both a passionate commitment to scientific methods and a passionate desire to help autistic children. I believe both these characteristics may be found in this book and that it will contribute to the future growth of applied behaviour analysis.

Sandy Hobbs
School of Social Sciences
University of Paisley

References

Hobbs, S. (2005) 'Beyond Rumor and Legend: Some Aspects of Academic Communication.' In G. A. Fine, V. Campion-Vincent and C. Heath (Eds) *Rumor Mills: The Social Impact of Rumor and Legend* (pp. 207–222). New York: Aldine.

Keenan, M., Kerr, K. P. and Dillenburger, K. (Eds.) (2000) *Parents' Education as Autism Therapists: Applied Behaviour Analysis in Context*. London: Jessica Kingsley Publishers.

Maurice, C. (1993) *Let Me Hear Your Voice: A Family's Triumph Over Autism*. New York: Knopf.

Skinner, B. F. (1953) *Science and Human Behavior*. New York: Macmillan.

Preface

Autism is considered the fastest growing serious developmental disorder while some reports indicate that a new case of autism is diagnosed nearly every 20 minutes (e.g. Princeton Child Development Institute 2005). Social impairments of children with autism are of particular concern because they prevent the normal interactions inherent in every social situation. Research findings suggest that when the rate of social initiations increases, social behaviour generally improves. Unfortunately, the treatment procedures available to make this happen are rather limited. Impairments in play and imitation skills have also been identified as key areas of any treatment programme. However, unless a specific training programme is designed to address these particular deficits children remain dependent on explicit cues for them to be able to engage in a sequence of activities that involve social interactions. Most of the effective procedures for enhancing the social skills of children with autism have used mainly typically developing peers with a variety of methods. The implication is that unless a child with autism attends a mainstream school setting variations of these procedures cannot be applied to the treatment of their social deficits. Bearing in mind the broad nature of each child's social development, the remediation of the social deficits that appear in autism remains one of the most daunting challenges for researchers and educators.

Applied behaviour analysis (ABA) has a long history of over four decades of significant and successful strategy development, verification and generalisation in the treatment of individuals with autism. One of the many effective behavioural strategies for dealing with autism is video modelling. Video is regarded as an expanding technological medium for bringing about behaviour change. It has considerable potential as an effective and socially acceptable form of intervention, mainly because it is widely used by typically developing children and adults for leisure, educational and business activities. The range of target behaviours and different methods by which this technology has been successfully implemented attests to its versatility as an educational tool for individuals with autism. For example, a variety of different behaviours can be presented in realistic contexts, it can be a useful medium for learners who cannot take advantage of print materials or complex language repertoires and it can efficiently display numerous examples of stimulus and response variations.

It has been extensively reported that autism is one of the most painful disorders for parents to understand and deal with. There is a great need for intervention plans that are based on empirical methods and which allow parents to become involved in the intervention process in their homes. This book is aimed at parents of children with autism and the large multi-disciplinary group of professionals working with these children. Its overall aim is to present the evidence for video modelling as a valuable technique for promoting social skills in children with autism. The book was inspired by the outcome of a series of successful research studies conducted by the two authors. Some data from these studies have already been published in peer-reviewed journals and at national and international conferences. Numerous professionals and parents have approached us with requests for more details about the design and implementation of this treatment procedure. Following these demands, we provide a text that gives a number of case examples supported by detailed diagrams and illustrations and step-by-step guidance on how to construct and assess the effectiveness of a video modelling intervention. Specifically, the overall objectives of this book include:

- the analysis of social deficits and a review of educational programmes for these deficits that are supported by scientific evidence

- an overview of the basic principles in any behavioural programme for the autism population

- an overview of the essential knowledge required for any behavioural research study

- the provision of a clear behaviour analytic account of modelling, exploring its definition, advantages and disadvantages and features specific to the treatment of autism

- an examination of the critical components of video modelling procedures that are effective in children with autism independently of their behavioural characteristics (e.g. imitation skills, disruptive behaviours, isolated play) and in the absence of any prompts.

Although we do not explicitly aim this book at the academic market it may well find its way into general, clinical and educational psychology courses, as well as social work, occupational therapy, health visiting, nursing and teacher training courses. We hope that this book will not only add to our existing knowledge base but will also have practical implications for those who care for children with autism in relation to their awareness of the prospect of effective treatment through applied behaviour analysis.

Christos Nikopoulos and Mickey Keenan

CHAPTER 1

Social Deficits in Autism

An Overview of Treatment Procedures

In the little world in which children have their existence, whosoever brings them up, there is nothing so finely perceived and so finely felt, as injustice.

Charles Dickens, Great Expectations *(1861)*

1.1 Introduction

Children with autism can be similar in many ways, displaying deficits in some areas of development and excesses in others (i.e. impairments of social interaction, communication and imagination). However, these behaviour characteristics can be different and unique for each child. Nonetheless, impaired social interaction is regarded as the hallmark feature of this disorder. Even during the first months of life, children with autism may not engage in simple social behaviours such as eye gaze, smiles or responses to parents' efforts at verbalisation and play interaction (Koegel and Koegel 1999). They may exhibit little if any eye contact, lack interaction with other children, spend time alone rather than with others, display behaviour that can be aggressive or exhibit minimal initiation and play skills.

A variety of different treatment procedures have been designed, assessed and evaluated to address the needs of children with autism. The overall goal is to change their developmental trajectory to more closely approximate that of their typically developing peers (Baron-Cohen 2004; Green, Brennan and Fein 2002). Interestingly, the development of social initiations from a child's viewpoint has been repeatedly identified as a key pivotal behaviour. That is, independent of the academic competence level of these children, naïve observers will not judge them as being pragmatically able to cope in mainstream environments unless they display initiations during their social interactions (Koegel, Koegel and Carter 1999). There has been a corresponding explosion of literature regarding the treatment of the social deficits in autism. This information, however, is a mix of science, anecdotes and unproven theories (Olley 1999). Accordingly, the aim of the following sections is to look more closely at deficits and then to explore the scientific evidence for interventions for these deficits.

1.2 Towards a definition of autism

Autism[1] is one of the most extensively and broadly discussed disorders, but a generally accepted definition is hard to find; more recently, though, the diagnosis of autism is becoming more standardised (Volkmar *et al.* 2004). Despite the fact that there are many definitions of autism (e.g. Baird, Cass and Slonims 2005; Rutter and Schopler 1992) all of them identify impaired ability for social interaction and communication, and idiosyncratic behaviours and deficits. The social deficits in particular became the reason that Leo Kanner (1943) chose the term 'autism' to describe that group of 11 children who demonstrated relatively common characteristics, different from those that appeared in the diagnosis of schizophrenia or childhood psychosis. Etymologically, autism derives from the Greek 'auto' which means 'self' (Allen 1992) and the term is used to describe a pervasive developmental disorder characterised by severe impairments in several areas of development including reciprocal social interaction skills, communication skills and the presence of restricted, repetitive and stereotyped patterns of behaviour, interests and activities (e.g. American Psychiatric Association 1994; Damasio and Maurer 1978; Happé and Frith 1996; Mundy *et al.* 1986; Sweeten *et al.* 2002). Furthermore, autism may be best regarded as a spectrum disorder (e.g. Gillberg 1992) because of the range of individual differences recorded in daily clinical practice (Hewitt 1998).

---

1   Autism is also called 'early infantile autism', 'autistic spectrum disorder', 'childhood autism', 'Kanner's syndrome' and 'classical autism'. The term 'autistic disorder' has been adopted by DSM-IV (American Psychiatric Association 1994) and it will be used interchangeably with the term 'autism' throughout this book.

1.3 Deficits in social behaviour

One of the most important aspects of human life is considered to be socialisation because of its impact on the development of attachment, peer relations, social skills or social competence. It forms the basis of all contacts between people and accounts for a major portion of their daily activity. It is important also for children's adaptive functioning and it constitutes a critical component in speculating about their mental health status (Ghuman *et al.* 1998).

Socialisation has been broadly defined as a judgement of general competence within society (Gresham 1986). However, difficulties in defining it have led to the use of terms like 'social reciprocity' or 'reciprocal peer interactions' (Strain and Shores 1977). Thus, social reciprocity or reciprocal peer interactions occur when children engage in social interactions with one another or when their actions support each other in their relationships.

Peer relations serve many important functions in children's development and lives generally (Dunn and McGuire 1992). In autism, however, it is reciprocity of social exchange that is missing more than anything else (Rutter, Mawhood and Howlin 1992; Volkmar and Pauls 2003), and is evident as a lack in both social responses and initiations to other people (Roeyers 1996). In fact, since autism was first identified by Kanner (1943), the characteristic of social deficits has retained a prominent position in diagnostic systems (e.g. DSM-IV, American Psychiatric Association 1994; ICD-10, World Health Organization 1992) and in rating scales (Morgan 1988) as the primary or central feature of autism (e.g. Groden and Cautela 1988; Stone and Lemanek 1990; Weiss and Harris 2001a). Even approximately 35 years later in his follow-up study Kanner observed that the children of his original study continued to experience significant difficulties in interpersonal relationships (Kanner 1971, 1973; Kanner, Rodriguez and Ashenden 1972). Importantly, all the subsequent definitions have continued to emphasise the centrality of delayed and deviant social development in the definition of autism along with other features, suggesting that social deficits may be the primary difficulties in autism (Koegel *et al.* 1992; Rutter 1978a, 1978b; Volkmar *et al.* 1993).

Indeed, many researchers maintain that social impairments are the core problem in autism and that social behaviours in this population are qualitatively and quantitatively different from those observed in other childhood disorders (e.g. Anderson *et al.* 2004; Quill 2000; Ruble 2001). Interestingly, it has been further suggested that social impairment may be a primary deficit in which secondary deficits such as communication or self-stimulatory behaviours may develop (Baker 2000). That is, although communication impairments are among the defining features of autism, the most important appear to be social rather than communication skills (Njardvik, Matson and Cherry 1999). In addition, although social skills may improve while some individuals interact with adults, many young children with autism still continue to exhibit little or no social interactions with their peers (Baker, Koegel and Koegel 1998).

Normally, pre-school-age children follow a predictable path of development, in which their social behaviours become more elaborate with increased age and experience, and they progress through this path with very little formal effort or intervention from their care providers (Guralnick 1986; Strain 1985). Recent evidence has demonstrated that infants with autism have a specific deficit in attending or orienting to social stimuli (Dawson *et al.* 1998; Hobson and Lee 1998; Swettenham *et al.* 1998). In the very first months of life, lack of reciprocal social interaction may prevent children with autism from adapting to complex social cues in the environment (Mundy and Markus 1997). Thus, children with autism who rarely engage in social interaction may have fewer opportunities to learn language than children who are more socially engaged and initiate more verbal interactions (Kaiser, Hester and McDuffie 2001). On the other hand, children with autism usually follow a significantly different path of social development in the sense that their acquisition of age-appropriate play skills, interaction abilities or peer friendships demands systematic and intensive endeavours from their primary caregivers (Groden and Cautela 1988; Strain *et al.* 1994). In addition, children with autism often engage in isolated activities, they can easily be distracted or attend to irrelevant aspects within a teaching environment, or lack interest in communicating with their peers (Gena and Kymissis 2001). In fact, in comparison to their peers, children with autism appear to interact socially with them for limited periods of time if any, make and accept fewer initiations, and spend more time playing alone (Koegel *et al.* 2001). To accommodate these social issues a variety of research programmes have addressed some specific behaviours including difficulties orienting to social stimuli (Dawson *et al.* 1998), acknowledging facial expressions (Celani, Battacchi and Arcidiacono 1999) or responding to another's distress (Bacon *et al.* 1998); difficulties in communicating through gaze (Willemsen-Swinkles *et al.* 1998), initiating social interactions (Hauck *et al.* 1995), establishing joint attention with others (McArthur and Adamson 1996), using appropriate greetings (Hobson and Lee 1998), sharing enjoyment or interest (e.g. Wetherby *et al.* 2004) or comprehending conversational humour (St. James and Tager-Flusberg 1994).

1.4 Social initiation

Typically developing children with deficits in social skills must learn not only to respond appropriately to the social initiations of peers but also to initiate a social interaction (Oke and Schreibman 1990). For children with autism initiating or beginning a social exchange with a peer is a skill that they typically do not display (Odom and Strain 1986). Indeed, research has shown that although children with autism can be taught how to respond to initiations (e.g. Odom *et al.* 1985), complex social behaviours such as initiating play and conversation typically remain at low levels (McDonald and Hemmes 2003; Pierce and Schreibman 1995; Richer 1976), especially when preferred items or activities are not involved (Krantz and McClannahan 1998). Thus, the promotion of social initiation remains one of the major targets in any intervention programme (Hauck *et al.* 1995; Rogers 2000; Schopler and Mesibov 1986).

In the literature, social initiation has been referred to as any motor or vocal behaviour directed to another person and is distinguished from a continuation of a previous social sequence (e.g. Brady *et al.* 1987; Hauck *et al.* 1995). Coding systems used in research (Lord 1984; Lord and Hopkins 1986; Lord and Magill 1989; Roeyers 1996) typically include at least two of the following behaviours:

1. talking with or shouting to a recipient
2. communicative gesture towards the recipient
3. showing or offering an object to a recipient
4. physical contact with the recipient such as touching or pushing gently
5. approaching the recipient
6. looking at the recipient
7. looking at an object that can be important in the interaction
8. laughing or smiling at the recipient.

These behaviours serve important functions when pre-school children interact. They include, for example, efforts to stop another child's action; actions to obtain permission from another child to participate in an activity; acquiring objects; directing the attention of another child; eliciting affection; gaining specific information or clarification; general initiations to engage in social contact or eliciting from a peer any other active response. Most of the above functions tend to be associated with directing others in play (i.e. behaviour requests) or obtaining the assistance of peers (Odom, McConnell and McEvoy 1992). Given that the level of social initiation in children with autism is a good predictor for a successful intervention (Koegel, et *al.* 1999b; Quill 2000) it is important that deficits in social initiation are addressed. Furthermore, social initiations are necessary for children with autism if they are to be judged as socially competent during interactions. Thus, research specifically designed to develop intervention strategies to teach social initiations as well as research to assess and define the types and numbers of initiations children need to exhibit in any social interaction will enhance our understanding of the best intervention procedures (Koegel 2000).

1.5 Interventions

At present, there is no cure for autism. Nor could there be. Autism is a summary label for describing specific behaviours, and a behaviour is not cured, rather it is changed. The question is 'To what extent and in what way, can behaviour be changed?' Accordingly, a number of interventions have been designed. A brief description of these interventions is outlined in the sections below under the following selection criteria:

1. these interventions are assigned to improve the social deficits of children with autism, and

2. these interventions are widely used in therapeutic settings or are reported in the literature and are listed by the two largest societies of autism: the Autism Society of America (ASA) 2005 and the National Autistic Society, UK (NAS) 2005.

Excluded are those interventions that do not refer to the enhancement of social skills directly or where there is no research evidence for their effectiveness. For example, facilitated communication (e.g. Bebko, Perry and Bryson 1996; Biklen 1990, 1992; Biklen and Schubert 1991; Montee, Miltenberger and Wittrock 1995; Mostert 2001), vitamin B6 and magnesium (e.g. Rimland 1999), 'greenspan' floor method (e.g. Greenspan 1992), medication (e.g. Posey and McDougle 2002, 2001; Santosh and Baird 2001) and secretin (e.g. Chez *et al.* 2000; Dunn-Geier *et al.* 2000; Esch and Carr 2004; Posey and McDougle 2000) lack scientific evidence for directly improving the social deficits of children with autism.

1.5.1 Son-Rise programme

1.5.1.1 BRIEF HISTORY

This method was developed by Barry and Samahria Kaufman in their efforts to help their son with autism. They designed an intensive stimulation programme based on 'an attitude of unconditional love and acceptance' (Kaufman and Kaufman 1976). In the initial stages, the method was implemented as a home-based programme. As soon as the Kaufmans realised that their son was functioning typically, they published their experiences (Kaufman 1981), which were also made into a film called *Son Rise: A Miracle of Love*. As the public interest in the method grew, they established the Option Institute and Fellowship in the United States in 1983. Since then, the Option Institute has offered training programmes for families with children with autism world-wide.

1.5.1.2 PHILOSOPHY – APPROACH

According to the Son-Rise philosophy the typical teacher pupil role is reversed and the pupil has to draw 'information', 'understanding' and 'insight' from the teacher. Gentle teaching, exaggerated responses and imitation are used to engage the child in an interesting social environment. Materials are placed in a therapy room out of the child's reach, and the child has to communicate with an adult in order to obtain access to these materials. The therapy room is designed to offer as little distraction as possible. Specifically, the Son-Rise programme claims to enhance the development of a child with autism by:

1. joining in a child's repetitive ritualistic behaviours, unlocking them, and therefore facilitating eye contact and social development

2. utilising a child's own motivation which sets the initial steps for education and skill acquisition

3. teaching through interactive play, and therefore promoting the social and communication skills

4. using energy, excitement, enthusiasm and continuous love, which in conjunction with a non-judgmental and optimistic attitude maximises the child's interest and attention

5. creating a safe, distraction-free environment, which facilitates teaching and learning (Autism Treatment Center of America 2004).

The Autism Treatment Centre of America provides an individualised one-week Son-Rise programme, which enables the parents to implement the techniques and to set up a programme at home. Additional advanced training programmes and supervision are also available (National Autistic Society 2000).

1.5.1.3 RESEARCH EVIDENCE

The proponents of this approach have published case studies claiming extremely positive outcomes through this approach, even curing their son (e.g. Kaufman 1981, 1994). Although some of the components of the programme (e.g. a child being imitated) have been investigated (e.g. Nadel and Peze 1993; Nadel *et al.* 1999), the whole approach lacks any systematic evaluation and research (e.g. Jordan, Jones and Murray 1998; Trevarthen *et al.* 1998; Williams and Wishart 2003). In other words, there is no scientific evidence to support it.

1.5.2 Picture Exchange Communication System (PECS)

1.5.2.1 BRIEF HISTORY

Although PECS was developed as a procedure to promote spontaneous communication in non-verbal children with autism (e.g. Magiati and Howlin 2003), published data have supported the improvement of social behaviours as well (Le and Charlop-Christy 1999). The social deficits of children with autism had been acknowledged when Andy Bondy and Lori Frost designed this procedure in 1987, within the Delaware Autistic Programme in the US (Bondy and Frost 1994). In fact, the general aim of PECS is to enable children with autism and other communication deficits to acquire key communication skills in a social exchange (Bondy 1996).

1.5.2.2 PHILOSOPHY – APPROACH

The PECS programme mainly combines the principles of a broad-spectrum behaviour analytic framework along with current understanding of the stages of a child's typical development. That is, behavioural procedures such as distinct prompting, reinforcement, error correction strategies and fading are used, while the selection of the stimuli is based on the developmental level of each child (Bondy and Frost 2001a; National Autistic Society 2000). The main function of the programme relies on teaching a child that communication is an exchange. In particular, the child is taught to make spontaneous social initiations by giving a picture or symbol. To enhance this, the child hands a picture to a person in exchange for receiving the item in the picture. When teaching spontaneous initiations, two trainers usually take part: one who responds to the child's social requests (the listener) and one who provides as much physical prompting as necessary and who does not interact with the child in any social manner. At any stage of the PECS training, the prompting is faded systematically. While the programme begins with highly motivating stimuli such as toys, food and activities in order to build requesting, it expands to labelling and to using abstract language (Quill 2000).

As soon as a reinforcer assessment has been completed and the preferred items have been identified, the PECS protocol consists of six phases:

1. How to communicate; the child is taught to pick up a picture of a preferred item, reach to a listener, and release the picture into the listener's hand.

2. Distance and persistence; the child learns to persist in his or her communicative efforts independent of any changes in the training environment that have deliberately been made.

3. Discrimination between symbols; the child is taught to discriminate between symbols in order that the messages become more concrete.

4. Using phrases; the child learns to construct a two-picture sentence and therefore the social approach necessary for communication is further enhanced.

5. Answering a direct question; the child is taught to answer a question as a prerequisite skill before commenting. For example, the student answers 'sunny' at the question 'what is the weather like?'.

6. Commenting; this phase concerns the development of spontaneous commenting contingent on an already learnt vocabulary. Thus, vocabulary is expanded while new words are gradually added. In the above example, the student might describe the weather in more details or explain the reasons why he or she liked such weather. (Bondy and Frost 2001a)

1.5.2.3 RESEARCH EVIDENCE

In the field of communication PECS has obtained a lot of respect and some research validates its usage. For example, Bondy and Frost (1994) reported that out of 85 non-verbal pre-school children PECS promoted the use of picture symbols for communication and the use of a combination of speech and picture symbols in 80 and 65 children respectively. Other studies have demonstrated the importance of using this procedure to enhance spontaneous initiations in verbal children with autism (Quill 1995a, 1997), or to increase word utterances in children with preverbal or limited functional speech (Ganz and Simpson 2004). In addition, the first pilot study on the evaluation of PECS conducted in the UK, named 'the Alice Project', produced some promising results (Baker 2001). Moreover, a study by Charlop-Christy *et al.* (2002) provided the first empirically controlled data on the effectiveness of the PECS programme, which further highlighted that children's social communicative behaviours increased after learning to use PECS. Nevertheless, further research is needed to assess the impact of PECS on social development and approach (Bondy and Frost 2001a) and to determine the optimal procedures for promoting social communication skills (Tincani 2004).

1.5.3 Daily Life Therapy (Higashi School)
1.5.3.1 BRIEF HISTORY

Daily Life Therapy was developed and pioneered by Kiyo Kitahara at the Musashino Higashi Gakuen School, in Tokyo, in 1964. (Kitahara 1983/84, cited in Trevarthen *et al.* 1998). This specific therapy is reported to be based on the Japanese educational principles and the philosophy that all children have potential for learning (Gurry and Larkin 1990). In 1987, the Boston Higashi School was established as the International Division of the Higashi School in Tokyo. Although the Boston school maintains its strong philosophical links to the original Japanese school, it differs in that the former has only children with autism, whereas the latter serves typically developing children as well (Quill, Gurry and Larkin 1989).

1.5.3.2 PHILOSOPHY – APPROACH

The Daily Life Therapy approach functions as a complete system that addresses both the content of the educational curriculum and the development of the social and emotional well-being of the children. According to Kitahara, Daily Life Therapy seems to focus on the social and behavioural aspects of autism and it relies on three central points:

1. Establishing a 'rhythm of life' and 'stabilising the child's weak emotions' concentrating on physical training.

2. Relieving the child from a 'spirit of dependence' through group-oriented education.

3. Promoting the stimulation of the intellect through continuous repetitions of the same actions and activities. (Quill *et al.* 1989)

In practice, Daily Life Therapy is an educational methodology based upon a development of group dynamics, rigorous physical education, arts and music, academic activity and vocational training. As far as possible, curricular activities are organised in groups and structured in order to enable the transmission of learning between the children through imitation (Quill *et al.* 1989). Academic activities such as language, mathematics, social studies or science are taught in relation to the typical school curricula to create inclusion opportunities for each child (Trevarthen *et al.* 1998).

1.5.3.3 RESEARCH EVIDENCE

Despite claims in the popular press about the Daily Life Therapy having many strengths as an effective approach for children with autism (e.g. Richardson and Langley 1997), it still lacks empirical validation (Larkin and Gurry 1998).

1.5.4 Treatment and Education of Autistic and related Communication handicapped CHildren (Division TEACCH)

1.5.4.1 BRIEF HISTORY

TEACCH is a complete programme of services for people with autism that combines several methods and techniques depending on each person's needs and emerging capabilities (Division TEACCH 2003). Founded by Eric Schopler, it was established as part of the department of Psychiatry at the University of North Carolina in the United States in 1966, initially providing services for a small number of children and their parents (Schopler and Reichler 1971). In 1972, the North Carolina General Assembly passed legislation which resulted in Division TEACCH becoming the first comprehensive community-based programme of services for people with autism and other developmental disabilities.

1.5.4.2 PHILOSOPHY – APPROACH

Division TEACCH recognises autism as an organic condition and, with close collaboration with the families, it delivers a flexible range of services to meet individual and family needs (Schopler 1997). The basic concept of TEACCH applies to the behavioural, developmental and ecological theoretical frameworks. It considers the sensory environment as a potential source of distraction and, therefore, a variety of environmental adaptations are used in a TEACCH classroom in order to help people with autism attend to tasks (Rogers 1999a). Also, the programme provides a lifelong continuum of services including assessment and diagnosis, individualised treatment procedures, special education, social skills and vocational training, consulta-tion, community collaboration and family support services (Erba 2000). TEACCH employs 'generalists' who may come from a variety of different dis-ciplines such as early intervention, psychology, nursing, speech and language pathology or social work (Lord, Bristol and Schopler 1993). However, and despite the claim that such generalists can take on the skills from their disciplines and integrate them into a holistic approach through training, such training is usually reduced to single short courses yielding uncertain outcomes (Jordan 2001).

Since the initial formulation of the Division TEACCH, seven essential programme components have been revised and evolved:

1. Service–research interaction; university-based research provides knowledge regarding new treatment procedures.

2. Parent collaboration; parents are treated as treatment collaborators, rather than causal agents of their child's disorder.

3. Administrative organisation; regional centres have been developed instead of having one central superclinic.

4. Clinical centres; TEACCH centres have been established across the US, Latin America and Europe to provide diagnostic assessments and educational programmes to families with children with autism.

5. Structured classrooms; adaptations of educational services implementing TEACCH have been used.

6. Continuum of services; a continuum of services for the entire autism spectrum and across the life span has been evolved.

7. Multi-disciplinary training; training has been offered to students, professionals, and parents, typically in an intensive one-week course. (Schopler and Mesibov 2000)

The general long-term goal of the TEACCH programme is for each person with autism to fit as independently as possible into society as an adult (Mesibov and Shea 2003). The TEACCH philosophy emphasises a positive and practical approach in terms of accommodating the environment to the related autism deficits in an effort to teach an individual with autism new skills. For example, areas that may cause sensory distractions are covered up, items or objects are put away, and work stations are designed to be free of any additional distractions (Rogers 1999b). The adapted environment enables the individual to utilise his or her strengths and to counterbalance areas of deficit (Schopler 1994). In this way, the strategies put forward by TEACCH do not address the difficulties related to autism directly, but they provide a 'prosthetic environment' in an effort to gain advantage over these difficulties (Jordan *et al.* 1998).

The major approach of TEACCH is the teaching structure, whereby both educational learning and prevention of behaviour problems are promoted in individuals with autism (Mesibov, Schopler and Hearsey 1994). This assumption was based on Schopler and Reichler's (1971) suggestions that children with autism, especially those at earlier developmental levels, needed a structured learning environment in order to learn new skills. Behavioural difficulties are compensated provided that they appear as the result of an individual's inability to understand and to cope with his or her environment. According to this perspective, visual skills and routines are used to create meaningful environments wherein people with autism can potentially react and understand. A social skills training model, in particular, emphasises the utilisation of cognitive social skills training approaches to teach social behaviours. These new skills are practised in individual sessions before they are generalised to group activities in the community, and eventually the individual's ability to understand social rules is enhanced (Olley 1986; Schopler and Mesibov 1986). Finally, a cornerstone of the TEACCH programme is the involvement of the parents as co-therapists who implement the treatment interventions at home (Ozonoff and Cathcart 1998).

1.5.4.3 RESEARCH EVIDENCE

Although TEACCH is regarded as one of the longest-established programmes with an international influence (e.g. Durham 2000; Fuentes, Barinaga and Gallano 2000; Preece *et al.* 2000; Roge 2000), there has been limited published evidence in terms of outcomes (Jordan *et al.* 1998). However, a few studies have demonstrated the effectiveness of the TEACCH programme in learning and behaviour generally (Schopler *et al.* 1971); compliance (Marcus *et al.* 1978), appropriate behaviour and communication (Short 1984); imitation, fine and gross motor skills and non-verbal communication (Ozonoff and Cathcart 1998); and reduction in stereotypic behaviours (Panerai, Ferrante and Caputo 1996). Nevertheless, many of the above studies lack experimental control and demonstrate only short-term gains in limited areas of development (Jordan *et al.* 1998; Ozonoff and Cathcart 1998) or are based on parental reports and questionnaires (e.g. Mesibov 1997; Schopler, Mesibov and Baker 1982; Sines 1996). Likewise, two uncontrolled studies showed mean IQ gains of 3–7 points for children in TEACCH between the ages of 3–4 and 7–9 years while 98 out of 142 children had no IQ change (Lord and Schopler 1988, 1989). Therefore, there is still a need for control studies to validate the TEACCH programme effectiveness as an ineffective, though benign, treatment can be harmful if it replaces a more effective treatment (Green 1996).

1.5.5 Auditory Integration Training (AIT)

1.5.5.1 BRIEF HISTORY

Auditory Integration Training was developed by Guy Berard, a physician in France, who first put forward the theory that the behavioural disturbances in autism could be caused by sensitivity to sound (Berard 1993). Although AIT had been used as a treatment since the 1960s, initially called 'Tomatis Effect', public interest grew after the publication of the book *The Sound of a Miracle* (Stehli 1991). The author of the book was a mother of a child with autism who claimed that her daughter made dramatic improvements after having undergone auditory training with Berard.

1.5.5.2 PHILOSOPHY – APPROACH

The philosophy of AIT is based on the assumption that children with autism usually experience areas of oversensitive hearing at a sensory level, which alters their ability to concentrate on the auditory environment. Thus, an environment overloaded with sounds is remediated by exposing an individual with autism to modified music, wherein the sensitive frequencies have been dampened. In this way, a systematic desensitisation or habituation of the individual to specific frequencies of sound is accomplished, allowing him or her to deal with everyday life in the family (Neysmith-Roy 2001), and also to gain in social awareness or verbalisation (Autism Society of America 2004).

In practice, AIT involves playing this modified music via headphones for 30 minutes twice a day for 10 days. The modification of the music is achieved in two ways: modulation and filtering. Modulation includes attenuation of high or low frequencies, whereas filtering includes attenuation of narrow frequency bands around sensitive frequencies for the individual with autism (Mudford *et al.* 2000).

1.5.5.3 RESEARCH EVIDENCE

Although anecdotal evidence (i.e. Stehli 1991) has shown that AIT can have dramatic results, a critical review conducted by Best and Milne (1997) as well as one by Mudford and Cullen (2005) classified this method as 'not proven' in terms of its effectiveness. In particular, seven studies have assessed the quantitative effects of AIT. In their two papers, Rimland and Edelson (1994, 1995) and one with their colleagues (Edelson *et al.* 1999) suggested that AIT was effective in reducing the aberrant and problem behaviours in children with autism. However, the investigators in the other four studies (Bettison 1996; Gillberg *et al.* 1997; Mudford *et al.* 2000; Zollweg, Palm and Vance 1997), reported no beneficial effects on the behaviours – including social behaviour – of people with autism. Moreover, a systematic review conducted for the Cochrane Collaboration further suggested that there is no clear evidence yet for AIT's effect on autism (Sinha *et al.* 2004). Therefore, the advocates of this approach have not only to develop the theoretical framework to explain why some individuals with autism may benefit from listening to AIT music, but also have to provide research evidence to support their claims (American Academy of Pediatrics 1998).

1.5.6 Applied behaviour analysis (ABA)

1.5.6.1 BRIEF HISTORY

The field of Applied Behaviour Analysis (ABA) is the scientific study of behaviour. Specifically, it is a science that seeks to use empirically validated behaviour change procedures in an effort to assist people in developing skills with social value (Baer, Wolf and Risley 1968; Skinner 1953). The science of behaviour formally started in 1938, when Skinner published his book entitled *The Behavior of Organisms* (Heward and Cooper 1987). However, the first demonstrations of the effectiveness of this treatment model in autism were provided in the 1960s with the studies of Ferster (e.g. Ferster 1961; Ferster and DeMyer 1961); Lovaas (e.g. Lovaas *et al.* 1966; Lovaas *et al.* 1967); Wolf (e.g. Baer *et al.* 1968; Wolf, Risley and Mees 1964; Wolf *et al.*, 1967) and Risley (e.g. Risley and Wolf 1966). In fact, Ferster (1961) first applied the behavioural principles to children with autism, illustrating that the observed behavioural excesses and deficits in this population were operants that were controlled by environmental consequences (Matson *et al.* 1996). Thus, he demonstrated that operant conditioning techniques such as positive reinforcement had positive effects and could foster learning in that population. However, it was Lovaas' landmark study (Lovaas 1987), providing empirical support for substantial and widespread gains in children with autism, which has caused a tremendous impact world-wide for educators and researchers (Rosenwasser and Axelrod 2001, 2002; see also Lovaas 1993 for an overview).

1.5.6.2 PHILOSOPHY – APPROACH

Applied Behaviour Analysis is defined as the science in which procedures derived from the principles of behaviour are applied to improve socially significant behaviours in a systematic way and to experimentally demonstrate that these procedures were responsible for the modification of the behaviours (Cooper, Heron and Heward 1987). Accordingly, ABA should not be regarded as a specific intervention technique, rather it is an overall science which delivers services to establish, guide and evaluate intervention programmes (Jensen and Sinclair 2002).

A behaviourally oriented approach includes a large number of conceptually consistent techniques that can be used in various combinations across different people and contexts (Romanczyk and Matthews 1998). With respect to autism a behavioural approach adopts a specific form of the general protocol wherein the following elements are involved:

1. Analysis and measurement; emphasis is placed on the definition of the behaviour in question and then an objective system is constructed to measure the frequency or duration of its occurrence.

2. Assessing the child; functional assessment and/or functional analysis are carefully administered which refer to the process of ascertaining empirically the controlling variables that enhance or inhibit the expression of a behaviour.

3. Developing an individualised curriculum; a sequence of long-term and short-term goals is set as a result of the assessment, reflecting the collective priorities of all people involved (e.g. parents, children and treatment providers), and adapted to the current developmental level of the child.

4. Selecting and systematically using reinforcers; an ongoing assessment is carried out to identify the functional reinforces that increase the motivation for learning.

5. Promoting generalisation; a specific and detailed plan is constructed so that the acquired new skills under particular conditions and settings will be expressed in different conditions and settings in the absence of a treatment.

6. Selecting intervention techniques with documented effectiveness; criteria for the selection of any intervention are based on controlled research evidence regarding specific skills, behaviours or conditions for individuals with similar diagnosis and characteristics that appear in the literature. (Anderson and Romanczyk 1999)

As long ago as 1981, ABA was identified as the treatment of choice for individuals with autism (DeMyer, Hingtgen and Jackson 1981). Specifically, from a behavioural analytic viewpoint, autism is a condition of behavioural deficits and excesses that, although may have a biological basis, are amenable to change through carefully constructive interactions with the physical and social environment. Moreover, it has been suggested that in order to understand autism, strengths as well as deficits must be carefully considered (Happé 1991; Yeung-Courchesne and Courchesne 1997).

In practice, a behaviour analytic treatment for autism focuses on teaching small, measurable units of behaviour in a systematic way. Every skill that a child with autism does not demonstrate is broken down into small steps (Richman 2001). Then, a specific cue or instruction, called an 'antecedent stimulus', is presented in order that each step is taught effectively. At the beginning, an additional antecedent called a 'prompt' may be used so that a child begins a specific behaviour. When target responses occur these are followed by specific consequences that have been found to act as reinforcers – reinforcers quite often vary from child to child. Then the prompts are gradually faded out dependent on the child's performance. Learning opportunities are usually repeated many times until a child performs a response readily in the absence of prompts. In each trial, a child's performance is recorded and evaluated according to specific and objective definitions or criteria. These data are graphed and give the therapist a picture of a child's progress as well as information about the effectiveness of a specific treatment technique. Training is structured in a way to meet a child's needs, learning style and pace (Green 2001).

Finally, it is worth mentioning that active family participation is a core element for any behavioural programme. Not only can a home-based behavioural treatment yield substantial behaviour and developmental changes (e.g. Anderson et al. 1987; Luiselli et al. 2000; Sheinkopf and Siegel 1998), but empowering parents with the knowledge and skills offered through ABA training can have a positive impact on the family as a whole (Dillenburger et al. 2002).

1.5.6.3 RESEARCH EVIDENCE

The list of studies published in peer-reviewed scientific journals demonstrating the effectiveness of behaviour analytic procedures with persons with autism is enormous. For instance, a decade ago Matson et al. (1996) counted more than 550 studies for the years from 1960 to 1995; since then the amount of published studies has almost doubled. This extensive research evidence has resulted in applied behaviour analysis being regarded as the best empirically evaluated intervention (Simpson 2001). In fact, in the US ABA has been recognised as the treatment of choice for people with autism by the surgeon general (US Department of Health and Human Services 1999), by the state governments in New York (Department of Health 1999) and California (Collaborative Work Group on Autistic Spectrum Disorders 1997), as well as a collaborative group in Maine (MADSEC Autism Taskforce 1999).

The general public interest in ABA grew after two main publications. The first was the most widely known study of Lovaas (1987) at the University of California, LA, while the second was Maurice's book *Let Me Hear Your Voice*, published in 1993, in which she described her children's recovery from autism. The Lovaas study reported on a two-year intervention of 19 young children with autism, aged under 40 months if non-verbal or under 46 months if verbal. Results from that study showed significant gains for the children in the intensive 40-hour group. Specifically, nine children (47%) of that group achieved normal educational and intellectual functioning in comparison to only 2.5 per cent of the control-groups children. Also, eight children (42%) in the intensive one-to-one group, who did not achieve normal functioning, still made significant gains in all areas of development. Two children of this group (11%) made limited gains. The evaluation tests within and across groups involved a wide range of variables, such as verbal skills, social adaptive skills, lack of toilet training, gross inattention, tantrums, play skills, self-stimulatory behaviours. Despite the remarkable success reported in that study, Schopler, Short and Mesibov (1989) raised some questions on the methodological aspects of the study, which have found little support.

A follow-up study for the children of the 40-hour group was conducted by McEachin, Smith and Lovaas (1993), in order to assess whether the improved quality of life as well as the significant changes in IQ and adaptive functioning had been maintained and endured through the years. Extensive assessment tools were used and the results demonstrated that eight out of the nine children showed normal educational and intellectual functioning. Specifically, the researchers stated that these children were indistinguishable from average children on tests of intelligence and adaptive behaviour. Other studies have shown similar results, which support the conclusion that ABA offers the best outcomes for children with autism. For example, Anderson *et al.* (1987) demonstrated that 54 per cent of the pre-school children who participated in their study progressed to regular kindergarten education. Other findings supporting the efficacy of an ABA treatment programme include Birnbrauer and Leach's (1993) study. In this study 45 per cent of the participants who attended a two-year treatment programme achieved substantial gains in IQ, language and adaptive behaviour tests. Harris and Handleman's (1994) study demonstrated similar gains in intelligence and language performance. Perry, Cohen and DeCarlo's study (1995) provided evidence about near recovery in two siblings, and the studies by Smith *et al.* (1997); Weiss (1999); Sheinkopf and Siegel (1998) and Eikeseth *et al.* (2002) replicated parts of the results of the original Lovaas study. Finally, other literature that demonstrates the effectiveness of ABA treatment programmes includes home-based behavioural treatments (e.g. Birnbrauer and Leach 1993; Lovaas 1987; McEachin *et al.* 1993; Smith, Groen and Wynn 2000; Weiss 1999), some aspects of parent-managed programmes (Dillenburger *et al.* 2004; Mudford *et al.* 2001; Smith *et al.* 2000), the May Institute (Anderson *et al.* 1987; Luiselli *et al.* 2000), broad-based ABA programmes (Green *et al.* 2002; Howard *et al.* 2005; Perry *et al.* 1995), or school-based treatment programmes (University of California, Los Angeles (UCLA), Eikeseth *et al.* 2002; Princeton Child Development Institute (PCDI), Fenske *et al.* 1985).

With respect to social behaviour, a large number of behavioural procedures have been effective in producing positive changes in children with autism. These procedures have mainly used typically developing peers in a variation of methods and combinations and could be summarised as follows:

- peer-implemented pivotal response training (e.g. Koegel *et al.* 1999; Koegel *et al.* 1999; Pierce and Schreibman 1995, 1997)

- peer-mediated social network (e.g. Haring and Breen 1992)

- script-fading procedure (e.g. Krantz and McClannahan 1993; Sarokoff, Taylor and Poulson 2001)

- peer-mediated intervention (e.g. DiSalvo and Oswald 2002; Goldstein *et al.* 1992; Kamps *et al.* 2002; McGrath *et al.* 2003; Strain 1983)

- self-management package (e.g. Koegel *et al.* 1992; Newman, Reineche and Meinberg 2000; Newman *et al.* 1995)

- use of a group-oriented contingency (e.g. Kohler *et al.* 1995)

- peer-mediated proximity (e.g. Roeyers 1995)

- the priming procedure (e.g. Zanolli, Daggett and Adams 1996)

- social stories (e.g. Del Valle, McEachern and Chambers 2001; Gray and Garand 1993; Hagiwara and Myles 1999; Kuoch and Mirenda 2003; Norris and Dattilo 1999; Rowe 1999; Smith 2001; Swaggart *et al.* 1995)
- peer incidental teaching (e.g. McGee *et al.* 1992)
- use of tactile prompts (Shabani *et al.* 2002; Taylor and Levin 1998)
- integrated play groups (e.g. Wolfberg and Schuler 1993)
- classwide peer tutoring (e.g. Kamps *et al.* 1994)
- video modelling (e.g. Sherer *et al.* 2001)
- photographic activity schedules (e.g. McClannahan and Krantz 1999).

In summary, ABA has a long history of over four decades of significant and successful strategy development, verification, and the promotion of generalisation (Heflin and Alberto 2001). This body of research substantiates the application of a range of successful behavioural strategies for decreasing behavioural excesses and for improving behavioural deficits (e.g. Hall 1997).

1.6 Synopsis

It has been thoroughly accepted that peer relations serve many important functions in children's development and lives. Essential components of any relation include both the responses to the social initiations of peers and the initiations of a social interaction; that is, social interaction is reciprocal. In autism, however, since it was first identified by Kanner, it is that reciprocity of social exchange that is missing more than anything else. Therefore, children with autism must learn not only to respond appropriately to the social initiations of peers, but also to initiate a social interaction. Furthermore, social initiations are necessary for children with autism so as to be judged as socially competent during interactions and to be able to enter the mainstream school settings. Consequently, various therapies or interventions have been designed to remedy specific symptoms in each individual and they often bring a substantial improvement. The most widely used programmes that address the social skills of children with autism include: the Option Institute's Son-Rise programme, PECS, Daily Life Therapy, TEACCH, Auditory Integration Training, and Applied Behaviour Analysis (ABA). Most currently available treatments for autism have not been evaluated in scientifically sound studies, or have been found ineffective or harmful in scientific studies (Green 2004). However, extensive research evidence published in peer-reviewed scientific journals has demonstrated that applied behaviour analysis is the best empirically evaluated intervention, making it the treatment of choice for people with autism.

CHAPTER 2

Applied Behaviour Analysis (ABA) in Autism

Basic Concepts in Practice and Research

Science moves, but slowly slowly, creeping on from point to point.

Alfred, Lord Tennyson, Locksley Hall *(1842)*

2.1 Introduction

In general, ABA focuses on the improvement of objectively defined and observable behaviours (Heward and Cooper 1987). It uses the methods of science (i.e. description, quantification and analysis) independently of the population being served by its procedures. This chapter examines how these scientific practices translate into a behavioural programme for the autism population. Also, it describes the basic concepts used in behavioural research in preparation for the research studies outlined in Chapter 4.

2.2 Diagnosis and applied behaviour analysis

Behavioural therapeutic approaches and programmes are based on a detailed investigation and assessment of an individual's strengths, needs and life circumstances. Therefore, an accurate diagnosis does not really add much to the intervention plans of a behaviour analyst. However, a diagnosis based on complete neuro-physiological and psychological examination could give essential information in:

1.   learning about causes and aetiology

2.   learning about signs that will permit earlier prognosis of children at risk for autism

3.   obtaining educational and other special benefits. (Cambridge Center for Behavioral Studies 2003)

2.3 The behavioural perspective on autism

The term 'autism' is not helpful in the explanation of an individual's condition. It is more properly used as a descriptive label that sums up how a person with autism is likely to behave. That is, sometimes he or she exhibits behaviours too often, 'behavioural excesses', and sometimes he or she exhibits behaviours too seldom, 'behavioural deficits'. Therefore, from a behavioural perspective autism is viewed as a syndrome comprised of these excesses and deficits. Examples of behavioural excesses in autism include stereotypic behaviours, self-injury and compulsions, whereas communication deficits, social deficits and inappropriate patterns of attention could be viewed as examples of behavioural deficits (Schreibman 1994). These excesses and deficits can be better analysed and understood when their functional relations to the environment are determined (Schreibman 1988). The context supporting this kind of analysis is usually referred to as the three-term contingency, otherwise called ABC (Antecedent – Behaviour – Consequence) which is an essential conceptual tool for any treatment provider (Schreibman 1994). Antecedents are the environmental events immediately preceding the behaviour are the consequences. Thus, when a particular behaviour is more likely to occur in the presence of one specific stimulus (antecedent), then this behaviour is said to be under the control of that stimulus. Similarly, when a particular behaviour is reinforced in the presence of a specific stimulus, then that stimulus may acquire control over the occurrence of that behaviour in the future. The technical term that is used to describe the control over a behaviour by a particular stimulus is *stimulus control*.

On some occasions, especially with challenging behaviours (e.g. Dixon, Benedict and Larson 2001; Fisher *et al.* 1998; Pelios *et al.* 1999), the observation and specification of the functional relation between behaviour and environmental events as just described is not clear. Then, these specifications are assessed or verified under a systematic manipulation of the hypothesised controlling variables. This assessment is typically referred to as a functional analysis of a specific behaviour, which consists of a more in-depth assessment of that behaviour (Cone 1997; O'Reilly 1997).

2.4 Key aspects of a behavioural programme applied to autism

The main aim of ABA is to structure individualised treatment programmes in order to bring out the best in each individual with autism. In general, there are three key aspects that constitute any behavioural programme. These aspects are in keeping with basic scientific practices. That is, data need to be collected. However, before we can collect data we need to define the phenomenon of interest. The act of defining in turn sets the occasion for measuring the phenomenon. With a measurement system in place it is then possible to determine the effects of an intervention. It is these findings that constitute the functional relation. In other words we would be in a position to say that the behaviour (i.e. the phenomenon) changes in a particular way when a specific intervention is introduced.

2.4.1 Keeping data

Behaviour analysts and other scientists work with data. These data refer to the quantitative results of deliberate, planned and usually controlled observation. Data collection gives information about a child's performance as well as the intervention effectiveness. Thus, the data shows whether an intervention needs to be adjusted. Keeping one's finger on the data pulse, so to speak, is usually referred to as 'data-based decision making'. Apart from ensuring that the effectiveness of a programme can be continually monitored, it also removes pressure from both the therapist and the child, as any problem is a task that needs to be analysed rather than being considered someone's fault. In addition, subjective factors of a child's performance such as fatigue, distraction, stress, depression are more easily identified when they impinge on the overall outcome of an intervention (Romanczyk 1996). An example of a data collection form is illustrated in Figure 2.1.

2.4.2 Defining behaviour

Bringing out the best in people with autism has been referred to as the main aim of an ABA programme, but what does it mean? Within the behavioural perspective of autism, this means the direct manipulation of the behavioural excesses and deficits. However, before an intervention takes place, it is necessary to 'operationally define' these excesses and deficits, otherwise

DATA COLLECTION FORM

Name: _____

D.O.B: _____

Behaviour/Task:

Procedure:

Data Collection

✓ = Correct response

x = Incorrect response

p = Prompting used

0 = No response

Date	Time	Trials (a set of 10)										Daily Data Summary		
												Correct	%	Comments
GENERAL COMMENTS												Total		
												Week's Summary		

Figure 2.1: An example of a data collection form

known as the overt target behaviour. In simple words, the question which needs to be addressed is: 'What is it that a behaviour analyst wants an individual with autism to learn?' Operational definitions are essential to begin to assess, change and evaluate interventions (Kazdin 2001).

Behaviour must be defined in an objective, behavioural and observable manner such that there will not be any doubt about its occurrence and its strength. Thus, for example, it is preferable to define a 'highly aggressive behaviour' as 'the child hits, kicks other children, or pulls another child's hair' (Schreibman 1994; see Table 2.1 for additional examples). Morris (1985) suggested that testing of the definition of a target behaviour occurs by giving a positive answer to questions such as, 'Can you count the number of times that the behaviour occurs in, for example, a 15-minute period, a one-hour

Table 2.1 Examples of operational definitions as opposed to common expressions employed for describing behaviours objectively

Common expressions	Operational definitions
Lack of social interest in people	A child does not socially interact with another person, when he or she does not emit any verbal or gestural behaviour and his or her body is not oriented toward a recipient of interaction while being within 1m away
Self-injurious behaviour (SIB)	A child's shoulders or hands make forceful contact with his or her hands, head, other parts of his or her body or with other objects
Stereotypic behaviour	A child's stereotypic behaviour comprises of hand waving, nose touching, body rocking, head movements, and tapping objects
Lack of verbal peer interaction	Verbal interaction includes verbal initiations as well as verbal responses to peer initiations. Thus, a child does not exhibit any vocal verbalisation related to a play activity and directed to another child and also he or she does not respond to any question or direction made by a peer
Display of aberrant behaviours	A child's aberrant behaviours comprise of scratching him or herself, hitting, kicking, pinching, pushing, or scratching others, as well as throwing objects and destroying materials
Display of destructive behaviours	A child pushes or presses his or her chin against his or her arm or against any part of another person's body
Resistance of change	A child resist environmental changes (i.e. transition to a new activity or environment) by emitting loud, vocal noises or speech produced at a very high intensity (i.e. screaming behaviour) and by biting, kicking, hitting, or throwing objects at a person nearby (i.e. aggressive behaviour)

period, or one day?' or 'Can you count the number of minutes that it takes for the child to perform the behaviour?' or 'Will a stranger know exactly what to look for when you tell him or her the target behaviour you are planning to modify?' In this way, developing clear definitions becomes a task of including information about what is and is not in any behaviour in as precise a way as possible.

2.4.3 Measuring behaviour

Once behaviour has been operationally defined, the next task is to be able to say how much of this behaviour occurs. An objective measurement of this specific behaviour will prevent any subjective judgements concerning the effectiveness of the treatment. In this way, the data will give information as to whether increases in positive behaviour or decreases in inappropriate behaviour have occurred or whether changes in non-treatment environments and maintenance of the desired behaviour have taken place (Houten and Hall 2001).

However, there are a number of difficulties that need to be addressed when dealing with the measurement of behaviour. These difficulties were identified by Skinner (1953, p.15) as follows:

> Behavior is a difficult subject matter, not because it is inaccessible, but because it is very complex. Since it is a process, rather than a thing, it cannot be held still for observation. It is changing, fluid, evanescent, and for this reason it makes technical demands upon the ingenuity and energy of the scientist. But there is nothing essentially insoluble about the problems which arise from this fact.

Importantly, a variety of techniques have been devised to help deal with such difficulties in measuring the target behaviour which will reflect any progress that has been made toward the behavioural goal.

In order to help establish a functional relation some data have to be collected. This is a fairly obvious statement and fortunately the way in which data are collected is also fairly obvious. Since behaviour can change across several different dimensions, questions such as how *often*, how *long*, how *soon* or how *strongly* it occurs provide guidance on the data needed to be collected. Thus, among others, the basic measurements include the *frequency* – how often a behaviour occurs, the *duration* – the length of time a behaviour lasts from beginning to end and the *latency* – the time taken from the onset of an event to the occurrence of a behaviour.

1. *Frequency.* Probably the most common measure of data collected in any behaviour modification programme is the number of times a behaviour occurs. This is because the behavioural goals often involve changing the dimension of how often a specific behaviour occurs. As Sarafino (2001) has suggested, frequency is an appropriate measure when the target behaviour has a clear start and end and it is performed in a fairly constant amount of time.

2. *Duration.* When the behavioural goal is determined by how long a particular behaviour lasts then duration is the most appropriate way of measuring that behaviour. This type of measurement is appropriate for assessing instances of behaviour that are ongoing activities, or that last for varying periods of time, or that are subject to a behavioural goal that concerns changes of that time (Sarafino 2001).

    Frequency and duration are two of the most basic dimensions of behaviour. Armed with data that relate either to frequency or duration a treatment provider can now make a precise scientific statement about the likelihood that a particular behaviour will occur across the day, or across the specific period of observation. However, there is also another important dimension of behaviour that is called *latency.*

3. *Latency.* The latency of a behaviour refers to the time taken for it to occur after the occurrence of a previous event. For example, one could measure the time taken for a child to engage in a social interaction when in the presence of other people. In practical terms we could be dealing with a summary label like 'shy'. The behaviour of a shy person might include latencies to engage in social interaction that would be much longer that the latencies of a person who is not shy. Once the latency is measured, it helps us to monitor the effectiveness of any procedure that might be used to help the person deal with their shyness. If the procedure is being effective we should see a decrease in the latency to engage socially with another person, depending upon the circumstances of course.

2.5 Basic concepts in behavioural research

As we have seen, collecting reliable data is essential in evaluating changes in behaviour for any behaviour management programme. The same applies to any experimental study. Research is carried out through well-controlled experiments. An experiment refers to the process in which the researcher manipulates one or more variables (e.g. an intervention) and measures the effects of this manipulation on one or more other variables (e.g. stereotypic self-injurious behaviour) in his or her effort to establish a functional relation between them. The variables the researcher controls are called independent variables, whereas those that vary freely are called dependent variables. Although there are many different types of experiments, these can be classified into two main categories; between-subjects designs and within-subject designs (e.g. Chance 1999). Traditionally, ABA employs within-subject designs, so-called intrasubject research, single-case or single-subject designs. In these experiments, a participant's behaviour is observed across time while interventions are either in effect or absent (e.g. Cooper *et al.* 1987).

Although intrasubject research is usually conducted with more than one participant, the data collected for the target behaviours are usually evaluated for each individual separately. The initial period during which a participant's behaviour is observed in the absence of the independent variable is called the *baseline period*, usually referred to as 'Condition A'. The *treatment period* follows the baseline in which a specific form of intervention is in effect (i.e. independent variable) and is usually referred to as 'Condition B'; other conditions would be labelled as C, D, E, etc.

Single-case research designs typically use graphic displays to visually present data collected in each condition. Graphic display is a simple method for organising, interpreting and communicating important data in a behavioural experiment and it can be as simple as a line graph (e.g. Leslie 2002). Specifically, lines are utilised to draw horizontal and vertical axes, condition changes and condition labels. Data points are plotted and data paths are identified. The horizontal axis represents the passage of time whereas the vertical axis represents values of the dependent variable (i.e. the dimension of behaviour being investigated). Typically, dashed vertical lines indicate the condition changes when properties of the independent variable are systematically modified. Condition labels provide brief descriptions of each experimental procedure in effect while each data point represents the occurrence of the behaviour under investigation during a session and across each experimental condition. Data paths are created when individual data points under each experimental condition are connected with a straight line. The trend of a data path is of a primary significance when analysing graphic displays as it demonstrates the relation between the independent and dependent variables of the experimental study (see Figure 2.2).

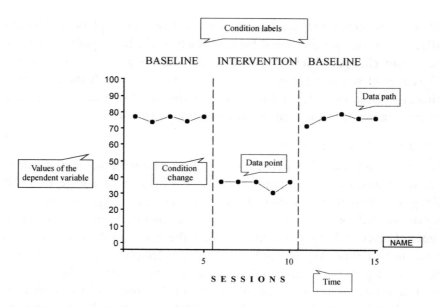

Figure 2.2: An example of a graphic display as used in single-case research designs depicting hypothetical data

2.5.1 Types of single-case experimental designs

One of the primary advantages of using single-case experiments in the science of behaviour analysis is that emphasis is given to controlling the extraneous differences among participants. Changes produced in each individual are assessed relative to their own unique performance prior to the introduction of an intervention. Every effort is made to directly control the extent of the changes possible for each participant. This practice contrasts with the traditional practice of 'controlling for' individual differences by randomly assigning participants to different groups and then hiding individual data in group averages. In behaviour analysis, then, the researcher works with individual variations in behaviour rather than trying to eliminate them (Chance 1999). The most common types of single-case experiments found in the behavioural literature are the *AB* designs, the *ABA Reversal* or *ABAB* designs, the *Multiple-baseline* designs, the *Changing-criterion* and the *Alternating-treatment* designs.

2.5.1.1 AB DESIGNS

The AB design is the simplest type of experimental design used in intrasubject research that consists of two conditions: the baseline (A) and the intervention

(B). Because there is only one baseline and one intervention phase this doesn't allow us to rule out the causal factors which might be responsible for the behaviour changes observed. However, the AB design is useful when the objectives of research are to determine the extent to which the behaviour changed (Sarafino 2001) and of course the findings from such a design are strengthened when it is used in a combination with others.

2.5.1.2 ABA OR ABAB REVERSAL DESIGNS

Reversal designs involve a series of experimental conditions that are alternated systematically over time. They have a distinct advantage over AB designs in that they can demonstrate a pattern of changes in the target behaviour that correspond to the presence or absence of the intervention. Two types of reversal designs are typically used: the ABA and the ABAB designs wherein a baseline (A) phase and an intervention (B) phase are repeated. That is, once the path of the target behaviour in baseline has been stabilised, then the intervention is introduced, until the target behaviour reaches a stable level again. At this point, the intervention is withdrawn (reversal phase) and the baseline condition is reinstated. This comprises the sequence of the experimental conditions in an ABA design (see Figure 2.3). When the intervention is re-introduced, then we have the formation of an ABAB design. The reversal phase allows us to assess whether behavioural changes occurred during intervention were indeed due to the independent variable in use. This is evident when a visible difference between the data paths in the A and B conditions is present and remains during the subsequent replication of these A and B phases. In a sense, the researcher repeats the experiment within the same study with the same participants. Thus, the researcher can provide clear evidence about the function of the independent variable on the behaviour under investigation by repeatedly alternating between A and B conditions.

Although the withdrawal of an intervention in a reversal design produces high levels of experimental control, there are some important considerations regarding its use. First, the effect of the independent variable during the intervention phase may not be fully or substantially reversible. That is, when the intervention is withdrawn, the behaviour changes might revert back toward baseline levels. For example, when an intervention of teaching a unit of behaviour such as social skills to some socially withdrawn participants is effective, then the target behaviour may fail to regress because it has been added to these participants' behavioural repertoire permanently. The second consideration refers to whether a withdrawal of an effective intervention may be undesirable or unethical for the individuals who participated in the study. It

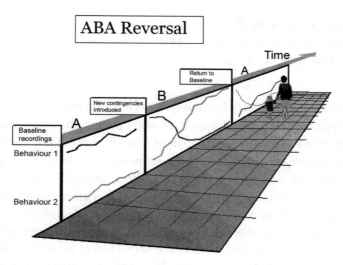

Figure 2.3: An illustration of the sequence of the experimental conditions in an ABA design

is for these reasons that reversal designs are not favoured in clinical practice. For example, there may be practical or ethical restrictions with withdrawing an effective intervention in eliminating a self-harmful behaviour. Fortunately, there are other designs within intrasubject research which effectively deal with these considerations.

2.5.1.3 MULTIPLE-BASELINE DESIGNS

Research using multiple-baseline designs essentially conducts a series of ABA designs wherein all baselines start simultaneously and proceed together for a while. However, there are three important advantages of the use of this type of designs over the typical reversal ones:

1. There are no reversal phases.

2. Introduction of the intervention is spread over a period of time across the separate AB designs which allows critical decisions to be made based on the data obtained.

3. A baseline phase in at least one AB design can extend beyond an intervention phase in another design which again provides the researcher with ongoing valuable information regarding the effectiveness of the intervention.

Thus, the sequence of three AB designs in a multiple-baseline design when baseline is 'A' and intervention is 'B' can be viewed in the following way:

First AB design: **A, B, B, B**
Second AB design: **A, A, B, B**   } Multiple-baseline design
Third AB design: **A, A, A, B**

One should see that changes in behaviour only occur when the intervention is introduced, irrespective of the duration of the baseline. In other words, changes of behaviour should only be apparent when Condition B is in effect. Multiple-baseline designs can be carried out across different behaviours, participants, or settings and hence, there are three important types: the *multiple-baseline across behaviours* design (see Figure 2.4 as an example) which examines changes across two or more behaviours of a single individual in a particular setting; the *multiple-baseline across participants* design which examines changes in the same target behaviour across two or more individuals in the same setting and the *multiple-baseline across settings* design which examines changes in the same target behaviour of the same individual across two or more different settings. These designs can become extremely powerful techniques as they do not require an undesirable withdrawal or reversal to the baseline condition. Therefore, multiple-baseline designs could be useful tools when a researcher wants to investigate the effectiveness of teaching strategies on the acquisition of skills such as social, play or language skills to children with developmental disorders.

2.5.1.4 CHANGING-CRITERION DESIGNS

Another useful technique for assessing experimental control of a behaviour change is the changing-criterion design. As the name implies, following a baseline, an intervention is introduced and the criterion for successful performance changes over time, usually becoming more rigorous (see Figure 2.5 for a detailed illustration). This design can be closely associated with the behavioural procedure of *shaping* with which a usually complex behaviour is established in an individual's repertoire by reinforcing successive approximations to the target behaviour. In each stage, reinforcement is dependent on the behaviours that are like some terminal or final target response (Grant and Evans 1994). Examples of using this type of design can be the assessment of the effectiveness of an intervention to teach vocal responses or to enhance generalisation of the already acquired verbal repertoire in children with learning difficulties.

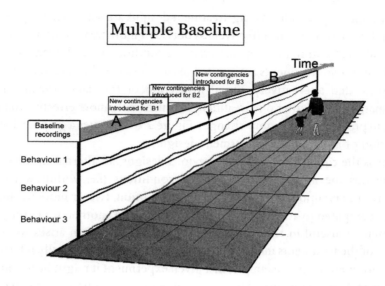

Figure 2.4: An illustration of the sequence of the experimental conditions in a multiple-baseline across behaviours design

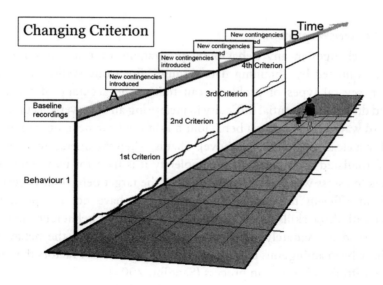

Figure 2.5: An illustration of the sequence of the experimental conditions in a changing-criterion design

2.5.1.5 ALTERNATING-TREATMENT DESIGNS

As the name implies, alternating-treatment designs are useful techniques for a researcher to examine the effectiveness of two or more treatments, when these are conducted within the same intervention condition with the same individual. That is, two treatments are applied in the condition but separated in time and presented alternatively. Visual inspection of the data provides useful information on whether one treatment is consistently more effective than the other in producing behaviour changes. Figure 2.6 illustrates a graphical representation of an alternating-treatment design.

As is the case for some of the previous designs, an alternating-treatment design has the advantage that reversal conditions (i.e. withdrawal of an effective intervention) are not necessary. In addition, two or more treatments can be compared to assess whether one is superior to another, something that is extremely useful in clinical practice. However, a problem arises when the effects of the treatments may 'interact', something which is usually referred to as an 'order effect'. For example, in a given experiment it might be found that treatment 'A' was more effective than treatment 'B' for a particular behaviour change. However, would this have also happened if only treatment 'A' had been introduced or alternatively if treatment 'B' had not been introduced at all?

2.5.2 Inter-observer agreement

Behaviour changes in any behavioural programme or research study are typically evaluated by obtaining data through direct observation methods. However, several types of problems can reduce the accuracy of the data collected due to the potential difficulty in measuring an observer's accuracy in a standard way. First, the target behaviour might not have been operationally defined in a clear way (see 2.4.3 above). That is, when the operational definition is formulated imprecisely or incompletely it is hard for two individual observers to assess whether or to what extent the target behaviour occurred. Second, insufficient training and practice might have not equipped the observer with those skills necessary in order to watch the behaviour carefully and to record it accurately. Third, an accurate recording of the behaviour might have been ambiguous because of distractions or other factors that may interfere with the observation process (Sarafino 2001).

Although these problems are addressed in a behavioural study by, for example, clarifying the definitions of behaviours precisely, or providing sufficient training to the observers, or even removing all the potential distractions,

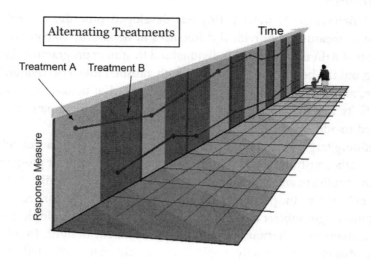

Figure 2.6: An illustration of the sequence of the experimental conditions in an alternating-treatment design

they may be impossible to eliminate entirely. Therefore, inter-observer agreement or reliability is typically measured as the basis for assessing the quality of the obtained data, which involves comparison of the data collected by two or more observers who record their data independently in order to ascertain their degree of consistency. Agreement data should refer to the dependent variables of any study. It is common that about 20 per cent of the observation sessions with at least one session per condition are assessed for inter-observer reliability. Also, a minimum criterion for the acceptability of inter-observer agreement can be an average of at least 80 per cent agreement, or can be as high as 90 per cent in the case of measuring permanent products (e.g. written forms). For frequency recording inter-observer agreement is calculated by dividing the number of agreements by the number of agreements plus disagreements and then multiplying the result by 100. For duration and latency recordings, percentage of agreement is computed by dividing the shorter duration or latency by the longer and multiplying the result by 100 (Cooper 1987a).

2.6 Synopsis

Applied Behaviour Analysis (ABA) has developed procedures specifically adapted to measuring individual differences in behaviour. Accordingly, the main aim of ABA is to structure individualised treatment programmes in order to bring out the best in each individual with autism. From a behavioural perspective, autism is viewed as a syndrome comprised of behavioural excesses and deficits, and therefore a large variety of treatment programmes has been designed to address these excesses and deficits.

Defining target behaviours operationally, measuring them accurately and keeping data constitute the key issues in any of these treatment programmes. The same applies to any experimental study implemented according to behavioural principles. In particular, behavioural research is carried out by employing single-subject designs such as reversal designs, multiple-baseline designs, changing-criterion and alternating-treatment designs. In addition, graphic displays are usually applied to present data collected in each condition of these designs visually. Finally, inter-observer agreement is typically measured as the basis for assessing the quality and reliability of the obtained data, as behaviour changes in any treatment programme or research study are evaluated by obtaining data through direct observation methods.

CHAPTER 3

Modelling from a Behavioural Point of View

Video Modelling in Context

There must be a beginning of any great matter, but the continuing unto the end until it be thoroughly finished yields the true glory.

Francis Drake, Dispatch to Sir Francis Walsingham *(17 May 1587)*

3.1 Introduction

Applied Behavior Analysis (ABA) is a strongly empirical scientific field that relies on the experimental analysis of behaviour. Specifically, it is a science that seeks to use empirically validated behaviour change procedures in an effort to assist people in developing skills with social value (Baer *et al.* 1968; Skinner 1953). Thus, ABA should not be regarded as a specific intervention technique, rather it is an overall science which delivers services to establish, guide and evaluate intervention programmes across different people and contexts (Jensen and Sinclair 2002). It regards any behaviour as functional and purposeful, which consists of a complex blend of factors relevant to the individual's strengths and limitations, physical status, personal history and the current social-environmental circumstances (Romanczyk and Matthews 1998).

Behaviour analysis has well-established roots in the field of conceptual training and programmed instruction (Grant and Evans 1994). Therefore, any treatment procedure is structured according to the established principles of the general philosophy of this science. Most of the treatment procedures are governed by a combination of these principles or, alternatively, more than one principle constitutes a treatment procedure. However, there are instances wherein a treatment procedure is formed by only one conceptual principle. Thus, within the general conceptual framework, behavioural principles could also be treated as treatment procedures. Positive reinforcement, prompting, shaping, chaining, fading and modelling, among others, are referred to as behavioural principles as well as specific procedures in any treatment (e.g. Leslie 2002). Modelling is regarded as one of the basic learning processes and it is also treated in the science of applied behaviour analysis as a procedure for teaching new behaviours and improving already acquired ones (e.g. Igo, French and Kinnison 1997; Leaf and McEachin 1999; Miltenberger 1997). Currently, however, there is no comprehensive behavioural description of the concept of modelling or observational learning. Instead it is most closely associated with social learning theory and social cognition.

Symbolic forms of modelling became logical outgrowths of the literature displaying the clinical efficacy of modelling procedures; video modelling being one of these forms. Video is regarded as a novel and expanding techno-logical medium for positive behavioural support. It has considerable potential as an effective and socially acceptable form of support, mainly because it is widely used by typically developing children and adults for leisure, educa-tional and business activities. The range of target behaviours and different methods by which this technology has been successfully implemented attests to its robustness as an approach for supporting appropriate behaviours in children with autism (Sturmey 2003). Accordingly, the purpose of this chapter is twofold. First, it aims to provide a clear behavioural analytic account for modelling exploring its definition, advantages and disadvantages, features and types. Second, it aims to provide a detailed report of the use of video modelling as an intervention procedure in autism.

3.2 Definition of modelling

Observational learning, modelling and imitation are three terms that in common language are used interchangeably. For instance, observational learning is sometimes equated with imitation; the observer watches a model perform a behaviour and then the observer does the same. Monkey see, monkey do! However, from a behaviour analytic perspective, there are some distinctions between them. In and of itself imitation cannot be regarded as a learning process (Pear 2001); that is, imitation of a model does not necessarily mean that (observational) learning has occurred, nor does a failure to imitate a model necessarily mean that learning has not occurred. As Catania (1998) has suggested, imitation cannot be used synonymously with observational learning because it does not imply that the observer has learned something about contingencies.

Two main theories of observational learning have been developed based on the social cognitive theory of Bandura (e.g. 1965, 1971, 1977, 1986) and the reinforcement theory of Miller and Dollard (e.g. 1967; see also Skinner 1969, for a similar analysis). Bandura suggests that observational learning can be explained through four processes that occur during or shortly after observation of a model. First, *attentional processes* take place while a person observes the relevant aspects of the model's behaviour and its consequences. Second, once that person is attending to these aspects of the model's behaviour, *retentional processes* follow. These are actions that the observer performs in order to evoke the modelled behaviour. That is, he or she may verbally represent the modelled behaviour or repeatedly perform that behaviour in some covert way. Third, the observer must have the *motor reproductive processes* necessary to perform the model's behaviour (i.e. he or she must be physically able to engage in the behaviour). Finally, *motivational processes* are essential, especially in determining whether a modelled behaviour will be imitated. According to Bandura, the observer must have an expectation that an imitated behaviour will produce reinforcement, otherwise he or she will not display it. Hence, reinforcement could affect the performance of the behaviour, but not the learning of it.

As an alternative to Bandura's theory, it is possible to explain observational learning within the behavioural framework. According to this view, Miller and Dollard (1967) argued that the changes in an observer's behaviour were due to the consequences of the *observer's* behaviour, not those of the model. They conducted a number of experiments that supported their theory. They demonstrated, for example, that imitation in children was a function of reinforcement. In one study, children could get candy from a machine if they manipulated the handle the right way, following a model's demonstration. In one condition, whenever the child imitated the model's behaviour, the machine provided candy. In another condition, children had to perform the opposite behaviour – *not* to imitate the model, in order for the machine to provide candy. In that way, the children learned to imitate the model when imitating paid off, and they learned *not* to imitate the model when imitating did not pay off (see Baer and Sherman 1964; Baer, Peterson and Sherman 1967 for further similar studies).

Bandura's theory has tremendous intuitive appeal, probably due to the fact that it captures the experience of observational learning as most people are familiar with it. However, it appears to have some problems as has been discussed elsewhere (e.g. Chance 1999; Gewirtz 1971). What, for example, is the explanatory value of including the term *retentional processes?* According to the theory, people seem to engage in a kind of covert practice of the observed skills. Yet animals such as bats, pigeons, rats can learn through observation. Is it logical to assume that such animals learn through the sort of retentional processes that Bandura describes? And if these species can learn without these rather complicated retentional processes, why are they regarded so essential to observational learning in humans?

Problems also exist with Miller and Dollard's theory (e.g. Bandura and Walters 1963) when you consider, for example, that if an observer receives reinforcement for imitating a model's behaviour, imitative performances occur even when the model is no longer present? For instance, one might see an advertisement for a film on one day and go to the cinema the next. The advertisement is no longer present, yet it still affects behaviour. Thus, although it has been shown that stimuli have their most powerful effects immediately, it is clearly the case that they may continue to affect behaviour long after they have disappeared. Moreover, on some occasions it can happen that imitation occurs in the absence of reinforcement of the observer's behaviour. In the previous example of the children who learned to imitate a model to get candy from a machine, later they imitated other models under other situations even though they received no reinforcement for imitating these models. If imitative behaviour occurs as a product of specific reinforcement, then why did the children imitate these models? An explanation of such behaviour can be given in terms of the concept of generalised imitation (see section 3.6.2 below). Generalised imitation proposes that reinforcement of a number of imitative behaviours can result in a general tendency to imitate modelled behaviour. That is, people learn through reinforcement not only to imitate a particular model emitting a particular response, but also to imitate *other* models emitting *other* responses. In everyday practice, observers learn, through reinforcement of their behaviour, to observe and subsequently imitate the behaviour of successful models and to avoid imitating the behaviour of unsuccessful models. They may even attend to models whose behaviour produces neutral consequences if imitating such models produces intermittent reinforcement. They may also observe and imitate modelled behaviour that is not reinforced if the model has characteristics often found in successful models (Chance 1999).

Bandura's and Miller-Dollard's theories of observational learning are in active controversy as explanations of the phenomenon. Possibly, the real difference between them lies in differing ideas about the nature of scientific explanation. Bandura's theory appeals to cognitive processes inside the individual, whereas the Miller-Dollard theory primarily explores the situation and the observer's learning history for an explanation. Therefore, a choice between these two theories becomes a choice between two different ideas about what constitutes scientific explanation.

Whatever the theoretical perspective adopted in analysing observational learning two main procedures are identified: modelling and imitation. First, in modelling the observer watches a model engaging in some behaviour. Second, in imitation this observer performs a pattern of new behaviours similar to those executed by the model that previously had not been in his or her repertoire (Ross 1981). However, in the literature these two procedures are usually used as one integrated unit, and therefore the observation of a behaviour and the subsequent imitation of it by a person are regarded as an example of modelling (e.g. Axelrod and Hall 1999). In this chapter a similar approach is adopted. Consequently, modelling can be defined as a procedure whereby a sample of a given behaviour is presented to an individual and then the behaviour of that individual is assessed to determine if he or she engages in a similar behaviour (Martin and Pear 2002). In more technical words, modelling takes place when one person, the model, performs a behaviour and this performance cues another person, the observer, to imitate that behaviour. Thus, modelling can be considered as an antecedent strategy in terms that the behaviour of the model exerts stimulus control over the observer's imitation of the modelled response (Cuvo and Davis 1998; Heflin and Alberto 2001) (see Chapter 2, section 2.3).

3.3 Advantages of modelling

Modelling as a treatment procedure can be a powerful tool both for learning new behaviours and improving already acquired ones. That is, a correct behaviour is demonstrated for the learner, the learner observes and imitates the model's behaviour which eventually replaces his or her previous incorrect behaviour (Miltenberger 1997). Also, research has demonstrated that modelling can produce rapid gains as it may take only one modelled instance for an observer to learn a new behaviour. Therefore, in many circumstances the procedure of modelling has the advantage of allowing the learner to demonstrate new responses without errors (Grant and Evans 1994).

Another advantage of modelling is the assumption that it is a natural method of teaching that occurs regularly in our everyday lives. People have the potential to act as models as any behaviour that they engage in may be imitated and, in a way, transferred by others to the next generations. A great amount of the behaviour that any socialised human has learned was initially developed by observing someone else engage in similar behaviour (Pear 2001). Through modelling, parents teach their children an enormous number of behaviours even from infancy. The child watches the behaviour of his or her parents initially and then of his or her peers, and afterwards tries the behaviour on his or her own. On occasions when it is not possible for a child to learn through this kind of observation (this issue usually concerns the most developmentally delayed children), a specific training programme usually takes place (Lovaas 1981). Also, modelling procedures have been used to solve a variety of behavioural problems. For instance, research literature has shown that modelling can be effective in teaching verbal behaviour and a wide variety of self-care skills, in reducing unreasonable fears, in improving communication or in preparing academic activities (e.g. Charlop, Schreibman and Tryon 1983; Freeman and Dake 1996; Maurice, Green and Luce 1996).

Finally, modelling represents a constructional approach to behaviour change in that it specifies desirable behaviours to be emulated. Thus, when someone uses modelling then he or she must have defined such desirable behaviours that are worth someone engaging in. The development of culture would probably be impossible without the influence of modelling and the world would be better if, every time that anyone used any form of punishment, the same person would also demonstrate an acceptable alternative to the punished behaviour (Baum 1994).

3.4 Disadvantages of modelling

People often forget how influential their behaviour can be on others and they underestimate the effects that their behaviours may have when they behave in undesirable ways (Martin and Pear 2002). Thus, the powerful characteristics of modelling that are advantageous also present some disadvantages. An important concern is the effects of modelled aggression and violence that the visual mass media usually show to viewers, especially when these are children. Interestingly, several published studies have shown that several types of aggressive behaviour suddenly increased when children had been exposed to violent movies (e.g. Bandura 1965; Bandura, Ross and Ross 1961, 1963). Specifically, the general conclusions of these studies were:

1. Children engaged in specific forms of aggressive behaviour, often identical to the ones previously shown in the films.

2. Increases in aggression usually remained after the violent films were no longer shown.

3. The amount of physical and verbally aggressive behaviours that the children exhibited to one another were related directly to the amount of time that had passed since the movie viewing.

Consequently, people's and importantly children's behaviour would be improved by increasing their exposure to admirable and interesting models who are interacting with others in a non-aggressive fashion, and by reducing their exposure to aggressive and violent models, especially when these models are presented heroically and are rewarded for their aggression (Grant and Evans 1994).

3.5 Features of modelling

Before describing the features of modelling as a procedure and how it is put into practice, it is worth reporting some general characteristics. First, the observer may satisfactorily imitate the new behaviour after the first exposure to the model's behaviour only when this new behaviour is one or two steps ahead of the observer's present level of competence. When a model's behaviour is several steps ahead of the observer's current abilities, then the observer is less likely to perform a similar behaviour successfully without practice (Baldwin and Baldwin 1986).

Second, a new behaviour can be learned more rapidly and efficiently by modelling than by shaping alone. There would be too many accidents if people were taught how to deal with the risks of, for example, exposed electrical wiring, guns, poisonous snakes or machine operation merely via differential reinforcement procedures (Baldwin and Baldwin 1986). In such situations, the existence of appropriate social models enhances learning and minimises the dangers of potentially fatal events (Bandura 1969).

Third, for modelling to occur, the observer has to be able to attend to the model's behaviour in order to demonstrate the same or a similar behaviour (Miltenberger 1997). In a training session, for example, attending can be defined as the observer staying seated, keeping hands on a table, looking at the model/trainer when his or her name is called and looking at the objects that the trainer may indicate (Striefel 1974). At this point, it is worth mentioning that although the demonstration of a same behaviour (i.e. exact imitation) may apply to a treatment session for increasing one's imitation skills, in everyday life modelling does not typically lead to exact imitations of the modelled behaviour. That is, the observer frequently introduces novel features into his or her effort to emulate a model's performance, reflecting unique aspects of the observer's behaviour repertoire or personality and different learning histories (Bandura and Walters 1963). Moreover, observers usually view a variety of different models demonstrating any given behaviour and therefore they tend to combine aspects of each model's performance into a new production, providing a phenomenologically unique behaviour (Bandura 1977).

As mentioned above, modelling comprises a part of the observational learning process. Also, these two terms are usually merely referred to as modelling, probably because the model plays such a crucial part in observational learning (Ross 1981). Therefore, there are issues or features found in the literature that, at the same time, are applied to both of them. Nevertheless, the overall idea remains the same: when an observer sees a model perform a behaviour that the observer has never done, the observer may learn how to perform the behaviour merely by watching. It is also true that different texts in the literature examine modelling from different perspectives, and therefore a variety of aspects is included in this behavioural procedure. However, most of them suggest that the origin of modelling as a learning procedure is unknown and may be expected to be difficult to prove (Deguchi 1984). Modelling as a learning procedure includes two main features: one-trial learning and inverse imitation (e.g. Baldwin and Baldwin 1986).

3.5.1 One-trial learning

In the behavioural literature, the term 'one-trial' has replaced the term 'acquisition simply through observation' which has been particularly described in the social cognitive theory (Kazdin 2001). Thus, one-trial learning implies that a relatively novel behaviour can be imitated by an observer following a single exposure to the model, without having received contingent reinforcement (Deguchi 1984). This can be explained by exploring the historical role of reinforcement for the emergence and control of one-trial learning. For example, research has demonstrated that new verbal behaviours can be imitated by children or even infants following a single demonstration during a modelling procedure, as long as other imitations are reinforced (Brigham and Sherman 1968; Poulson *et al.* 1991). The imitative operant performance of an observed behaviour will occur immediately or it will be delayed. It should be pointed out here that there is no need for any further explanation regarding the proximal distance between the immediate and delayed imitative behaviours, as both phenomena are distributed on a simple continuum of time. That is, if the emergence of a delayed performance can be attributed to the reinforcement history of an observer, and also can be controlled by an environmental manipulation, then delayed performance can be explained and ascribed to those historical events rather than to a mediating cognitive process (Deguchi 1984). Thus, from a behaviour analytic perspective, a proximal causation is not employed to fill in possible temporal gaps between acquisition and performance. Rather, specific historical environmental events have to be investigated to explain the control of an observer's behaviour by a model's behaviour or its observed consequences (Masia and Chase 1997).

There are several factors that may contribute to the fact that an observer will imitate the behaviour of a model in one trial:

1. *Viewing the consequences of a model's behaviour.* As stated previously, viewing the type of consequences that a model's behaviours obtain strengthens or weakens the observer's probability for an imitative response (Ross 1981). That is, the consequences of the modelled behaviour can function as discriminative cues for similar consequences for an observer's later imitation (Deguchi 1984). Thus, a modelled behaviour is more likely to be attended to and then imitated only if it functions as a reinforcer for the observer's behaviour (Bandura 1965). Other people's actions tend to become discriminative stimuli for someone engaging in similar actions when these actions receive positive or negative reinforcement. When a child watches someone open a door to go outside, he or she will perform the same behaviour in order to receive the same reinforcement from going outside (Martin and Pear 2002). This function of the modelled consequences, also called 'vicarious reinforcement', has been used for interpreting the concept of social influence in specific behaviours (e.g. Garlington and Dericco 1977). On some occasions, however, people attend and display appropriate behaviours without being directly exposed to the contingencies of a model's behaviour, when that behaviour has been shaped by prevailing contingencies (Skinner 1978).

2. *Consequences of the observer's behaviour.* The consequences of imitating a model's behaviour will also influence the observer to imitate a model's behaviour (Miller and Dollard 1967). If a specific behaviour

produces one kind of consequence for a model, while a very different kind of consequence for an observer, the latter consequences will eventually affect the likelihood of an imitative response. For example, if a model is playing a computer game at high levels of competence and therefore enjoys playing it, an observer is likely to try the same game. However, if the observer is consistently unsuccessful, he or she is likely to abandon the game. Ultimately, people tend to do what works for them independently of whether it worked for a model (Chance 1999).

3. *Viewing a model's emotional responses.* Sometimes, there are reinforcers that reflect the emotional status of a model. That is, an observer might attend and imitate those behaviours and activities of a model that have delivered signs of pleasure to the latter. For example, if a model is smiling or showing other signs of happiness while reading a book, an observer may notice the book as something worth looking into, even though it is merely a speculation what reinforcers had caused the model so much apparent pleasure (Baldwin and Baldwin 1986).

4. *Characteristics of a model.* An observer may attend to and imitate a model's behaviour even though he or she does not have access to reinforcers or signs of pleasure delivered to a model. This may happen when an observer respects, admires or likes a model and therefore the behaviours of a high status model can act as an antecedent to an observer's imitative responses (Bandura 1969; Perry and Furukawa 1988). People tend to imitate competent or well-known people because the behaviours emitted by these people have usually got more reinforcing effects than imitating incompetent or unpopular people. For example, many of the behaviours of a famous singer such as mannerisms, styles of dress, or idioms can become discriminative stimuli for further imitative performances. Furthermore, people also learn to discriminate which subsets of the model's behaviours can be reinforcing to imitate, and which are not. Thus, an observer may imitate the way an attractive model dresses, but not imitate the way that the model spends his or her spare time. From a behavioural perspective, the model's actions obtain conditioned reinforcing properties, and therefore an observer's

similar actions receive conditioned reinforcement[1] (Martin and Pear 2002). Thus, merely by viewing the model's behaviour the observer is provided with vicarious reinforcement for paying attention to the model's performance. This has been the main reason that researchers have suggested that the characteristics of a model might be a critical component for the effectiveness of a modelling procedure (e.g. Dowrick and Jesdale 1991).

5. *Similarity between the observer and the model.* In cases where an observer views two different behaviours exhibited by two models respectively, then he or she tends to attend and imitate the behaviour of the model that is more similar to him or her (assuming that other variables are equal). Therefore, it is quite common that people interact according to similar interests, similar ages, similar jobs or hobbies. It seems that similarity increases the likelihood that an observer will acquire modelled information through observational learning (Kornhaber and Schroeder 1975). On the contrary, studies have shown that the above aspect may not be applied to the early imitation stages in infancy. That is, early imitation does not vary as a function of familiarity or similarity with the model, and therefore infants may imitate equally a stranger and their parents (Meltzoff and Moore 1992).

6. *Similarity of a behaviour.* There is a tendency that an observer is more likely to pay attention and imitate a model's behaviour when they are both engaged in similar tasks. A common example would be when people 'are following the leader' due to similar sets of behaviours occurring in their everyday lives. Peterson (1968), however, demonstrated that similarity of response per se between observers and models was not necessary for the performance of behaviours in the absence of any extrinsic reinforcement.

7. *Reinforcement for attentiveness.* As mentioned previously, attentiveness is a critical prerequisite for imitation. The skill of attending can be modified or increased by the use of differential reinforcement,

---

1   Conditioned reinforcement involves reinforcers that have acquired their reinforcing properties after they have been paired with primary reinforcers (e.g. food, water etc.). For example, a stimulus (e.g. a coloured card or any token) which has been paired with food in the training of a child with autism may also be reinforcing for the child's correct responses even when the child does not appear to be hungry.

prompts or rules, especially when these happen in everyday social situations (Cooper 1987b). Hence, increase in an observer's level of attentiveness may also increase the probability that the observer will imitate a modelled behaviour.

8. *The simplicity of the modelled behaviour.* The modelled behaviour must be consistent with the current competence of the observer. If the observer has to imitate a rather complex behaviour, which demands skills that he/she does not have, then the observer may not be able to attend the model (Kazdin 2001). For example, this can become obvious when children are taught a foreign language, and entire sentences are broken down into small phrases or even words. In this way, children imitate one phrase or word before moving on to the next, and eventually they are able to imitate the whole sentences. This technique is usually referred to as guided imitation (e.g. a shaping or a chaining procedure applied to modelling). It has been used by Lovaas and his colleagues to teach a non-verbal child with autism to imitate words (Lovaas *et al.* 1966).

9. *Past reinforcement of a similar behaviour.* Skinner (1974) has suggested that when an organism imitates another by behaving as the other behaved, then contingencies of both survival and reinforcement must be carefully considered. Indeed, past reinforcement for imitating a particular model or type of behaviour increases the probability of performing the modelled behaviour when discriminative stimuli and contexts are similar to those wherein reinforcement occurred in the past (Leslie and O'Reilly 1999). Thus, an observer's imitative response is regarded to be functionally controlled by the model's behaviour in terms that the behaviour of the observer is due to past reinforcers for imitation, and not to other factors (Skinner 1974). For example, a police officer who runs after a thief is not imitating the running behaviour, rather he is trying to catch him due to the fact that the same type of behaviour has been reinforced in the past. This type of learning is a process that begins early in life, when people learn to discriminate which kind of models and behaviours should be imitated in appropriate contexts. Thus, due to differential reinforcement, people learn that not all types of behaviour should be imitated, but that imitation of particular types of behaviour should be avoided.

10. *Variability of contexts.* Contexts can also become discriminative stimuli for the performance of imitative behaviour, as the same

behaviour can be reinforced in one setting whereas it can be punished in another. For example, a child's imitation of his or her parent's profanity at home may be punished, indicating that the home is a context for not imitating this type of behaviour. However, the child's profanity may receive numerous reinforcers at school while in interaction with peers. Therefore, interaction with peers at school becomes a discriminative stimulus for imitative swearing (Baldwin and Baldwin 1986).

3.5.2 Inverse imitation

On some occasions, an observer performs a response that cannot be classified as an imitation but as an inverse imitation, because he or she does the opposite to the model's behaviour. In this way, an observer may learn from a model by not imitating the model. Indeed, imitation may even serve as evidence that observational learning did not occur (Chance 1999). People usually exhibit inverse imitation when there is reinforcement for behaviour that complements or differs from the model's performance (Skinner 1953). For example, the movements of two people when they dance together must compliment each other in order to produce reinforcing results. Also, inverse imitation is reinforced when the observer does anything that clearly differs from the model's behaviour. Reinforcement for being different, rather than for complementing the model is responsible for the emergence of a contrary behaviour. Inverse imitation of this type often occurs when observers disfavour the model, see that the model's behaviour is followed by punishments or they receive strong compatible reinforcers for demonstrating to others or to themselves that they are behaving differently from the standard models. For example, members of the Mafia tend to behave differently from the police officers, because any behaviour exhibited by a police officer is likely to be punished by the Mafia members (Baldwin and Baldwin 1986).

3.6 Types of modelling

Typically in the science of behaviour analysis, modelling has been used along with other procedures. A commonly cited example of modelling was reported by Jones (1924). The work of Jones was significant because she explored a number of different ways of overcoming anxiety in children, only one of which was modelling. Since then, a number of different types of modelling has been developed and elaborated. However, in this section the most popular and widely used types of modelling from the autism literature will be explored. The selection of this population is based on the fact that learning through modelling usually has to be taught to children with autism (Weiss and Harris 2001b). These techniques include:

1. exact and behaviour-feature imitation

2. generalised imitation

3. peer modelling

4. self-modelling

5. video modelling.

3.6.1 Exact and behaviour-feature imitation

When people think of imitation they are usually familiar with those instances of behaviour that belong to exact imitation; the observer's behaviour is identical to the model's behaviour. Thus, when all of the features of the model's behaviour are imitated, then exact imitation occurs. Nevertheless, modelling processes tend to include imitation of only some features or properties of a specific behaviour. When some of the properties of the model's behaviour are imitated, this process is called behaviour-feature imitation (Grant and Evans 1994). Moreover, behaviour-feature imitation can occur even when the modelled response and the imitative response do not seem to share any detectable topographical properties.[2] From this perspective, researchers have tried to analyse unusual or atypical responding as an indication of creative behaviour (Grant and Evans 1994).

It is important that behaviour-feature and exact imitation are discriminated, especially when they are used in the training of children with autism. This is essential because the pattern of behaviour-feature learning in children is a key means of language teaching, as it can help the children both to learn through imitation and to recombine behaviour features to form novel responses, and therefore to promote response generalisation. This type of modelling has been extensively used within the behavioural analytic training manuals for individuals with autism (e.g. Freeman and Dake 1996; Maurice *et al.* 1996).

---

2   Topography of a behaviour refers to the physical features that comprise this particular behaviour. For example, when the behaviour of interest is walking around a room, the topographical properties of this particular behaviour comprise the movements of this person's legs and arms, his or her pace, direction, speed etc.

3.6.2 Generalised imitation

This process refers to instances wherein an individual imitates a new response on the first trial without reinforcement, after having received reinforcement for imitating a number of behaviours in the process of developing an imitation repertoire (Baer and Deguchi 1985; Baer *et al.* 1967). Specifically, Baer *et al.* reported that it is not only possible to reinforce the imitation of particular actions, but it is also possible to reinforce a general *tendency* to imitate. They called this tendency *generalised imitation*. The tendency to imitate models is the product of experience (learning history). People learn to observe and then imitate successful models because doing so has produced positive reinforcement, but people may also learn to observe and imitate models even when their behaviour is not reinforced. Kymissis and Poulson (1990) have suggested that the behavioural analytic accounts of imitation have concentrated on the concept of generalised imitation. Earlier, these researchers had defined generalised imitation as a behaviour that:

1. is topographically similar to that of a model

2. is controlled by virtue of the fine-grained topography of the model's behaviour

3. occurs in the absence of environmental consequences for its occurrence, or occurs under consequences that are reduced from those during training. (Poulson and Kymissis 1988)

Holth (2003), however, argued that the term *generalised* can be a redundant or even a deceptive term, as any instance of true imitation implies properties of controlling relations in which there has not been a direct reinforcement history.

In the area of autism, promoting generalised imitation is an essential goal in any behavioural teaching curriculum for children with autism, especially when generalisation of the acquired new skills receives much concern and programming (e.g. Tryon and Keane 1986; Young *et al.* 1994). The development of this specific behaviour in children with autism is considered as primary, because training does *not* involve teaching of any single behaviour. Following this avenue, Poulson *et al.* (1991) demonstrated that generalised imitation could be taught in infants between 9 and 12 months old.

It also is worth mentioning that at least three variables must be considered when a treatment provider tries to control the performance of generalised imitative responses. These include:

1. The manipulation of environmental events such as the presence of the treatment provider, instructions, characteristics of and schedules of reinforcement applied to the model (Bandura and Walters 1963).

2. The arrangement of the discriminative stimuli in such a way that the required responses will be involved (Peterson 1968; Peterson and Whitehurst 1971).

3. The delivery of consequences such as reinforcement (Baer *et al.* 1967).

3.6.3 Peer modelling

When a modelling procedure occupies models that are close enough to the skills, age or status of the observers, instead of an expert model, then it is referred to as peer modelling. Peer modelling begins at a young age and it stands as a powerful social influence. This is the main reason of the effectiveness of peer modelling, and studies suggest that it is highly desirable for everybody to have opportunities to observe peers who are skilled, especially in areas in which people tend to be deficient (Grant and Evans 1994).

Peer modelling has received considerable attention in the treatment of children with autism (e.g. Charlop *et al.* 1983; Egel, Richman and Koegel 1981; Lanquetot 1989). For example, it has been effective in increasing social interactions (Garfinkle and Schwartz 2002) and spontaneous verbalisations (Charlop and Walsh 1986), in promoting response chains (Werts, Caldwell and Wolery 1996), or in enhancing generalisation (Carr and Darcy 1990).

3.6.4 Self-modelling

Advances in technology and specifically in audiotape, videotape and computers have given people opportunities to observe themselves in ways that were previously impossible. This technology has made the use of self-modelling possible, which is defined as the positive behaviour change that results from watching oneself on videotapes performing exemplary behaviours (Morgan and Salzberg 1992). Self-modelling has been applied as a therapeutic tool in a variety of populations in an effort to improve performances and skills (e.g. Brown and Middleton 1998; Dowrick 1999; Meharg and Woltersdorf 1990). In autism, self-modelling has been suggested as an effective technique in reducing challenging behaviours (Dowrick and Buggey 2000), in training correct verbal responses to questions (Buggey *et al.* 1999) and spontaneous requesting (Wert and Neisworth 2003), in learning new linguistic structures (Hepting and Goldstein 1996), or in promoting spontaneous requesting. In addition, self-modelling has been effectively used in facilitating parents' interactions with their children with autism (Reamer, Brady and Hawkins 1998).

3.6.5 Video modelling

Video modelling is defined as the instances of modelling in which the model is not a live one, but one that is videotaped, in an effort to change existing behaviours or learn new ones (Dowrick 1991). Initially, an observer discriminates a model's behaviour and, afterwards, he or she demonstrates that specific behaviour in natural settings (Morgan and Salzberg 1992).

Video modelling as a treatment procedure has been effective in a variety of situations, both with typically developing children and those with developmental disabilities (e.g. Charlop-Christy, Le and Freeman 2000; Nikopoulos and Keenan 2004a). For example, published studies using children with autism have demonstrated that video modelling can be effective in teaching generalisation of purchasing skills across community settings (e.g. Haring *et al.* 1995), functional living skills (Shipley-Benamou, Lutzker and Taubman 2002), perspective taking skills (Charlop-Christy and Daneshvar 2003; LeBlanc *et al.* 2003), verbal and motor responses (D'Ateno, Mangiapanello and Taylor 2003) and generative spelling (Kinney, Vedora and Stromer 2003), in promoting social interaction and reciprocal play (Nikopoulos and Keenan 2003, 2004a, 2004b) in enhancing conversational skills (Charlop and Milstein 1989; Sherer *et al.* 2001), in increasing play-related comments of children with autism towards their siblings (Taylor, Levin and Jasper 1999), or in reducing disruptive transition behaviour (Schreibman, Whalen and Stahmer 2000).

3.7 Some contemporary developments

An approach to observational learning or modelling should not be criticised or justified only by its level of explanation. It should be judged in terms of its contribution to a science and a technology of human development (Deguchi 1984). However, apart from the two main theories of Bandura and Miller-Dollard, a few more developments have been reported in the literature in relation to the behavioural principles responsible for the effects of modelling. First, modelling can be considered as an antecedent strategy, as discussed earlier, which exerts a high degree of stimulus control over people's performances (e.g. Heflin and Alberto 2001). Moreover, it can be considered as an 'elaborate prompt' because it helps the person perform a new or infrequent behaviour and because it may provide a lot of information such as how to perform the behaviour, when to do it, and what the consequences are likely to be (Sarafino 2001). Second, modelling could be explained within the paradigm of *establishing operations* (e.g. Nikopoulos and Keenan 2004a). The term *establishing operation* is referred to as an environmental event, operation or stimulus condition that affects an organism by momentarily altering the reinforcing effectiveness of other events as well as the frequency of occurrence of that part of the organism's repertoire relevant to those events as consequences (e.g. Michael 1993, 2000). Consequently, a modelled behaviour can alter the reinforcing effectiveness of the stimuli involved and thus facilitate the occurrence of an imitative response. According to Skinner (1957), any rule-governed behaviour is under the control of verbal discriminative stimuli. He also suggested that:

> any movement capable of affecting another organism may be verbal... Audible behaviour which is not verbal (e.g. clapping, gestures, pointing, writing, typing) also could count as a verbal stimulus as long as 'the speaker stimulates the skin of the observer. (p.14)

Thus, a third explanation might be that a modelled behaviour could serve as a verbal discriminative stimulus that affects subsequent responding and therefore modelling could be examined as an example of rule-governed behaviour. That is, when a model performs then he or she probably emits a verbal behaviour or provides a verbal description of a contingency that stands as a rule/instruction for the observer to imitate that specific behaviour. Finally, a paradigm of observational learning or modelling could be better interpreted through the examination of those behavioural analytic processes such as intermittent reinforcement, stimulus discrimination and generalisation, functional and functional equivalence classes (Masia and Chase 1997).

3.8 Video modelling as a therapeutic and educational tool

The therapeutic and educational uses of live modelling as an effective training tool have been described since at least the 1920s (Jones 1924). It seemed that symbolic forms of modelling (i.e. audiotaped, videotaped and filmed) became logical outgrowths of the literature displaying the clinical efficacy of live modelling procedures (e.g. Nelson, Gibson and Cutting 1973; Rosenthal 1977). Interestingly, research evidence showed that there were no significant differences between the symbolic and the live models in the learning process (Bandura and Barab 1973; Meharg and Woltersdorf 1990).

Video modelling as a treatment procedure has been effectively used within a large number of distinct disciplines and in a variety of different ways (Hosford and Mills 1983; Steinke 2001). In medicine, for example, a video intervention-prevention package was used in the assessment of patients with asthma, which integrated video technology with qualitative research methods, and it was proposed as having great potentials for revealing new understandings of a number of environmentally and socially mediated chronic conditions, such as obesity, function-limiting disabilities, human immunodeficiency virus infection, and others (Rich, Lamola, Amory and Schneider 2000; Rich, Lamola, Gordon and Chalfen 2000). Likewise, video modelling strategies have been designed and used in patient education in order to decrease anxiety, pain and sympathetic arousal while increasing knowledge, co-operation and overall coping ability. The researchers in those studies proposed that although no panacea, a well-designed video education programme could occupy an important and singular position in patient education systems (Gagliano 1988). Video modelling has also been used in nursing practice and education (Chang and Hirsch 1994), in increasing self-care behaviours in elderly caregivers (Clark and Lester 2000) and in reducing social anxiety and self-impression in cognitive psychology oriented studies (Harvey et al. 2000).

In psychotherapy, video modelling has been suggested as a therapeutic tool in the treatment of eating disorders (Vandereycken, Probst and van Bellinghen 1992), obsessions (Agababa and Gallois 1985), phobias (Ollendick and King 1998), conduct disorders in children (Brestan and Eyberg 1998), in work with incest survivors (Katz-Charny and Goldstein 1995), and in the treatment of childhood sexual trauma survivors (Arauzo, Watson and Hulgus 1994; Zelenko and Benham 2000).

In behavioural research, video modelling has been proposed as an effective treatment tool in residential electricity conservation (Winett et al. 1982), in enhancing social behaviour in pre-school children with low levels of social responsiveness (Keller and Carlson 1974; O'Connor 1969, 1972), in teaching self-protection techniques (Poche, Yoder and Miltenberger 1988), teaching employment-related skills to adults with severe mental retardation (Morgan and Salzberg 1992), teaching domestic skills with an embedded social skill to adults with severe mental retardation (Bidwell and Rehfeldt 2004), developing a simple meal preparation skill in adults with moderate and severe learning difficulties (Rehfeldt *et al.* 2003), establishing compliance with dental procedures in persons with learning difficulties (Conyers *et al.* 2004), or in increasing community involvement of a man with learning disabilities (Houlihan *et al.* 1995). Also, videotapes have been used in increasing the efficiency of consultation time and treatment integrity in the treatment of aggression (Egan, Zlomke and Bush 1993), or as a feedback intervention to increase the on-task behaviour rate in students with emotional/ behavioural disorders (Walther and Beare 1991).

In addition, video modelling has been employed in parent training to help parents identify their children's behaviour problems (Webster-Stratton 1990) or in the teacher training as an interactive approach (Goodwin and Deering 1993). Further, video modelling has been applied as a prevention tool to AIDS and to AIDS-related perceptions (Rye 1998) or as an intervention to improve breast cancer clinical trial knowledge and beliefs (Curbow *et al.* 2004).

Video modelling has also proven effective with the typical population, for example, in the acquisition of motor skills for physical activities and sports (e.g. Emmen *et al.* 1985; Hager *et al.* 2004) or in increasing normal pre-school children's social interaction and social play involvement (Ballard and Crooks 1984). Finally, in the area of autism video modelling has concentrated on teaching a variety of different skills (e.g. Charlop-Christy and Daneshvar 2003; D'Ateno *et al.* 2003; Schreibman *et al.* 2000) and video technology was used for a retrospective analysis for the identification of early symptoms such as sensory-motor and social behaviours, communication and attention in infants who subsequently were diagnosed as having autism (Adrien *et al.* 1992, 1993; Baranek 1999; Maestro *et al.* 1999).

3.9 Video as a visually cued instruction in autism

Visually cued instruction refers to the use of those cues such as objects, photographs, pictographs, written scripts or videos, in order to prepare, prompt or promote social expectations. Visual cues provide tangible and concrete information without the relevant abstract language being necessary in order that individuals with autism attend to, organise or became aware of social events (Quill 1997).

During the last decades, there has been an obvious shift in emphasis from language-based instruction to more visual instructional supports as a catalyst for learning in children with multiple disabilities and autism spectrum disorders (e.g. Bondy and Frost 2001b; Coucouvanis 1997; Jolly, Test and Spooner 1993; Quill 1997; Tissot and Evans 2003). For example, Hodgdon (1995) documented that individuals with autism often experience difficulties in attending to, regulating or understanding auditory inpute and therefore visual prompts appeared to enhance their communication process. Indeed, structured teaching programmes that highlight visual stimuli instead of auditory stimuli in the treatment of children with autism have been recommended by other researchers (e.g. Prizant and Rubin 1999; Schopler, Mesibov and Hearsey 1995).

Visually cued instructions have been successfully implemented to increase adaptive behaviours (Newman et al. 1995), and to decrease maladaptive behaviours in children with autism (Quill 1995b). Furthermore, visual instructions have been used to facilitate receptive language, joint attention and communicative gesturing, and to teach how to follow activity schedules, whereby various vocational skills (Sowers et al. 1985) and home living skills were also taught (Krantz, MacDuff and McClannahan 1993). In addition, visual prompts constitute a significant part in the structure of TEACCH programme for many years (Bryan and Gast 2000; Schopler and Mesibov 1994; Schopler, Mesibov and Kunce 1998).

Research studies have provided evidence that children and adults with autism are more able to attend to or remember visual materials than spoken language or social materials (e.g. Bernard-Opitz, Sriram and Sapuan 1999; Dawson et al. 2000; Minshew et al. 1992; O'Riordan 2004). It seems that this observed pictorial superiority has a connection with atypical development of language in autism. Kamio and Toichi (2000) argue that since the pictorial semantic system is superior to the verbal one in typically developing children, this particular system is most frequently used by children with autism who typically display deficits in spoken language in order to process information from their environment. Furthermore, it has been evidenced that children with autism sustain attention to graphic information at the same level as typically developing peers (Garretson, Fein and Waterhouse 1990). Thus, sustained attention to concrete visual or graphic cues relevant to social or communication information can enhance attention and awareness of social and language messages in children with autism (Quill 2000).

Visual instructions can highlight sequences of events that children with autism have to follow as the visual picture remains present until the whole sequence is completed (Mesibov 2003). Temple Grandin (1996), currently an assistant professor with autism at the Colorado State University, characteristically stated the following about her visual thinking skills:

> Many nonverbal people with autism can understand speech, and some are capable of reading and writing. I learned how to write proper English because my parents spoke proper English with almost no slang. To determine correct grammar I 'played a video' in my mind to see if the sentence sounded like mom or dad. (Quill 1995b, p.38)

Finally, the popularity of television and video media relative to books suggests that many people prefer watching and listening to reading (e.g. Salomon 1984). Thus, by taking advantage of the tendency of children with autism to better follow visual instructions, the use of videotapes can become one promising means of training. Instructional videotapes are easily duplicated and exported and, properly packaged, may be useful to agencies with limited financial resources and technical expertise (Neef *et al.* 1991).

3.10 Potential advantages of video modelling in autism

Video modelling seems to offer many advantages to individuals with autism (Corbett and Abdullah 2005; Krantz *et al.* 1991; Lasater and Brady 1995). First, video models can present a variety of different behaviours in realistic contexts (e.g. DeRoo and Haralson 1971; Haring *et al.* 1987). That is, a videotape can be designed to provide a high degree of similarity between the real experience and the experience shown in that videotape. Thus, individuals with autism are expected to display more appropriate behaviours than they would have using other training techniques in simulated settings (Alcantara 1994).

Second, video may be a useful medium for learners who cannot take advantage of print materials or of complex language repertoires (Browning and White 1986). That is, symbol presentations or simple sequences of actions would be included in a well-constructed video in such a way that it could enhance the imitation skills of individuals with autism.

Third, video can efficiently display various examples of stimulus and response situations, taking advantage of the observed attentional skills of children with autism to graphical presentations (Garretson *et al.* 1990). Also, it has been reported that children with autism favour viewing themselves in video, even the same scenes repeatedly (Krantz *et al.* 1991). Thus, observational learning skills in children with autism are further developed as they can repeatedly review a model's behaviour during a treatment procedure, and these children may discriminate cues in their environment that are needed to function independently (Bryan and Gast 2000).

Fourth, a video modelling procedure can lead to new intervention strategies in such a way that individuals with autism could control their severe behaviour problems (e.g. Greelis and Kazaoka 1979; Schreibman *et al.* 2000).

Fifth, the use of video strengthens internal consistency and reliability in data collection. It allows for more confident comparisons of data across learners and sessions such as recording of sequences or correct responses or assessment of complex behaviours (Morgan and Salzberg 1992; Powers and Handelman 1984). In other words it facilitates standardisation of behaviour measurement.

Sixth, video modelling promotes discrimination training for the target children or their families, by including error models. In this way, not only does training in the correct responses take place, but it is also relatively easy to show which responses are to be avoided (e.g. Reamer *et al.* 1998).

Seventh, the video medium provides new opportunities for addressing the generalisation deficits displayed by children with autism. For example, Daoust *et al.* (1987, cited in Dowrick 1991) demonstrated that by employing delayed consequences through the use of video, generalisation across settings and people was established.

Finally, video modelling serves as an efficient cost-effective tool in the treatment of individuals with autism. That is, the video recording of a model's actions just once would negate the high cost of live models employed in many kinds of training programmes (Racicot and Wogalter 1995).

3.11 Synopsis

Modelling is a powerful tool both for teaching new behaviours and for improving already acquired ones. Modelling occurs when a sample of a given behaviour is presented to an individual and then that individual engages in a similar behaviour. It includes two main features:

1. One-trial learning; a relatively novel behaviour can be imitated by an observer following a single exposure to the model, without having received contingent reinforcement.

2. Inverse imitation; an observer may perform a response that is the inverse of the model's behaviour on occasions when there is reinforcement for behaviour that complements or differs from the model's performance.

Modelling has been widely used in treatment programmes for individuals with autism, mainly in a form of exact or behaviour-feature imitation, generalised imitation, peer modelling, self-modelling and video modelling.

Video modelling as a treatment procedure has been effectively used within a large amount of distinct disciplines and in a variety of different ways. Similarly in autism, video modelling has been implemented in a variety of forms, uses and contexts, and has been proved effective in teaching a variety of different skills. Video modelling as a visually cued instruction can serve as an efficient cost-effective tool in the treatment of individuals with autism, as it presents a variety of different behaviours in realistic contexts and displays numerous examples of stimulus and response variations. Also, video may be a useful medium for learners who cannot take advantage of print materials or of complex language repertoires, which can promote the discrimination and generalisation training in individuals with autism. Video modelling procedures can lead to new intervention strategies in such a way that children with autism can control their severe behaviours. In terms of programme delivery, video modelling facilitates standardisation of data collection and treatment integrity.

CHAPTER 4

Implementation of Video Modelling in Autism

Through the unknown, we will find the new.

Charles Baudelaire, Les Fleurs du Mal *(1857)*

4.1 sing video modelling with children with autism
A brief overview

During at least the last three decades video modelling has been used in the treatment of individuals with autism in a variety of different forms and contexts, in combination with other behavioural procedures or not. Thus, in 1982, Steinborn and Knapp first reported empirical evidence on the use of video modelling as a treatment procedure for a child with autism. They used a behavioural training programme and a classroom-based model of a traffic environment in order to teach a child with autism pedestrian skills. Specifically, they used video recordings to familiarise the child with traffic at local intersections and their results revealed positive effects of the treatment package which generalised to the natural environment with minimal training.

A few years later, Haring *et al.* (1987) investigated the generalisation of purchasing skills across community settings to youths with autism using videotape modelling. Their results showed that in conjunction with interactive *in vivo* training, video modelling was effective in increasing independent functioning and social responding in three community settings for all three students. Also, they argued that although they did not control for potential sequence effects, video modelling procedures would be a promising addition to the behavioural strategies for promoting generalisation. However, another study by Haring and his colleagues (1995) provided further support for the effectiveness of direct community instruction combined with videotape modelling in promoting generalisation of shopping skills. Moreover, a study by Alcantara (1994) further evaluated the effects of a videotape instructional package (i.e. viewing videotapes, on-site prompting and reinforcement) on the acquisition and generalisation of purchasing skills in community settings. The results of that study revealed that a videotape instructional training package can be an effective strategy for teaching community survival skills. There were, however, a few concerns about the correlation of the treatment package with prior *in-vivo* training on the items that the children were expected to purchase in the community stores.

In 1989, Charlop and Milstein used video modelling to teach script conversations to three boys with autism who attended an after-school programme. After training, not only did the children's conversational skills generalise to different toys, unfamiliar persons and different settings, but new responses increased that were not included in the videotapes. It should be noted, however, that conversations were not initiated by the children, but by therapists, unfamiliar adults or siblings who, instead, provided the questions to them (Stevenson, Krantz and McClannahan 2000).

In 1999, Taylor *et al.* conducted two experiments in order to increase play-related statements in two children with autism towards their siblings. In both experiments the procedures comprised of two main phases, video viewing and practice *in vivo*; subsequently changes in behaviour were assessed in probe sessions with the participants' siblings. That is, in the first experiment a child with autism initially watched scripted play comments between his sibling and an adult. Then he participated in practice sessions using the same stimuli in the presence of an adult. In their second experiment, the researchers presented brief segments of video models of play comments between an adult and his sibling to another child with autism, who afterwards practiced the acquisition of play comments while playing with an adult. Both of these studies revealed that video modelling was an effective intervention for teaching children with autism to make scripted and unscripted play statements while playing with their siblings. In the same year, Buggey and his colleagues (Buggey *et al.* 1999) used videotaped self-modelling to promote responding in three children with autism. Specifically, they investigated the

effectiveness of this video-based procedure in the acquisition and maintenance of appropriate verbal responses to questions and their results showed
that the three participants substantially increased their rates of appropriate
responding to questions during play situations.

In the following year, two studies were published. The first study was
conducted by Schreibman *et al.* (2000), who demonstrated that video implemented as a priming technique[1] could be effective in reducing or eliminating
the disruptive behaviour of three children with autism in transition situations.
The results of the second study by Charlop-Christy *et al.* (2000), revealed that
video modelling was not only an effective method for teaching children with
autism a variety of skills (e.g. expressive labelling, spontaneous greetings, conversational speech) which generalised across persons, settings and stimuli, but
it was also superior to *in-vivo* modelling. Following this line of research,
Sherer *et al.* (2001) replicated previous findings in enhancing conversational
skills in children with autism and, more importantly, they demonstrated that
using a model was equally as effective as using self as a model. In the
following year, Shipley-Benamou *et al.* (2002) implemented an instructional
video modelling technique to teach functional living skills such as making
orange juice, preparing a letter to mail and putting the letter in the mailbox,
pet care, cleaning a bowl and table setting to three children with autism. They
concluded that instructional video modelling was effective in promoting skill
acquisition across all children which maintained after a one-month follow up.

In 2003, there were five more published studies which provided evidence
on the efficacy of video modelling. Specifically, it was used to teach perspective taking to three children with autism (Charlop-Christy and Daneshvar
2003). Similar results were obtained by LeBlanc and her colleagues (LeBlanc
et al. 2003). D'Ateno *et al.* (2003) taught a pre-school girl with autism verbal
and motor responses during three play activities (having a tea party, shopping
and baking). Another study using a computer format in combination with
video rewards examined generative spelling in a girl with autism (Kinney *et al.*
2003). The acquisition of that skill helped the girl to acquire literacy skills
commensurate with her general school placement. In the final article of that
year, Sturmey (2003) concluded that video technology can be a powerful tool

---

1   According to the authors of that paper, in priming, a child is provided with an
     opportunity to preview future events in a way that reduces disruptive behaviours, as
     these events become more predictable. Thus, priming could be regarded as a
     technique to control antecedent events or even to set up establishing operations.

for teaching appropriate adaptive behaviour, independent play and academic tasks to children with autism.

In 2004, three more publications were added. Dauphin, Kinney and Stromer (2004) evaluated an intervention package comprised of video-enhanced activity schedules and matrix training in order to teach a child with autism sociodramatic play. Results of that study provided evidence about the efficacy of video-enhanced activity schedules to teach this kind of play, as opposed to the use of matrix training which was shown to facilitate generative learning outcomes. Coyle and Cole (2004) examined videotaped self-modelling to decrease the rates of off-task behaviour in three children with autism. They demonstrated that the intervention package produced considerable decreases in off-task behaviours during the period of intervention which were maintained during follow-up. Simpson, Langone and Ayres (2004) used a computer-based instruction programme with embedded video clips to promote social skills such as sharing, following teacher directions and social greetings in four children with autism. Specifically, children were taught how to discriminate examples from non-examples of social behaviours displayed in the video clips. Results showed that this training package was effective in teaching individuals with autism a few social skills in their natural environment.

Finally, the effectiveness of video modelling with or without self-management was further demonstrated in compliment-giving behaviours of children with high-functioning autism (Apple, Billingsley and Schwartz 2005). Interestingly, results from that study suggested that self-management could be used as a means to produce social initiations when video modelling alone fails. In conclusion, it is worth emphasising that experimental control in all of the above studies was demonstrated through the employment of single-case research methodology such as multiple baseline designs or ABA reversal and multiple-treatment designs.

4.2 Experimental analysis of video modelling procedures

It has been well evidenced that the social impairment of children with autism may be their most important deficit both in responding appropriately to the social initiations of others and also in initiating a new social interaction (e.g. Ingersoll, Schreibman and Stahmer 2001; Koegel et al. 1992; Roeyers 1995). Specifically, the behaviour of engaging in social initiation is crucial for enhancing social interaction (Haring and Lovinger 1989) as this component affects directly the overall levels of social behaviour (e.g. Strain, Kerr and

Ragland 1979). Accordingly, five research studies, reported in detail below, assessed the effectiveness of video modelling in promoting social skills in children with autism. Before outlining these studies, however, it is essential to briefly introduce some common issues that were adopted in all of them.

4.2.1 Basic guidelines for designing video modelling procedures

Below is an overview of the general instructions and guidelines that were taken into consideration. These guidelines are an amalgam of procedures common to much of the previous research and lessons drawn from the studies as they evolved:

1. After a task analysis, each component of a specific task should be videotaped. The number of sequences to be shown needs to be gauged for a particular child experimentally.

2. Preferably one model should be used.

3. Simple behaviours demonstrated by the model should be about 30–40 seconds maximum.

4. At the initial stages, the setting viewed in the videotape should be the same as the setting in which the child will demonstrate the imitative behaviour. Thereafter, different settings could be used.

5. The treatment provider has to be sure that the videotape shows a close-up of the action he or she wants the child to imitate.

6. The child should be allowed to watch each video clip at least once.

7. The child has to be allowed to have at least two or three minutes to demonstrate the modelled behaviour. Whether or not the child has imitated the videotaped behaviour, the treatment provider could occasionally provide him or her with praise or a small piece of food for behaving well unless disruptive or challenging behaviours are in place.

8. The child should watch the same modelled sequence again if he or she fails to imitate the behaviours; this should be done at least three times.

9. The treatment provider must keep data for every trial and let the child have at least three successful trials before he or she moves to the next video clip.

10. Programming for maintenance and generalisation of the imitative behaviour must take place across settings, stimuli, people and time.

4.2.2 Selection criteria for participants, stimuli and models

One of the main objectives of this series of studies was to examine the critical components of video modelling procedures that are effective in children with autism independently of their behavioural characteristics (e.g. imitation skills, disruptive behaviours, isolated play etc). Consequently, there was no exclusion criterion as long as the participants were children with a primary diagnosis of autism. Pseudonyms are used instead of the real names of the children.

In all of the studies, research stimuli comprised mainly of toys appropriate to the developmental age of the children, such as a trampoline, a wooden train, a ball, a set of tambourines. These toys were selected because all children were familiar with them and this also meant that guidance and instructions on how to play with them, which was never given at the time in the studies, would not confound the effects of the independent variables being studied.

The models used throughout were a familiar adult, an unfamiliar adult or an unfamiliar peer, who were selected according to the characteristics indicated by other research studies (e.g. Grant and Evans 1994; Martin and Pear 2002). The behaviour of the models on the videotapes was as natural as possible, avoiding a slow or exaggerated pace (cf. Biederman *et al.* 1999). Adults and peers were used as previous research has suggested that children with autism could learn equally well from both types of models (Ihrig and Wolchik 1988). Because it has been suggested that the use of audio in conjunction with visual information may maximise the effects of modelling (Racicot and Wogalter 1995), an audio component (i.e. 'Let's play', 'Let's move the table' or 'Let's sit down') was included.

4.2.3 Measuring the behavioural characteristics of the children

The Childhood Autism Rating Scale (CARS; Schopler, Reichler and Renner 2002) has been suggested as a valid and reliable behavioural rating scale widely used in the diagnosis of children with autism and pervasive developmental disorders (Stella, Mundy and Tuchman 1999). Here, it was used in order to classify the children in the mild to moderate range (a score of 30 to 36 points) or in the moderate to severe range (from 37 to 60 points) of autism. CARS has been shown to have high reliability and validity (Ozonoff and Cathcart 1998), and incorporates all five important diagnostic systems: the

Kanner criteria (1943); the Creak points (1961); the definition of Rutter (1978a and 1978b); the criteria of the National Society for Autistic Children (NSAC) (1978) and the DSM-IV criteria (American Psychiatric Association 1994). In fact, a recent study demonstrated a complete agreement between DSM-IV and CARS and a clear superiority to the Autism Behavior Checklist (Rellini *et al.* 2004) or to the Autism Diagnostic Interview-Revised (Saemundsen *et al.* 2003). CARS includes the following 15 items:

1. relating to people
2. imitation
3. emotional response
4. body use
5. object use
6. adaptation to change
7. visual response
8. listening response
9. taste, smell, and touch response and use
10. fear or nervousness
11. verbal communication
12. non-verbal communication
13. activity level
14. level and consistency of intellectual response
15. general impressions.

Collectively, ten children scored within the severe range of autism (range, 38 to 52 points) and 8 children within a mild–moderate range of autism (range, 31 to 36.5 points). It was found that the areas of relating to people, imitation, verbal and non-verbal communication were affected more severely in all children. Finally, a Likert-type scale/questionnaire (e.g. Sommer and Sommer 1997) with a specified section for comments (see Appendix) was designed and given to the teachers and caregivers in order to provide any additional information concerning the behavioural characteristics of the children.

4.2.4 Pre-training for TV watching

An important prerequisite for modelling to be effective is that the learners attend to the specific behaviours being modelled (Cooper 1987b). Hence, children were required to be able to watch TV for at least one minute before experiencing the video modelling procedures. Thus, at the beginning of each study, all children were assessed as to whether they were able to attend to various TV morning zone programmes for the specified period of time. For the children who did not meet that criterion, specific training based on verbal instructions, physical guidance and modelling was provided. Positive reinforcement in the form of edibles and praise was used throughout this training. Generally, except for two children in the first study, all of the other children were able to watch TV for at least a couple of minutes consecutively.

4.2.5 Delivery of consequences to the children

During all sessions in all studies no specific consequences were provided by the researcher. For example, instructions such as 'Let's do the same' were not given at any time following the video viewing (cf. Charlop and Milstein 1989) nor was there any previous training on the video display (cf. Taylor *et al.* 1999). This was done in order to avoid contaminating the video modelling intervention with other factors. However, the plan was that when challenging behaviours occurred it would be necessary to intervene if the situation became dangerous for the child's safety; this never occurred. In addition, during the intervals between all sessions (approximately 5 to 8 mins) and across all conditions, including baselines, each child was taken out of the research setting to an outside playground area. The researcher observed each child to ensure for his or her safety without providing any particular consequences. General social praise was given to each child along with edibles on some occasions in order to maintain general participation within the research context (Tryon and Keane 1986). Importantly, the researcher did not mention anything in relation to the video, nor did he give any instructions to the child about the behaviour required.

4.2.6 Video recording of the sessions

It has been proposed that accurate measuring and recording of target behaviours can be further enhanced by videotaping behaviours and then making direct assessments from the taped recordings (e.g. Sarafino 2001). Hence, all sessions in all studies were video recorded using a camcorder mounted on a tripod with a wide-angle lens. Also, whenever possible, the camcorder was placed out of the reach of the children and was covered with a cloth to make it invisible to them.

4.2.7 Study 1: Promoting social initiation in a play context[2]

In the first study, the general notion of promoting social skills and particularly social initiation in children with autism by using video modelling was systematically examined.

4.2.7.1 METHODOLOGY

Seven children, six boys and one girl, ages 9–15 years, participated in this study. These children attended a residential school for children with developmental and learning disabilities and they had been diagnosed with autism by independent agencies according to the DSM-IV criteria (American Psychiatric Association 1994). In addition, all of them had also been diagnosed with either profound mental retardation or just mental retardation. Their scores on the CARS were between 39 and 52 points, indicating a severe range of autism.

Aspects of their behaviour was analysed across five different categories: expressive language, receptive language, play and social skills as well as other behaviours (e.g. stereotypes, challenging behaviours etc.). Data for the *expressive language* category showed that three children were non-verbal, two had only echolalic speech, one child had some speech consisting of either single words in response to visual prompts or simple requests, and the last one had frequent speech but mainly inappropriate or directed to nobody in particular. *Receptive language* for two children was limited to a few words, for three children to very simple two-word instructions and two of them could respond to a few words and familiar instructions. All of the children had restricted toy *play skills*. Specifically, two children demonstrated very little appropriate toy play without direct supervision and continuous prompting, preferring solitary activities. Two other children were interested only in manipulating (not playing) a narrow range of toys whereas one child lacked interest in toys apart from a few specific puzzles. The toy play skills for the two remaining children were limited to some books, drawings, paintings, puzzles and a few games on the computer while one of them transferred from one activity to another very quickly without actually completing any activity. As for their *social skills*, most of the children either almost totally lacked any response or interaction with people or lacked social and emotional reciprocity with other children (unresponsive to people). The social behaviour of one child was slightly different; she could seek adult attention without, however, interact-

---

2   Extensive analysis and description of this study appear in Nikopoulos and Keenan (2003).

ing with other children. In addition, none of the children engaged in any eye contact as an indication of non-verbal social behaviour. Finally, all of the children had very limited concentration spans, four of them displayed a variety of stereotyped and repetitive motor mannerisms (e.g. hand flapping, wringing of hands, spinning objects, playing with sand) and also sometimes exhibited challenging behaviours; one child's general behaviour was passive for most of the time (not doing anything in particular), and another child could also become aggressive to others. It is also important to mention that from all of the assessments it emerged that all the children had restricted non-verbal imitation repertoires.

This study took place in two adapted rooms of the school which were unknown to the children. In the first room was a 14-inch television and, 1.5 metres away, a chair had been placed for viewing the video. In the second room, a variety of toys was spread on the floor; they included a ball, a set of tambourines, a basin with sand and other toys in it, a trampoline, a toy with two hammers for hitting pop-up monsters, a plastic tea set, as well as a few cones and footstools.

The children's performance was recorded throughout while in both rooms for six different behaviours:

1. video watching
2. social initiation
3. appropriate play
4. object engagement
5. disruptive behaviours and
6. other behaviours (see Table 4.1).

A variation of a multiple baseline across participants design and an A-B design was used across the seven children. The procedure comprised the baseline and the video modelling conditions. A graphical presentation of the general procedure during baseline, video modelling with the first toy and generalisation probe with the second toy can be seen in Figure 4.1. The purpose for establishing a baseline was to assess the children's performances in the absence of any video presentation. This would provide an objective method for evaluating the effects of the video modelling training. There were two kinds of baselines: those with all toys present and those with only the modelled toy present (i.e. the toy viewed in the videotape or, generally, the one placed near the researcher's seat). Thus, during the baseline sessions, both the child and the researcher entered the room with the toy(s) and the

Table .1 The operational definitions of the behaviours for hich measurements ere ta en to assess the effect of the video modelling procedures

Dependent measurements	Operational definitions
Video watching	This was defined as each child's eyes being directed to the TV screen for as long as the video was playing. A mirror which had been hung a few metres away enabled the measurement of the total duration of the time each child spent watching the TV. Whenever a child withdrew attention for five consecutive seconds, then a prompt (e.g. the verbal instruction 'watch the TV') was provided.
Social initiation	This has been defined elsewhere as 'approaching a person and giving or showing him or her an object, prompting someone to engage in an activity, pointing to or reaching toward an object, or verbalising one or more understandable words' (Krantz et al. 1993, p.137). In this study, social initiation was defined as each child approaching the researcher, emitting any video modelled verbal (e.g. 'Let's play') or gestural behaviour (e.g. taking him by the hand), establishing eye-contact, and leading him towards any toy to play with. Also, a social initiation was scored as being imitative whenever it was emitted within the first 25 seconds of entering the research room. This decision was determined by two factors: first, previous research has suggested that following a model's presentation, the imitative behaviour has to occur within about 10 seconds (Cooper 1987a), and second because 15 seconds had elapsed before the researcher sat on the chair and the model explored the room.
Appropriate play	This was defined as the time spent by each child playing with the researcher using any toy in the manner for which it was intended. Total duration and a 10-second partial interval recording systems were used to measure this behaviour.
Object engagement	Whenever a child engaged in isolated play with any toy laid on the floor a 10-second partial interval recording system was used to measure this object engagement behaviour.
Disruptive behaviours	A separate system (i.e. 10-second partial interval recording system) was used for measuring the time that children engaged in disruptive behaviours. These included self-injurious behaviour, stereotypic object manipulation, tantrums, hitting objects, shouting words in an inappropriate way.
Other behaviours	Any behaviour that could not be scored according to any of the above categories was defined as other behaviour (e.g. looking through the window, sitting on the table or floor without doing anything, stereotypic speech). Again, a 10-second partial interval recording system was used to measure the time spent engaged in this behaviour.

A total duration recording system is often used to measure the total amount of time an individual engages in the behaviours under investigation during a pre-determined period of time. Sometimes, though, interval recording is used to measure whether these behaviours of interest are just present or absent within specific time intervals. Hence, a 10-second partial interval recording system simply meant that the behaviours under investigation were recorded as simply present or absent at any time during the specified 10-second interval (Cooper 1987a).

Study 1

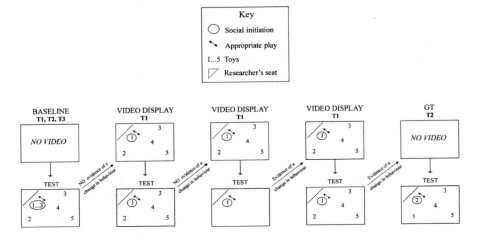

Figure 4.1: *Graphical presentation of the general procedure during baseline, video modelling intervention with the first toy and generalisation probe (GT) with the second toy for all children. The modelled toy in each condition was either T1, T2 or T3*

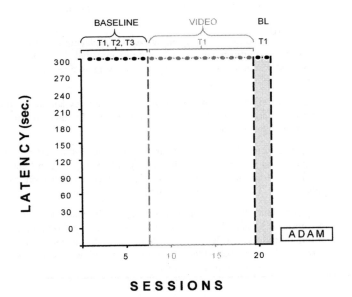

Figure 4.2: *Latency with which Adam emitted a social initiation towards the researcher during the two kinds of baselines. The modelled toy was either T1, T2 or T3. Shaded area indicates the condition when only one toy was present . Reproduced from C. Nikopoulus and M. Keenan (2 3) Promoting social initiation in children with autism using video modelling'. Behaviour Interventions Journal 18, 87 1 8, © 2 3 John iley   Sons Limited. Reproduced with permission*

researcher approached the chair to sit down. Both the researcher and the child remained in the room for five minutes unless the child emitted a social initiation, played with the researcher using any toy in an appropriate way, and completed that play in less time. Prior to the next session (trial) each child had a short break of five to eight minutes in an outside playground area. To keep the discussion simple, data will be presented in detail for only one child (i.e. Adam in this study), although reference may be made to some findings for the other children. A similar strategy has been adopted for all subsequent studies. Those interested can read the original papers where all the data are presented. Thus, Figure 4.2 shows the two kinds of baselines for Adam. During both baselines (i.e. sessions 1–7: all toys present, and sessions 20–21: one toy present), Adam did not emit a social initiation response with any of the toys. Specifically, during baseline sessions 35 per cent of intervals were occupied by object engagement and other behaviour occupied 63 per cent of intervals (see Figure 4.3).

Afterwards, children were required to view one of the three 35-second videotapes; in other words, the video modelling condition commenced. The only difference between these three videotapes was the fact that a different model was depicted in each of them. A typically developing peer acted as a model in the first videotape, an unfamiliar adult in the second videotape and a familiar adult in the third videotape. Some children viewed the first, some the second and some the third videotape. In each videotape, the researcher was shown entering the room with the toy(s) along with one of the models and going to sit on a chair. The model spent a few seconds wandering around the room and then approached the researcher, taking him by the hand saying, 'Let's play' and leading him to a particular toy which was closer to the researcher's seat. Afterwards the researcher and model played together with that toy for about 15 seconds (see Figure 4.4). The same videotaped scene was constructed across all five different toys; that is, while the scenario remained constant, the model played with the researcher with each of the five toys.

After the children had viewed the videotape, they were guided to the room shown in the video where the behaviour was assessed in the same way as it had been assessed in baseline. As in the baseline, there were two kinds of assessments following the video presentations: those with all toys present and those with only the modelled toy present (i.e. the toy viewed in the videotape). The main reason for having two kinds of baselines and therefore two kinds of assessments in the video modelling condition was to evaluate whether the presence of more than one toy in a play setting could affect the children's imitative performance (cf. Pierce, Glad and Schreibman 1997).

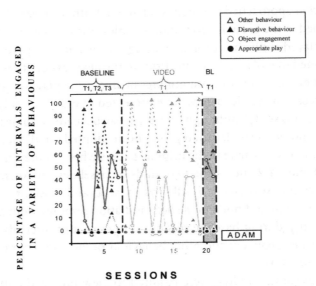

Figure 4.3: Percentage of 1 -second intervals of appropriate play, object engagement, disruptive and other behaviours for Adam during baseline conditions. The modelled toy was either T1, T2 or T3. Shaded area indicates the condition when only one toy was present

Figure 4.4: An example of a 35-second video display in which a familiar adult, a peer or an unfamiliar adult engaged in a simple social activity using a particular toy with the researcher

Within a maximum of five minutes each child was assessed as to whether he or she was able to emit a social initiation response and to engage in an appropriate play with the researcher within the first 25 seconds (see Figure 4.5). When this performance occurred in three consecutive sessions he or she was transferred to the next condition in which another toy was used. This criterion of emitting a social initiation response within the first 25 seconds and in three consecutive sessions, however, had to occur only when a child was assessed in the presence of all toys. On occasions wherein the criterion was met in the presence of only one toy (see Figure 4.6), an additional assessment with all the toys present was conducted before each child experienced that next condition. For Adam, when the video modelling procedure was initially implemented with a familiar adult as one of the two models and all toys present, he did not emit a social initiation after 12 sessions (see Figure 4.7). In the presence of only one toy, however, Adam met the criterion of performing the modelled behaviour during the first 25 seconds in 3 consecutive sessions within 10 sessions (Condition T2). Following a similar performance with all toys present (session 32), imitative responding did not occur when video modelling for the second toy was implemented (sessions 34–36: all toys present). However, successful responding now occurred at session 49, after Adam had experienced a condition with only the second modelled toy left in the room (sessions 37–48). When video modelling for the third modelled toy

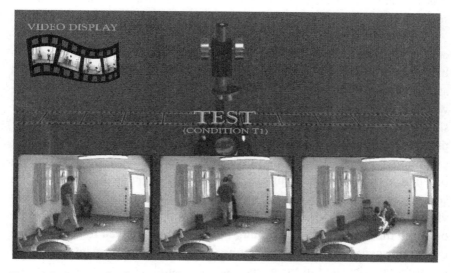

Figure 4.5: An example of a successful assessment test during Condition T1 (all toys present). As in the video, each child initially approached the researcher (first picture from the left), then emitted a social initiation by saying 'Let's play' and or taking him by the hand and establishing eye-contact (second picture), and finally led him towards any toy to play with (third picture)

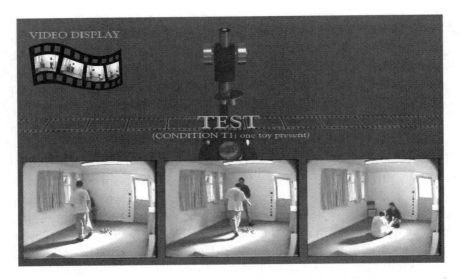

Figure 4.6: An example of a successful assessment test during Condition T1 (only one toy present). As in the video, each child initially approached the researcher (first picture from the left), then emitted a social initiation by saying 'Let's play' and or taking him by the hand and establishing eye-contact (second picture), and finally led him towards any toy to play with (third picture). This responding was followed by another assessment with all the toys present, before the child experienced the next condition

was implemented (sessions 51–54) the criterion was met within only 4 sessions (see Figure 4.8).

An important aspect of any behaviour analytic programme is the assessment for generalisation of the behaviour changes. That is, once an intervention has produced the desired changes in the target behaviour then an additional assessment takes place in the absence of the intervention to determine whether the behavioural change is permanent and generalises to other situations. In the current study, there were three kinds of generalisation assessments: across *toys* (GT), across *settings* (GS) and across *peers* (GP). With a few exceptions, all generalisation assessments were identical to those during baseline, in that there was no prior video presentation. First, the generalisation sessions across toys were conducted with toys that had not been previously viewed in the videotape by the children. Second, a different room from the one used during the video modelling training was employed for the sessions examining generalisation across settings. Third, another peer instead of the researcher participated in the generalisation sessions across peers. Follow-up measures were obtained after one and two months had elapsed since the last generalisation assessments. These follow-up assessments were exactly the

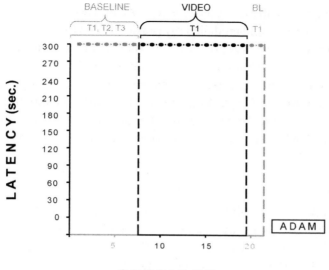

Figure 4.7: Latency with which Adam emitted a social initiation towards the researcher during the first implementation of video modelling with all toys present. 'Promoting social inititaion in children with autism using video modelling'. *Reproduced from C. Nikopoulus and M. Keenan (2 3) Promoting social initiation in children with autism using video modelling'.* Behaviour Interventions Journal 18, 87 1 8, © 2 3 John iley   Sons Limited. Reproduced with permission

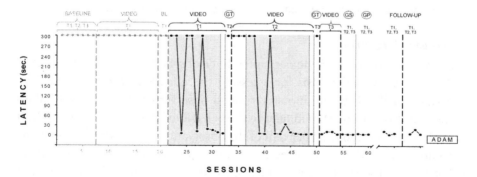

Figure 4.8: Latency with which Adam emitted a social initiation towards the researcher following the initial introduction of the video modelling condition in which only one toy was present. The modelled toy was either T1, T2 or T3. Shaded areas indicate those occasions when only one toy was present and GT, GS, and GP indicate the generalisation sessions across toys, settings and peers, respectively. Reproduced from C. Nikopoulus and M. Keenan (2 3) Promoting social initiation in children with autism using video modelling'. Behaviour Interventions Journal 18, 87 1 8, © 2 3 John iley   Sons Limited. Reproduced with permission

same as those during all the baseline sessions. Adam's responding did not generalise either to the second modelled toy (session 33: all toys present) or to the third toy (session 50: all toys present). Importantly, this performance generalised across settings (Condition GS: sessions 55–57) and across peers (Condition GP: sessions 58–60) and maintained after one and two-month follow-up periods (see Figure 4.8). Finally, it is worth mentioning that the percentages of intervals containing object engagement and other behaviour decreased, so that by about session 45 appropriate play predominated thereafter (see Figure 4.9).

Social validation

Broadly defined, social validation refers to the process of assessing whether treatment objectives, procedures and effects are important and acceptable to 'consumers' (Runco and Schreibman 1987). That is, the society or 'consumers' validate the social significance of the goals, the social appropriateness of the procedures and the social importance of the effects of any intervention (Wolf 1978). In this context, ten mothers of school-aged children participated in the social validation of the treatment outcome. These mothers were not familiar either with the children or with the purposes of the study; however, they had been provided with the definitions of the behaviours in interest. They watched videotaped vignettes depicting baseline and intervention sessions and they had to identify those scenes in which the child emitted a social initiation and afterwards played appropriately with the researcher. These vignettes were selected and presented in a random order.

Inter-observer agreement

As mentioned in the previous chapter, inter-observer agreement measures in ABA are used as the basis for assessing the quality of the obtained data, because of the difficulty in measuring an observer's accuracy in a standard way. Agreement data should refer to the behaviours in interest of any study. It is common that about 20 per cent of the observation sessions with at least one session per condition are assessed for inter-observer reliability. A minimum criterion for the acceptability of inter-observer agreement can be an average of at least 80 per cent agreement, or it can be as high as 90 per cent in case of measuring permanent products (e.g. videotapes) (Cooper 1987c). In this study, inter-observer agreement was assessed on 31 per cent of all observations. The second observer was naïve to the conditions of this study and he recorded data from at least one session for each child during each

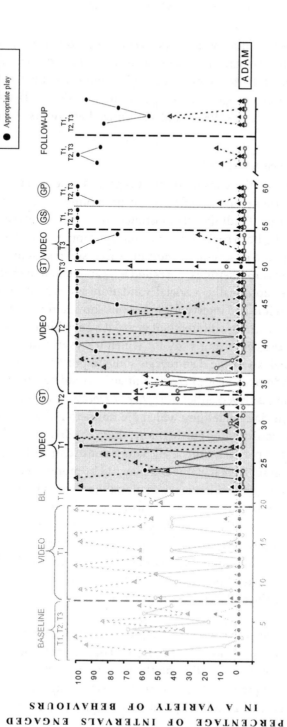

Figure 4.9: Percentage of 1-second intervals of appropriate play, object engagement, disruptive and other behaviours for Adam following the initial introduction of the condition in which only one toy was present. The modelled toy was either T1, T2 or T3 and shaded areas indicate those occasions when only one toy was present. GT, GS and GP indicate the generalisation sessions across toys, settings and peers, respectively

condition. Average reliability was 95 per cent (range 89–100%) across all children. Specifically, the percentage agreement across each behaviour respectively was: (1) Social initiation 100 per cent; (2) Appropriate play 97 per cent (92–99%); (3) Object engagement 94 per cent (90–97%); (4) Disruptive behaviours 93 per cent (89–98%) and (5) Other behaviours 93 per cent (91–96%).

4.2.7.2 FURTHER CONSIDERATIONS

The main objective of the current study was to examine whether a video modelling intervention could be effective in promoting social initiation in children with autism. Findings demonstrated that this intervention was effective in enhancing both social initiation and appropriate toy play for most of the children (four out of seven). In addition, successful responding in these children generalised across settings, peers and toys and maintained at one and two-months follow-up. Finally, a social validation assessment using video vignettes of the baseline and intervention sessions showed that mothers identified those scenes in which children had emitted a social initiation and had played with the researcher using a toy for which it was intended.

A thorough analysis of the data reveals some important issues. First, the failure of three children to engage in social initiation could be attributed to the fact that all of them displayed either *disruptive* or *other* behaviours most of the time throughout the day, something which did not permit them to watch the video presentation consistently. Furthermore, these children were non-verbal and did not engage in play activities at all. This is consistent with a suggestion that abnormalities in social behaviour and play can be more severe in children with autism with very limited language than in those who have some speech (Lord and Pickles 1996). However, the performance of these three children is instructive for the use of video modelling because it indicates that the likely success of this intervention is closely dependent upon the prior elimination of behaviours that interfere with the development of imitation skills. This suggestion is reinforced by the finding that almost all instances of social initiation and play emitted by the children were those that had been previously viewed on the videotape.

Second, it was noted that whenever appropriate play increased, children's competing behaviours reduced respectively. That is, behaviours such as isolated play with any toy, or sitting on the floor without doing anything in particular, or stereotypic speech or isolated object manipulation decreased substantially (i.e. near to zero levels) and were replaced by appropriate play.

Third, it became evident that social initiation was more likely to occur when a single stimulus – only one toy – was present. That is, with the video display remaining the same – all toys depicted – across all conditions, the target behaviour was initially reached in the presence of a single toy. A possible explanation of this finding could be that a play environment with more than one toy distracted the children from discriminating the required modelled actions (cf. Pierce *et al.* 1997).

Finally, it is not that clear to what extent the selected play materials per se influenced the target behaviour. For example, three out of four children spent only a short period of time playing with the trampoline, probably due to its physical strength demands. In addition, we do not know whether the presence of an adult (i.e. researcher) during the training conditions influenced the target behaviour even though this behaviour generalised across other peers.

4.2.7.3 RECAP

Children were taken to one room to view a 35-second video of one of three models, either a familiar adult, a peer or an unfamiliar adult, engaged in a simple activity using a particular toy with the researcher. After the model had emitted a social initiation, he or she played with the researcher using a toy, which was varied across conditions, for about 15 seconds. Then, each child was taken into the research room (the same room as that shown in the video) while the researcher engaged in the same behaviour as shown in the video. Within a maximum of five minutes each child was assessed as to whether he or she was able to emit a social initiation response and engage in an appropriate play with the researcher within the first 25 seconds. When this performance occurred in three consecutive sessions he or she was transferred to the next condition in which another toy was used. However, if this criterion was met when only one toy was present, another assessment with all the toys present was conducted, before each child experienced that next condition.

4.2.8 Study 2: Generalisation of social initiation and reciprocal play in a simplified play context[3]

Results of Study 1 revealed an important finding; social initiation was more likely to occur when a single stimulus (i.e. a toy) was present. In that study, the children viewed a short videotaped scene depicting the setting in which,

---

3   Extensive analysis and description of this study appear in Nikopoulos and Keenan (2004b).

afterwards, they would be assessed for imitating the modelled actions. Thus, the same setting was used both for the video recording and the subsequent assessment. Also, the children viewed the modelled scene recorded from the same corner as they would be expected to in reality. That is, if someone wanted to examine the video recording of the modelled actions and the video recording of a child successfully imitated those modelled actions, then he or she would notice that the only difference in the latter videotape would be the presence of a child instead of a model. In light of the above, a reasonable research question is: Could video modelling be effective in promoting social initiation and reciprocal play when specific components of the video (e.g. angle) were different? Similarly: Could video modelling be effective when the setting in which the video was first viewed was different from the setting in which it was tested?

We have already seen that another defining characteristic of autism is the presence of inappropriate play. This has led to the development of play-based curricula and intervention strategies to teach play skills to children with autism (Sigafoos, Roberts-Pennell and Graves 1999). Also, it has been well documented that the behaviour gains obtained by children with autism often do not generalise in the absence of training, especially when it is based on traditional prompting and reinforcement procedures (e.g. Charlop-Christy et al. 2000; Lovaas, Koegel and Schreibman 1979; McGee, Krantz and McClannahan 1985).

To summarise, the present study was designed to examine whether success with one toy using video modelling could increase the probability of success with new toys in the absence of video; whether alteration of video display components (e.g. angle, environment etc.) could influence the effectiveness of video modelling and finally whether increases in reciprocal play are facilitated when social initiation occurs.

4.2.8.1 METHODOLOGY

Two boys and a girl, ages 7.5, 8.5 and 10.5 years, participated in this study. They all met the DSM-IV criteria for autism (American Psychiatric Association 1994) and their scores on the CARS were 33.5, 36.5 and 36.5 points respectively; all were within the mild-moderate range of autism.

Features of their *expressive language skills* could be summarised as echolalic speech, some incomplete sentences and verbalising of actions while interacting with objects, though all of the children were able to follow simple and familiar instructions rather well. As for their *play skills* with toys, two of the children lacked interest in toys and preferred solitary activities while the third child spent most of his spare time in 'reading' rather than playing with toys or engaging in social games. *Socially,* they performed limited interactions with other children and there were marked impairments in the use of non-verbal behaviours. On the other hand, their interaction with adults was more advanced, though mainly in the form of compliance. Other aspects of these children's behaviours included limited concentration span, occasional extremely active behaviour, non-functional routines or rituals, a persistent desire to follow set patterns of behaviour as well as repetitive and stereotyped patterns of behaviour.

Three different rooms at the children's school were used; the room shown in the videotape, the research room and the generalisation room. All rooms were like typical classrooms with all the relevant stimuli present along with a few toys, apart from some heavy furniture, which could obscure children's movements. These toys were easy to use and included a wooden train, a ball, a game involving plastic frogs being made to 'eat' coloured balls, a set of tambourines and a trampoline. Finally, a 17-inch television and a chair had been located in an arranged area outside of the research room for the children's videotape viewing.

All sessions were videotaped for a later in-detail analysis of the data collection regarding video watching, social initiation, reciprocal play, object engagement and other behaviours (see Table 4.1 for operational definitions of these behaviours and how they were recorded).

A multiple baseline across participants design was used for the three children. The general procedure during baseline, video modelling and generalisation conditions is depicted in Figure 4.10. During baseline sessions (Condition T1–5), both the researcher and the child entered the research room without previously viewing any videos. The researcher then sat on a chair while one of the five toys had already been placed near his chair. Each child was assessed in the presence of each of the five toys at least once while these were randomly alternated across sessions. The termination of each baseline session was determined by two factors: either after a maximum of five minutes had elapsed or after a child had emitted a social initiation response and played with the researcher using the toy near the chair in less time.

When a steady trend had been established across a number of baseline sessions, then video modelling was implemented. This type of trend can be seen in Figure 4.11, where baseline data for social initiation and total time engaged in reciprocal play with each toy have been plotted for one child (Sheryl). Sheryl did not emit a social initiation and neither did she play with

Study 2

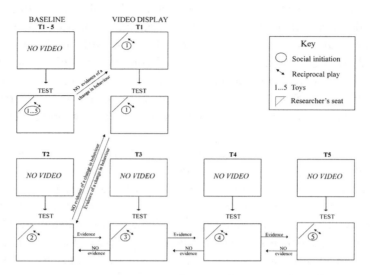

Figure 4.1 : Graphical presentation of the general procedure during baseline, video modelling intervention and generalisation across toys for all children

the researcher using any of the toys. In the video modelling condition, children were initially directed to sit and watch the 30-second videotape. In that video, a model (a typically developing peer) was shown to engage in a simple social play with the researcher using a specific toy (i.e. the frog game; see Figure 4.12).

Afterwards the children were taken into the research room. In that room, the same toy as shown in the videotape (i.e. the frog game) had been placed in the same location as in the video. Importantly, the researcher's behaviour remained similar to that at baseline and also there was no reference to the video or to the behaviour engaged in at any time. Rather, he only responded to initiations and did not provide any prompts to try to get the child to continue playing. When a child succeeded in emitting a social initiation and playing with the researcher within the first 15 seconds in three consecutive sessions (see Figure 4.13), he or she was transferred to the next condition in which another toy was used. For example, data for Sheryl revealed that she emitted a social initiation within the first five seconds of each session and played with the researcher for the rest of the session (approximately 295 seconds; see Figure 4.14). Consequently, she experienced condition T2.

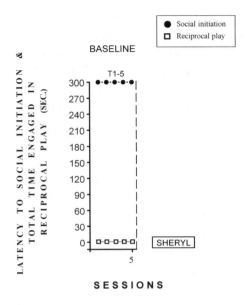

Figure 4.11: Latency with which Sheryl emitted a social initiation towards the researcher as well as the total time engaged in reciprocal play during baseline. Reproduced from C. Nikopoulos and M. Keenan (2 4) Effects of video modelling on training and generalisation of social initiation and reciprocal play by children with autism'. European Journal of Behavior Analysis 5, *1 13. Reproduced by permission of Norwegian Association for Behavior Analysis*

Figure 4.12. An example of a 3 -second video display in which a peer engaged in a simple social activity with the researcher in the presence of one particular toy each time

However, if a child failed to emit a social initiation within the specified time (15 seconds) in three consecutive sessions, then he or she experienced the preceding condition. While that child's performance in the previous condition was successful, it would be anticipated that this additional practice would facilitate a successful responding in the condition that the above criterion failed to be met. This procedure of transferring a child from one condition to another remained in place until he or she was assessed with the fifth consecutive toy in Condition T5.

The effectiveness of video modelling was further evaluated through *generalisation* assessments across toys, settings and peers. Thus, after children had experienced the only video modelling condition (Condition T1), they were assessed to see whether their successful imitative performance (i.e. social initiation and reciprocal play) could generalise across other *toys*. Specifically, four different toys were used, each one in a different condition. The order of the toys across children varied. That is, in Condition T2 a child was assessed either in the presence of a ball or a set of tambourines or a trampoline or in the presence of a train (see Figure 4.15). These conditions were exactly the same as in the baseline as children had not viewed any video prior to these assessments. As in Condition T1, similar results were obtained during Condition T2 in which Sheryl emitted a social initiation and played with the researcher using another toy (a ball) in the absence of any prior video display (see Figure 4.16). During the next condition (i.e. T3), however, responding did not initially generalise to a different toy (tambourines). When Sheryl experienced a return to the preceding condition (Condition T2) just once, the criterion performance was met during Condition T3 within the minimum three sessions. Thereafter, Sheryl's social initiation response remained at very low levels using either the trampoline or the wooden train. In addition, the total time engaged in reciprocal play was near a mean of 292 seconds whenever a social initiation had been emitted (see Figure 4.17).

Next, during generalisation across *settings* (GS) each child was assessed across all toys, but in a different room. In essence, this condition was also exactly the same as baseline as it occurred in the absence of any video display. Afterwards, in the sessions examining generalisation across *peers* (GP) each child was assessed across all of the five toys as in baseline, though a different researcher participated. Finally, follow-up measures were obtained one and three months after the final measurements had been taken. Each child was assessed across all five toys once in the same setting as the one used during all the baseline sessions. Again, successful imitative responding for Sheryl using all five toys

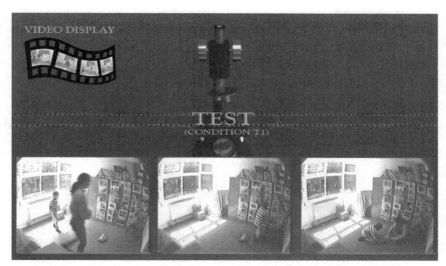

Figure 4.13: An example of a successful assessment test during Condition T1. As in the video, initially each child entered the room (first picture from the left), then he or she approached the researcher, emitted a social initiation by saying 'Let's play' and or taking him by the hand and establishing eye-contact (second picture), and finally led him towards any toy to play with (third picture)

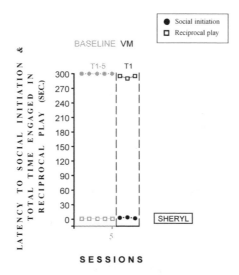

Figure 4.14: Latency with which Sheryl emitted a social initiation towards the researcher as well as the total time engaged in reciprocal play during the video modelling condition. Reproduced from C. Nikopoulos and M. Keenan (2 4) Effects of video modelling on training and generalisation of social initiation and reciprocal play by children with autism'. European Journal of Behavior Analysis 5, 1 13. *Reproduced by permission of Norwegian Association for Behavior Analysis*

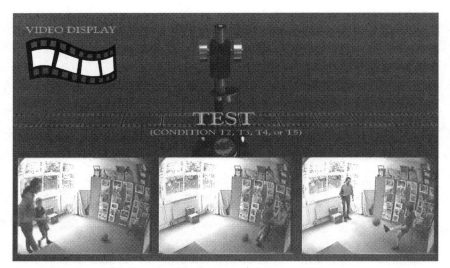

Figure 4.15: An example of a successful assessment test during Conditions T2, T3, T4 or T5. In the absence of any prior video display, initially each child entered the room (first picture from the left), then he or she approached the researcher, emitted a social initiation by saying 'Let's play' and or taking him by the hand and establishing eye-contact (second picture), and finally led him towards any toy to play with (third picture)

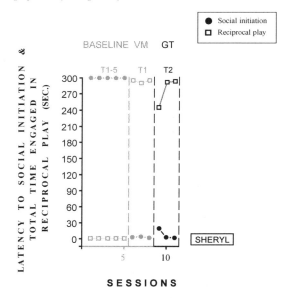

Figure 4.16: Latency with which Sheryl emitted a social initiation towards the researcher as well as the total time engaged in reciprocal play during the first generalisation across toys condition (GT). Reproduced from C. Nikopoulos and M. Keenan (2 4) Effects of video modelling on training and generalisation of social inititation and reciprocal play by children with autism'. European Journal of Behavior Analysis 5, 1 13. Reproduced by permission of Norwegian Association for Behavior Analysis

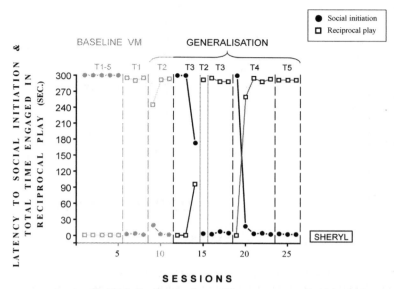

Figure 4.17: Latency with which Sheryl emitted a social initiation towards the researcher as well as the total time engaged in reciprocal play during the remaining generalisation across toys conditions (GT). The toy used in each of them is referred to as T2, T3, T4 or T5

generalised across settings (GS) and across peers (GP), and it maintained at one-month and two-month follow-up periods (see Figure 4.18).

4.2.8.2 FURTHER CONSIDERATIONS

Despite the concerns about whether or not individuals with autism display impairments in imitation skills (e.g. Harris and Weiss 1998; Hobson and Lee 1999; Jordan and Powell 1995), it appeared that video modelling as a treatment strengthened those imitation skills for all three children. That is, all children's imitative responding of emitting a social initiation and engaging in reciprocal toy play enhanced following a short video presentation. More importantly, video modelling promoted the generalisation of successful responding across four other different toys, settings and peers and maintained at one and three-month follow-up in the absence of a video display or any other kind of prompting.

Social validity of the study was obtained from eight school-aged children who watched videotaped vignettes of baseline and intervention sessions, and who were asked to identify the children with whom they would be more likely to play. These school-aged children picked those scenes where the children played with the researcher (i.e. the intervention sessions).

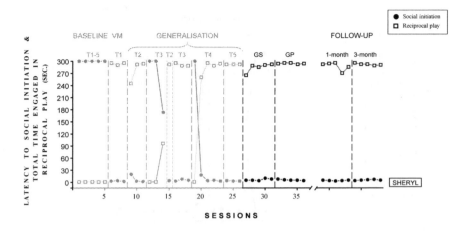

Figure 4.18: Latency with which Sheryl emitted a social initiation towards the researcher and the peer as well as the total time engaged in reciprocal play across generalisation across setting (GS) and peers (GP). Data for the two follow-up assessments are also depicted. Reproduced from C. Nikopoulos and M. Keenan (2 4) Effects of video modelling on training and generalisation of social inititation and reciprocal play by children with autism'. European Journal of Behavior Analysis 5, 1 13. *Reproduced by permission of Norwegian Association for Behavior Analysis*

The effectiveness of the video modelling procedures was further validated through an inter-observer agreement assessment, which was carried out for all the four dependent measurements in about 43 per cent of sessions across all conditions. Specifically, total inter-observer reliability was 97 per cent (range, 92–100%) and the percentage agreement across each depended measurement respectively was: (1) Social initiation 100 per cent; (2) Reciprocal play 98 per cent (93–100%); (3) Object engagement 96 per cent (92–99%); (4) Other behaviours 94 per cent (92–97%).

Although the impact of video-based modelling on generalised behaviour change has rarely been examined (Reamer *et al.* 1998), here successful responding of the children generalised across stimuli (i.e. toys), settings and peers following only three video modelling sessions in Condition T1. This generalised responding could probably be attributed to two factors. First, the imitation of the modelled behaviour (i.e. social initiation and play) had been reinforced by playing which increased the likelihood of a similar behaviour occurring in the future under similar environmental contingencies (e.g. a room, a toy, a video display, people etc.). Second, the use of a medium such as a video which permits all the important elements (i.e. toy, model and researcher) to be captured close enough together in terms of the two-dimensional TV screen might have helped in the discrimination of the modelled behaviour.

Finally, two important issues from the previous study were further verified here. That is, social initiation was more likely to be imitated in the presence of a single stimulus (i.e. only one toy) and also all the competing behaviours reduced substantially as soon as social initiation and reciprocal play occurred for all children.

4.2.8.3 RECAP

Children were required to view a 30-second video of a typically developing peer engaged in a simple activity using a particular toy with the researcher for about 15 seconds. After watching this video sequence once, each child was taken into the research room (different from the one displayed in the video) by the researcher and experienced Condition T1. When a child succeeded in emitting a social initiation response within the first 25 seconds in three consecutive sessions during that condition then he or she was transferred to the next one. Subsequent conditions (T2, T3, T4 and T5) were exactly the same as Condition T1 except that no video was displayed and a different toy was used in each condition. The criterion for each child to be transferred from one condition to another was to emit a social initiation response in three consecutive sessions until he or she was assessed with the fifth toy in a row in Condition T5.

4.2.9 Study 3: Training of social initiation and reciprocal play

The successes reported in Studies 1 and 2 could have been influenced by the location of the modelled toy near the researcher's seat. Thus, a possible question that needs to be addressed is: What would happen if the location of the toys shown in the video was different from the location of the toys during testing in the research setting?

It has been documented that when a context controls a specific behaviour, that control is unlikely to be exerted by the situation as a whole. Instead, certain stimuli present in the situation may be responsible for that control. But often it is difficult to identify those contingencies that exert control over a specific behaviour (Weatherly, Miller and McDonald 1999). To complicate matters, we must bear in mind that individuals with autism also engage in stimulus overselectivity (Lovaas and Koegel 1979; Lovaas et al. 1971; Schreibman and Lovaas 1973). Overselectivity has been used to describe a restricted stimulus control during the acquisition of responding to complex stimuli (Rincover and Ducharme 1987). For example, if a child is being taught how to discriminate a fork from a spoon he or she may focus on the colour (a very salient aspect) rather than the shape of each. Hence, he or she may experience much difficulty when trying, in real life, to decide which utensil to use. Consequently, Study 3 was especially designed to investigate whether the location of the stimuli would affect children's responding.

4.2.9.1 METHODOLOGY

One child (i.e. Victor) who was attending a school for learning and developmental disabilities and had been diagnosed with autism by outside agencies participated in this study. Victor was an 11-year-old boy with some speech mainly in the form of one or two-word responses to simple questions. According to the CARS he was classified within the severe range of autism, having scored a total of 38 points. He rarely interacted with other children or developed peer relationships, and if he interacted with adults at all it was mainly in the form of compliance. Victor displayed very little play skills as most of the time his general behaviour was extremely passive and he engaged in nothing in particular. Other aspects of his behaviour included lack of eye-contact, limited concentration span, impairments in the use of non-verbal behaviours and lack of spontaneous seeking to share enjoyment or interests.

Across a number of conditions, his performance was measured with respect to video watching, social initiation, reciprocal play, object engagement and other behaviours (see Table 4.1 for operational definitions). In reversal research designs (e.g. ABA) (see Chapter 3 for the respective description), the intervention is withdrawn in order to reinstate the baseline conditions. However, there are occasions when either the behaviour change is permanent (e.g. when teaching a skill) or when withdrawing the intervention is undesirable or even unethical. Consequently, for the purposes of the current study an AB design was used for assessing the effectiveness of video modelling on social behaviour. Importantly, the administration of this design was done in such a way that it obtained the essential properties (e.g. verification and replication)[4] of a reversal or a multiple baseline design; cause-effect relationships were identified through an extensive evaluation of video modelling across a number of intervention assessments.

---

4   Verification is achieved when it can be demonstrated that the responses in the baseline would have remained unaffected had the independent variable (e.g. a treatment procedure) not been introduced. On the other hand, when the independent variable produces changes in the baseline responding then *replication* requires a repeated demonstration of these changes contingent upon further manipulations of this independent variable (Heward 1987).

Data for baseline, intervention and generalisation sessions across another child were collected in the research room, while data for generalisation across settings were collected in the generalisation room. Figure 4.19 shows the general procedure during baseline and video modelling conditions with the first toy. In addition, all baseline and generalisation sessions were conducted in the absence of any video presentations. Specifically, at the beginning of each baseline session (Condition T1–3a,b,c,d) the researcher guided the child (i.e. Victor) into the research room and he approached the chair to sit down. One of the three toys had been already located either 1.5 metres away from the chair (i.e. as shown in the video) or near the corners of the room. All three toys were used in either locations and hence Victor experienced a total of six sessions during the baseline assessment. Victor, however, did not meet criterion with any of the toys independently of their location. In this condition other behaviours occupied all the intervals with no sign of object engagement or reciprocal play at all (see Figures 4.20 and 4.21).

Since a stable trend of the data had been identified after the completion of these baseline sessions, a video modelling procedure was introduced. At first, the Victor was required to watch a 30-second videotape. The videotape presented a typically developing child (model) and the researcher engaging in a simple toy play, after the former had emitted a social initiation towards the latter (see Figure 4.22).

Study 3

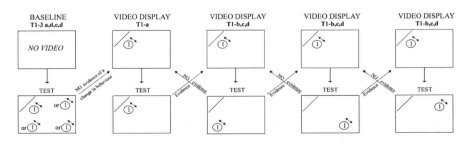

Figure 4.19: Graphical presentation of the general procedure during baseline and video modelling intervention with the first toy for Victor

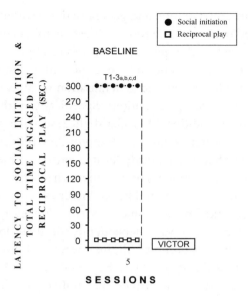

Figure 4.2 : Latency with which Victor emitted a social initiation towards the researcher as well as the total time engaged in reciprocal play during the baseline

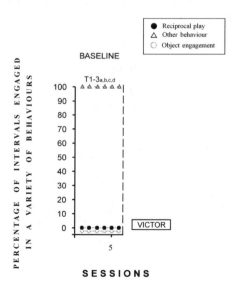

Figure 4.21: Percentage of 1 -second intervals of reciprocal play, object engagement and other behaviours for Victor during baseline

Figure 4.22: An example of a 3 -second video display in which a peer engaged in a simple social activity with the researcher in the presence of one particular toy on each occasion

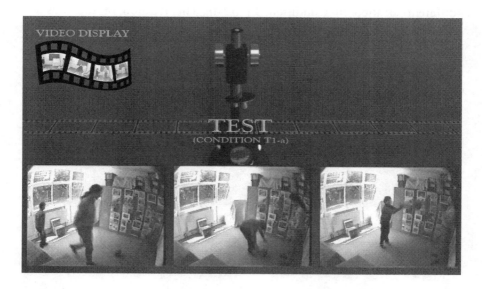

Figure 4.23: An example of a successful assessment test during Condition T1-a. Victor initially entered the room (first picture from the left), then emitted a social initiation towards the researcher by saying Let's play' (second picture), and finally played with him using the modelled toy, which was placed in the same location as in the video (third picture)

Across a number of conditions the same video was used but on each occasion a different toy was used. However, the location of each toy (1.5 metres away from the researcher's seat) remained constant in all videos. Following the video presentation, both the child and the researcher entered the research room and the assessment was conducted in the same way as in baseline. Importantly, the researcher did not mention anything concerning the video, nor did he give any instructions to the child about the behaviour required.

The toy used during all conditions was the respective toy presented in the video, which in Conditions T1-a, T2-a and T3-a was laid in the same location (see Figure 4.23 as an example of Condition T1-a). During Conditions T1-b,c,d, T2-b,c,d, and T3-b,c,d the location of the toy was varied. That is, in each of these conditions the toy had been placed in a different location on the floor of the room. In this way, the child viewed a video depicting a toy near the researcher's seat and then he detected the same toy in a different location. Thus, as there were at least three sessions in each of these conditions (i.e. T1-b,c,d, T2-b,c,d and T3-b,c,d), the child was assessed while the toy had been located in three different places (see Figure 4.24 as an example of one different location in Condition T1-b,c,d). The location of the toys was randomly varied across sessions and conditions to control for order effects.

Figure 4.24: An example of a successful assessment test during Condition T1-b,c,d. Victor initially entered the room (first picture from the left), then emitted a social initiation towards the researcher by saying 'Let's play' (second picture), and finally played with him using the modelled toy (third picture), which was placed in a different location to that shown in the video

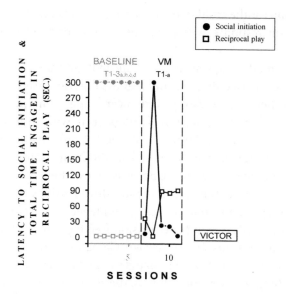

Figure 4.25: Latency with which Victor emitted a social initiation towards the researcher as well as the total time engaged in reciprocal play during the first video modelling condition in which the modelled toy was placed in the same location as shown in the video

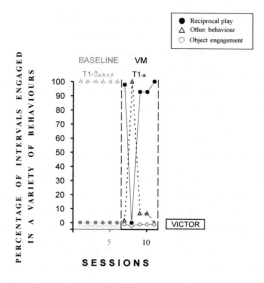

Figure 4.26: Percentage of 1-second intervals of reciprocal play, object engagement and other behaviours for Victor during the first video modelling condition in which the modelled toy was placed in the same location as shown in the video

Also, the criterion for the child to be transferred across conditions was to emit a social initiation response within the first 25 seconds in three consecutive sessions.

When video modelling was first introduced (Condition T1-a), latency to social initiation decreased dramatically and the criterion was met within five sessions. Other behaviours dropped to near 5 per cent per session and reciprocal play predominated at a level of 95 per cent with an average of about 75 seconds per session (see Figures 4.25 and 4.26). Similar results were obtained when the toy had been placed in different locations (Condition T1-b,c,d), wherein criterion performance was met within six sessions. Thereafter, criterion was met within the minimum three sessions across all conditions, with an exception in Condition T2-a, while reciprocal play increased to an average of about 102 seconds per session (see Figures 4.27 and 4.28).

Generalisation sessions across *settings* (GS) and across *peers* (GP) were conducted to ensure that the child's changes in behaviour would persist after the video modelling intervention. Thus, in the absence of any video presentation the procedures in generalisation across settings and peers were exactly the same as in baseline. However, a different room and a different peer were employed in each respective condition. Likewise, the two follow-up measures (i.e. one and two-month) were conducted identically to the baseline sessions, though in the research room. Importantly, during generalisation across settings and peers as well as after one and two-month follow-up periods, Victor's performance remained at the same levels as during video modelling conditions. That is, latency to social initiation was set at a level of about 15 seconds and reciprocal play at an average of approximately 132 seconds per session (see Figures 4.27 and 4.28).

4.2.9.2 FURTHER CONSIDERATIONS

Data from this study demonstrated that video modelling could be effective in promoting social initiation and reciprocal play when a single stimulus (i.e. one toy) was present, independently of the differences between the settings and the location of the stimuli in the video and *in vivo*. In terms of other concurrent behaviours, data revealed that all the competing behaviours reduced substantially as soon as social initiation and reciprocal play occurred. The accuracy of these results was assessed through an inter-observer reliability assessment. Average levels of reliability were as high as 96 per cent (range, 93–100%). In addition, successful responding generalised across settings and peers and these results were maintained at one and two-month follow-up. Furthermore, the results of the social validity assessment showed that eight

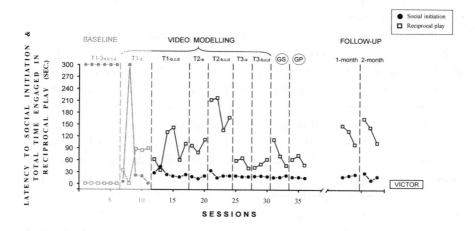

Figure 4.27: Latency with which Victor emitted a social initiation towards the researcher as well as the total time engaged in reciprocal play across all remaining video modelling, generalisation and follow-up conditions. GS and GP indicate the generalisation sessions across settings and peers respectively

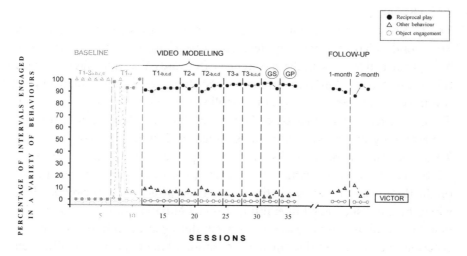

Figure 4.28: Percentage of 1-second intervals of reciprocal play, object engagement and other behaviours for Victor across all remaining video modelling, generalisation and follow-up conditions. GS and GP indicate the generalisation sessions across settings and peers, respectively

typically developing school-aged children would play with the child as he behaved (i.e. playing reciprocally with the researcher) during the video modelling conditions.

It has been suggested that the transfer of stimulus control probably requires the manipulation of antecedent conditions by introducing an alternative stimulus, which may result in the occurrence of a desired response and increased reinforcement (Taber *et al.* 1999). In the current study, the child's successful responding initially was under the control of the video display (antecedent). Thereafter, this successful responding remained even during the assessments wherein the modelled toys were laid in a different location (i.e. Conditions T1-b,c,d, T2-b,c,d and T3-b,c,d) as well as during all generalisation assessments (video was not present). No alternative stimulus was added to the video display. Instead, the only requirements for that child to emit a social initiation and afterwards to play with another person (i.e. researcher and generalisation peer) were the presence of one toy in any location and an initial short training using a videotape showing a social interaction between two models. This was a significant finding for using a video display in a treatment session since children with autism may engage in overselectivity in their responses to complex stimuli and their behaviour tends to be under restricted stimulus control (e.g. Lovaas and Koegel 1979).

4.2.9.3 RECAP

The first step of the video modelling procedure was for the child to view a 30-second video of a typically developing peer engaged in reciprocal play using a particular toy with the researcher. Afterwards, the child was taken into the research room (different from the one displayed in the video) by the researcher and experienced one of the following conditions; T1-a/T1-b,c,d, T2-a/T2-b,c,d or T3-a/T3-b,c,d. The toy used during all conditions was the respective toy presented in the video, which in Conditions T1-a, T2-a and T3-a was laid in the same location, as opposed to Conditions T1-b,c,d, T2-b,c,d and T3-b,c,d in which the respective toy was laid in different places on the floor from that shown in the video. As occurred in all previous studies, when the child succeeded in emitting a social initiation response within the first 25 seconds in three consecutive sessions during any condition, he met the criterion to be transferred to the next condition in the sequence. Finally, each session was terminated when the child had emitted a social initiation and had completed playing (i.e. by saying 'stop' or 'finish' or walking away from the toy) with the researcher. However, if the child had not engaged in reciprocal play, then the session ended after five minutes had elapsed.

4.2.1 Study 4: Construction of a prolonged activity schedule [5]

A major finding of Study 2 was that the target behaviours (i.e. social initiation and reciprocal play) generalised across four other different toys in the absence of video display, while there was only one stimulus (i.e. one toy) present in the research room. That is, without children previously watching any video, they were assessed as to whether they emitted a social initiation and afterwards played with the researcher using the only toy available (which was varied across sessions) within the time limits of one session. Each session terminated whenever play with each respective toy had been completed. Therefore, the next logical step would be the design of an intervention that would promote generalisation of these two behaviours (social initiation and reciprocal play) across other different toys without the session being terminated. In other words, would children emit numerous social initiations to play with the researcher (i.e. a sequence of behaviours) using a variety of toys that are available in the room in one session? This possibility would set up the ground of designing a prolonged activity schedule using short video clips.

Results of the first study, however, showed that most of the children experienced difficulties in imitating the model's behaviours while in a setting with a variety of toys available (i.e. multiple stimuli). In that study, these difficulties were overcome when the research setting was adapted in terms of presenting one stimulus at a time. This manipulation, though, would not facilitate the establishment of a prolonged activity schedule as only one toy would be available each time. Potentially, an alternative route for promoting children's imitative responses in an environment with a variety of toys would be to simplify the video display by reducing the number of behavioural components depicted in it. Consequently, the current study was designed to examine whether a video modelling intervention can be effective in building a sequence of behaviours in settings with multiple stimuli (i.e. a variety of toys) by simplifying the components of the video display but still using the same unit of two behaviours, social initiation and play. This study attempted also to replicate a previous finding showing that components (i.e. angle, environment etc.) could be altered without diminishing the effectiveness of video modelling.

---

5   Extensive analysis and description of this study appear in Nikopoulos and Keenan (2004a).

4.2.10.1 METHODOLOGY

Three boys with autism (one of them had also been diagnosed with Attention Deficit Hyperactivity Disorder) aged 7, 8.5 and 9 years old, who were attending a school for learning and developmental disabilities, participated in the current study. Their scores on CARS were within the range of mild-moderate autism, having a total of 31, 32 and 35.5 points, respectively.

In terms of their *language* skills, all children were verbal, though quite often their speech was either out of context or directed to themselves. However, they responded to simple everyday instructions relatively well. They displayed limited interest in toys, demonstrating rather limited *play* skills. In the *social* domain, all children had difficulties in developing any peer relationships appropriate to their developmental level and their interaction with adults was mainly in the form of compliance. Finally, stereotyped and restricted patterns of interest such as preoccupation with parts of objects, set patterns of behaviour and interaction, or limited concentration span were some other aspects of these children's behaviours.

Figure 4.29 depicts a graphical presentation of the procedure of this study. A multiple baseline design across the three children was used and data were collected for three main responses: video watching, social initiation and reciprocal play (see Table 4.1).

Initially, during the baseline sessions (Condition T1–5) both the child and the researcher entered the research setting in which the five toys had already been placed on the floor in the same manner as would later be shown in the video. However, there was at least one session in which each of the toys had been placed near the researcher's seat. Each session was terminated when either a child had completed playing (i.e. by saying 'stop' or 'finish' or walking away from the toy) or after a maximum of five minutes, whichever occurred first. Representative data for one child (i.e. Matthew; the second child in the sequence of the design) are depicted in Figure 4.30. During baseline there were no recorded instances of social initiation for Matthew after nine sessions.

Once a stable trend had been established in baseline, the video modelling intervention (Condition T1-a) was implemented for the first child (i.e. Ian); both the other two children remained in baseline. Initially, Ian viewed the 35-second videotape once, in which a typically developing peer (the model) was shown emitting a social initiation and then playing on the trampoline (the modelled toy) with the researcher for about 15 seconds (see Figure 4.31). Then he was taken into the room containing the toys as in the video and experienced Condition T1-a (see Figure 4.32). When Ian succeeded in emitting a

Study 4

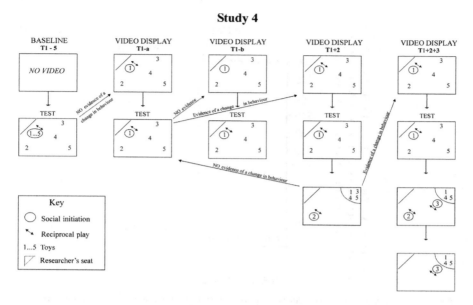

Figure 4.29: Graphical presentation of the general procedure during baseline and video modelling intervention for all children

social initiation response within the first 25 seconds in three consecutive sessions – a stable trend of the data was established – he was transferred to the next condition (Condition T1+2). However, if he failed to meet this criterion, Condition T1-b was introduced. In this condition, he was required to watch a simplified version of the videotape before being assessed. That is, the part of the tape showing the model playing with the researcher was erased leaving only the scene in which the model emitted a social initiation to the researcher (see Figure 4.33). Here, if a stable trend was identified, then he experienced Condition T1+2. In the meantime, video modelling (Condition T1-a: full version of the videotape) was introduced for the second child, Matthew. Social initiation for Matthew did not occur in the first three sessions after exposure to the video (Condition T1-a). When Condition T1-b was introduced (i.e. the simplified video presentation) latencies to social initiation decreased across trials using the modelled toy (trampoline). The time engaged in reciprocal play varied between 45–100 seconds (see Figure 4.34).

In Condition T1+2, when Ian (the first child) had completed playing with the researcher using the modelled toy (the trampoline as in Conditions T1-a or T1-b), the researcher removed that toy along with three others (i.e. tambourines, the frog game and wooden train) and he returned to his chair.

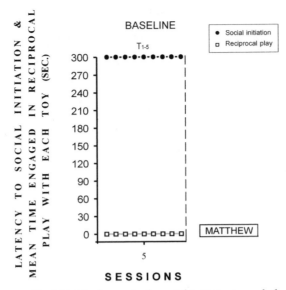

Figure 4.3 : Latency with which Matthew emitted a social initiation towards the researcher and the mean time engaged in reciprocal play with each toy during baseline. Reproduced from C. Nikopoulos and M. Keenan (2 4) Effects of video modelling on social initiations by children with autism'. Journal of Applied Behavior Analysis 37, *93 96. Reproduced by permission of the Society for the Experimental Analysis of Behavior, Inc.*

Figure 4.31: An example of a 35-second video display in which a peer engaged in a simple social activity using a particular toy with the researcher

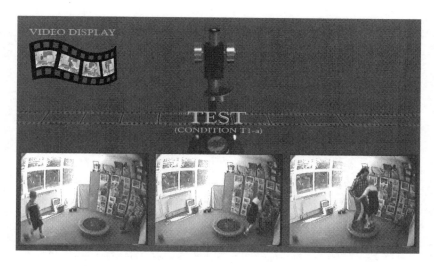

Figure 4.32: An example of a successful assessment test during Condition T1-a. As in the video, each child initially approached the researcher (first picture from the left), then emitted a social initiation by saying 'Let's play' and or taking him by the hand and establishing eye-contact (second picture), and finally led him towards any toy to play with (third picture)

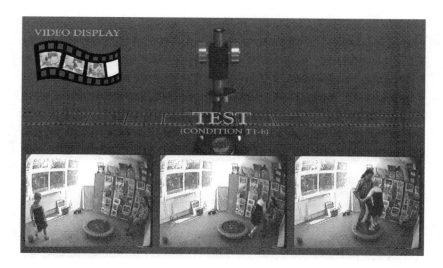

Figure 4.33: An example of an assessment test during Condition T1-b. Following a video display of a peer emitting a social initiation only, each child initially approached the researcher (first picture from the left), then emitted a social initiation (second picture), and finally led him towards any toy to play with (third picture)

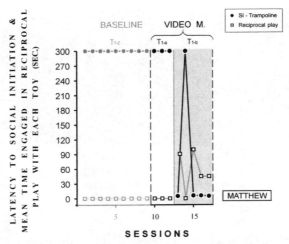

Figure 4.34: Latency to social initiation (SI) towards the researcher for Matthew as well as the mean time engaged in reciprocal play with each toy during the first video modelling condition. Shaded area indicates those occasions in which he viewed the simplified video presentation. Reproduced from C. Nikopoulos and M. Keenan (2 4) Effects of video modelling on social initiations by children with autism'. Journal of Applied Behavior Analysis 37, 93 96. *Reproduced by permission of the Society for the Experimental Analysis of Behavior, Inc.*

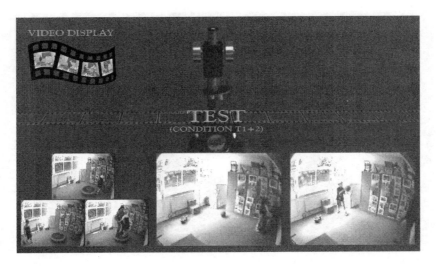

Figure 4.35: An example of a successful assessment test during Condition T1 2. As in the video, each child initially approached the researcher (first picture at the bottom left of the cluster), then emitted a social initiation (top picture in the cluster), and led him towards any toy to play with (third picture at the bottom right of the cluster). Afterwards, he emitted another social initiation (large centre picture in the figure) and engaged in reciprocal play with the researcher using a different toy (large picture on the left) in the absence of any prompts

Therefore, only one toy (the ball) still remained in the room. This toy was placed in the same location across all trials during this condition (see Figure 4.35). Again, when Ian met the criterion of emitting a second social initiation and playing with the researcher using the second toy (ball) he was transferred to the next condition (Condition T1+2+3). Meanwhile, if a stable trend in Matthew's (the second child) performance was established during the first video modelling condition he was transferred to the next condition (Condition T1+2). For Matthew, here, during the first session, social initiation was directed only at play with the modelled toy. Thereafter, however, his latencies reduced and there was a marked increase in the time engaged in reciprocal play. Interestingly, the first toy played with on each occasion was the modelled toy (see Figure 4.36). In addition, it was at this time when video modelling was introduced for the third child following a continuous data collection in baseline.

In Condition T1+2+3, when Ian (the first child) had completed interactive play using the trampoline, the researcher removed that toy and another two (i.e. the frog game and wooden train) and he returned to his chair. Consequently, two toys (ball and tambourines) now remained in the room, placed again in the same location across all trials. Whenever a child emitted a second social initiation response followed by play with one of the remaining toys (ball or tambourines) that toy was removed and the researcher returned to his chair (see Figure 4.37).

The session terminated when both the child and the researcher had played with all three toys. Meanwhile, when each of the other two children met the criterion in the condition they were assessed, they then experienced the following condition. In this condition, Matthew initiated play with all the toys and the mean time engaged in reciprocal play with each toy across trials was slightly lower than the time observed in the previous condition; on each occasion the toy initially selected was the modelled toy (see Figure 4.38). If a child failed to emit a social initiation response in three consecutive sessions during Conditions T1+2 and T1+2+3, then the preceding condition was re-introduced. If a child succeeded in emitting a social initiation response when he was returned to that condition the criterion for moving to the next condition was reduced to one session, instead of three, containing a social initiation response. This is better illustrated in Figure 4.39 which shows data for Ian, the first child in the sequence of the design. In Condition T1+2+3, Ian initiated play only with the modelled toy and the time engaged in reciprocal play with it averaged 33 seconds. Hence, Condition T1+2 was re-introduced.

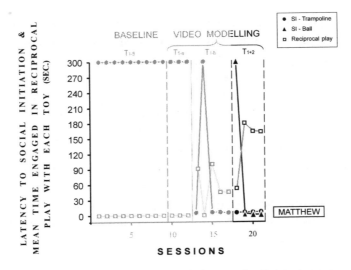

Figure 4.36: Latency to social initiation (SI) towards the researcher for Matthew using two different toys as well as the mean time engaged in reciprocal play with each of these toys. Reproduced from C. Nikopoulos and M. Keenan (2 4) Effects of video modelling and social initiations by children with autism'. Journal of Applied Behavior Analysis 37, 93 96. Reproduced by permission of the Society for the Experimental Analysis of Behavior, Inc.

Figure 4.37: An example of a successful assessment test during Condition T1 2 3. There are three clusters of pictures, and each cluster has a bottom left, a top, and bottom right. Each child initially approached the researcher (cluster 1, bottom left), then emitted a social initiation (cluster 1, top), and led him towards any toy to play with (cluster 1, bottom right). This was the sequence of the two models' behaviours previously showed in the video. Afterwards, in the absence of any prompts (e.g. a video or researcher's instructions), he emitted a second social initiation (cluster 2, bottom left), moved towards a different toy (cluster 2, top), and played with the researcher (cluster 2, bottom right). Finally and again in the absence of any prompts, he emitted a third social initiation (cluster 3, bottom left) and led the researcher towards another toy to play with (cluster 3, top and bottom right)

There, Ian's performance improved and the time engaged in reciprocal play with each toy was about 163 seconds. When he was returned to Condition T1+2+3 this performance was maintained for the first two trials, though there was a relatively large decrease in time engaged in reciprocal play with each toy on the last trial.

In the current study there were two types of generalisation assessments; those across toys and those across settings. Prior to both types of generalisation there was no video presentation. Thus, during generalisation tests across *toys*, when each child had played with the researcher using the trampoline, the frog game, the ball or the tambourines, he was assessed in the presence of a new toy, the wooden train. As in all previous video modelling conditions, the rationale for removing the toy with which a child had used for playing with the researcher following a social initiation response remained the same. The tests for generalisation across *settings* (Condition GS) were conducted in another room, unknown to the children, and the procedures were the same as those described for Conditions T1, T1+2 and T1+2+3 respectively. That is, each child had to emit one, two or three social initiations before playing with the researcher using the trampoline, the ball, or the tambourines.

Finally, two follow-up assessments were obtained after one and three months. Procedures during follow-up tests were similar to video modelling conditions in that a number of toys remained in the room after the modelled toy was removed. That is, in the absence of any video viewing the procedure at the first follow-up session was identical to Condition T1; the second follow-up session was identical to Condition T1+2; the third follow-up session was identical to Condition T1+2+3. The setting during all follow-up sessions was the same setting used during baseline sessions. Across all generalisation and follow-up assessments, Matthew's latencies to social initiation were relatively low across all the remaining conditions and during each trial the trampoline was played with first. Time engaged in reciprocal play with each toy was similar to previous conditions, although there was an increase during the three-month follow-up compared to the one-month follow-up (see Figure 4.40).[6]

---

6   In all designs of this study and in sessions that were terminated when each child had played with only one toy, the modelled toy (i.e. Conditions T1-a and T1-b, first session in GS and follow-ups), the mean time is synonymous with the overall time engaged in reciprocal play.

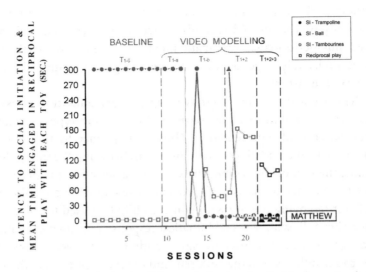

Figure 4.38: Latency to social initiation (SI) towards the researcher for Matthew using three different toys as well as the mean time engaged in reciprocal play with each of these toys. Reproduced from C. Nikopoulos and M. Keenan (2 4) Effects of video modelling on social initiations by children with autism'. Journal of Applied Behavior Analysis 37, 93 96. *Reproduced by permission of the Society for the Experimental Analysis of Behavior, Inc.*

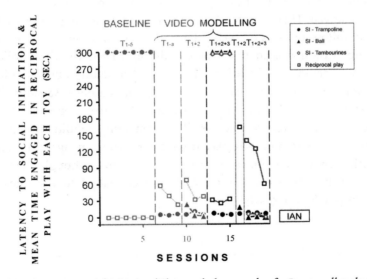

Figure 4.39: Latency to social initiation (SI) towards the researcher for Ian as well as the mean time engaged in reciprocal play with each toy. Initially, Ian failed to meet the criterion performance using three different toys (first introduction of Condition T 1 2 3). However, this occurred when the previous condition (i.e. T 1 2) was re-introduced for one session

4.2.10.2 FURTHER CONSIDERATIONS

The results of this study showed that a video display divided into its components enhanced both social initiation and reciprocal play in three children, which generalised across different stimuli, establishing a prolonged activity schedule. The successful responding in these children was not influenced by the different settings in the video and *in vivo*, and gneralised across settings and toys and maintained at one and three-month follow-up periods.

Furthermore, a social validity assessment with the participation of 25 undergraduate psychology students and five teachers in special education revealed that they recognised those video vignettes in which children had emitted a social initiation and had played reciprocally with the researcher. Specifically, these people, who were not familiar either with the children or with the purposes of the study, watched videotaped vignettes that consisted of three baseline and three intervention sessions, presented in random order. Each of the baseline scenes depicted a different toy near the researcher's seat and also there was one scene from each intervention condition. The observers were given the definitions of the behaviours that they had to identify and they were asked to recognise those scenes in which the child emitted a social initiation

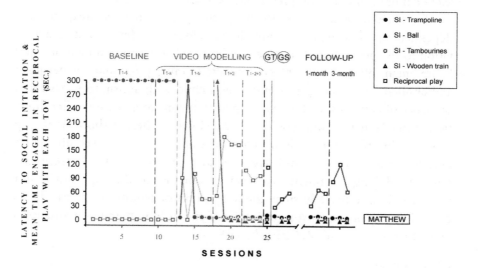

Figure 4.4 : Latency to social initiation (SI) towards the researcher for Matthew as well as the mean time engaged in reciprocal play with each toy during the generalisation sessions across toys (GT), settings (GS) and the two follow-up assessments. Reproduced from C. Nikopoulos and M. Keenan (2 4) Effects of video modelling on social initiations by children with autism'. Journal of Applied Behavior Analysis 37, 93 96. Reproduced by permission of the Society for the Experimental Analysis of Behavior, Inc.

and afterwards engaged in play with the researcher. In addition, the observers had to identify how many social initiation responses were included in each of the videotaped scenes. Finally, for the inter-observer agreement, a total mean agreement was 98 per cent (range, 94–100%), while the percentage agreement across social initiation was 100 per cent and across reciprocal play 96 per cent (range, 94–99%).

One of the main findings of the first study, which was also replicated in the second, was that the children were more likely to perform the target behaviours (i.e. social initiation and reciprocal play) in the presence of one stimulus (i.e. one toy). In this study, however, the same target behaviours were effectively displayed by children with autism, but in the presence of multiple (i.e. at least five) different stimuli. This was achieved by modifying the video display that was viewed by the children, instead of adjusting the research setting. That is, the video display was divided into its two major components (i.e. social initiation and reciprocal play), which eventually facilitated the imitative responding independently of the number of the present stimuli. It seemed that such a simplified video presentation helped the children to focus on the behaviours of interest, facilitating the observed attentional skills of these children to graphical presentations (Garretson et al. 1990).

To conclude, research has shown that changes in behaviour are quite often dependent upon the treatment provider to deliver cues, demonstrating a limitation to the generality of treatment effects for these children (Stahmer and Schreibman 1992). Thus, unless a specific training programme is designed and applied, these cues are essential for a child with autism to engage in a sequence of activities, without waiting for someone to give him or her directions (McClannahan and Krantz 1999). However, here a short video clip proved to be effective in building a sequence of behaviours and children with autism benefited, very quickly (i.e. after three sessions), from the video modelling treatment. This was a remarkable accomplishment for these children, especially since the acquisition of lengthy response chains comprises one of the most significant difficulties in individuals with autism (MacDuff, Krantz and McClannahan 1993).

4.2.10.3 RECAP

Initially, each child viewed a 35-second video of two people engaging in a simple social activity using a particular toy. Afterwards, he was taken into the research room (different from the one displayed in the video) and experienced Condition T1-a. There, if a child emitted a social initiation within the first 25 seconds and played with the researcher in three consecutive sessions, he was transferred to Condition T1+2; otherwise, to Condition T1-b. This condition (T1-b) was exactly the same as Condition T1-a except that the part of the video shown the model playing with the researcher had been erased. Condition T1+2 was exactly the same as Condition T1-a with the exception that all the toys (including the modelled toy) but one (a ball) were removed when a child and the researcher had completed playing with the toy shown in the video (i.e. a trampoline). Then the researcher returned to his chair and without any reference to the video waited for the child to emit a social initiation response using that other toy. Therefore, apart from the modelled toy there was one additional opportunity for each child to emit a social initiation to the researcher using another toy. Again, when each of the two social initiations occurred within the first 25 seconds in three consecutive sessions, the child experienced Condition T1+2+3. Condition T1+2+3 was exactly the same as Condition T1+2 with the exception that all the toys (including the modelled toy and the ball) but one (the tambourines) were removed when a child and the researcher had completed playing with the two toys (i.e. the modelled trampoline and the ball). Thus, each child had three opportunities to emit a social initiation and play with the researcher. The rationale for the researcher returning to his chair and waiting for the child to emit a social initiation as soon as he had completed playing using a toy remained with each of the two other remaining toys. During Conditions T1+2 and T1+2+3 if a child failed to emit the respective number of social initiations in three consecutive sessions, then he experienced the preceding condition, just once.

Finally, each time that the toys were removed, an additional five minutes was allowed for the child to exhibit the target response. That is, in Condition T1+2, two different additional toys were used and the whole session could last up to 10 minutes. In Condition T1+2+3, three different toys were used and each session could potentially last up to 15 minutes.

4.2.11 Study 5: Teaching complex social sequences

Successes demonstrated in all previous studies were primarily based on the imitation skills of children with autism. This finding adds to the debate that individuals with autism usually present difficulties in most imitation tasks (e.g. Brown and Whiten 2000; Dawson and Adams 1984; Heimann et al. 1992; Receveur et al. 2005; Rogers et al. 2003; Stone, Ousley and Littleford 1997; Venn et al. 1993), although children with autism may perform as well as typically developing children on some simple tests of imitation of actions using objects (Beadle-Brown 2004; Charman and Baron-Cohen 1994;

Ingersoll, Schreibman and Tran 2003). Previous video scenes, however, were limited to one set of behaviours (i.e. social initiation and reciprocal play), which the children, afterwards, had to display in a real context. The next logical step would be to investigate whether a sequence of topographically different activities[7] could be included in a video modelling procedure. It would be useful, for example, to examine how many sequences of behaviour could be included in individual video clips so that effective activity schedules would be constructed using video clips instead of booklets of pictures (cf. McClannahan and Krantz 1999). This possibility would offer a time-efficient and personnel conserving teaching tool (Charlop and Milstein 1989).

The present study, then, was designed to examine whether video modelling could build a sequence of behaviours not necessarily belonging to the same topographical response class; whether a video of three different behaviours could be imitated when a history of one imitative behaviour has been established; if video modelling could be effective in building a sequence of behaviours that were not included in the children's repertoires (i.e. social initiation was not a component of the video) and also whether increases in imitative responding are facilitated when social initiation occurs.

4.2.11.1 METHODOLOGY

Three boys and one girl whose ages ranged between 6.5 and 7.5 years participated in this study. They attended a school for learning and developmental disabilities and had been diagnosed with autism (one of them also with epilepsy). Their scores on the CARS were 31 and 34.5 points (mild-moderate range of autism) as well as 41.5 and 44 points (severe range) respectively.

Under the *expressive language domain*, two children displayed echolalic speech most of the time; one child had some speech, mainly through the use of incomplete sentences, and the fourth child could speak quite frequently, though her speech was not always consistent and resembled delayed echolalia. Their *language understanding* was limited to one or two-word instructions and they also used a few basic non-verbal behaviours to communicate. Three of the children engaged mostly in solitary activities involving construction toys, jigsaws, bicycles, making bubbles or riding a bicycle, and

---

7   Topography refers to the form of a particular operant behaviour or the way in which it is configured in space and time (e.g. the specific movements involved) (e.g. Pear 2001). In this study, topographically different activities could be a social initiation leading not only to playing with a toy, but also to carrying out other simple tasks.

dressing up activities whereas one of these two displayed very restricted *play skills*. *Socially*, limited interactions with adults or other children as well as lack of a development of any peer relationships appropriate to their developmental levels were the main characteristics for the three children. The fourth child lacked any interaction or response with other people even in the form of non-verbal behaviours. In addition, all of the children showed restricted patterns of interest and set patterns of routines and behaviours. They sometimes became extremely active and aggressive to others, they lacked eye-contact and their concentration span was very limited. Two of the children displayed some stereotyped and repetitive motor mannerisms (e.g. whole body movements, tapping furniture with a hard object), while non-functional routines or rituals as well as restricted patterns of interest with books or a computer occupied most of the daytime of one child. One child tended to request or to ask the same things all the time and occasionally she followed set patterns of behaviour, rituals or routines.

The children's performances under baseline and video modelling conditions were measured in a semi-naturalistic room of their school. Thus, in contrast with all the previous studies, here children viewed the videotapes and were assessed during all conditions in the same room shown in the videotapes. This was because there was only one room available. In terms of the stimuli (objects) available in that room, there was a camcorder, a television, two chairs, a ball, a table and two rags. During all conditions the children's behaviours that were recorded included video watching, social initiation, reciprocal play, object engagement, other behaviours (see Table 4.1 for operational definitions) and imitative responding. *Imitative responding* was defined as each child engaged in any of the three activities previously depicted in the videotape in the same or similar way as the model had done. A latency recording system was used for measuring this behaviour; recording for the second or the third activity in the sequence commenced as soon as the preceding had been completed.

Two research designs were used throughout: a multiple baseline across three children and an AB design for one child. Two major phases were identified in the current study: baseline and video modelling divided into five different conditions. A graphical presentation of the general procedure during baseline and video modelling conditions is given in Figure 4.41. During baseline sessions and in the absence of any video presentations or references to the television (it was hidden behind a curtain in the same room), both the researcher and each child entered the room, while the former went and sat on the chair. Each child's performance was recorded within a maximum of five minutes per session. Figure 4.42 depicts the baseline data collected for one of the children (i.e. Paul; the third child in the sequence) who was assessed within a multiple baseline design. Paul's latency to social initiation was at the highest level of 300 seconds. Similar performance was recorded for the set of the three imitative activities (i.e. imitative response) during the third, sixth, eighth, eleventh and fourteenth sessions.

Afterwards, in the video modelling sessions each child was first guided to view one of the 20–37-second videotapes once, in the same room that the subsequent assessment would take place. Then the researcher covered the television and sat on his chair. Similarly, each child was assessed as to whether the video presentations changed his or her behaviours within a maximum of five minutes.

The main video modelling conditions were referred to as S-1, S-1,2 and S-1,2,3. 'S' stands for *social initiation* while the figures reflect the total number of different activities shown in the videotape. In Condition S-1, each child viewed a videotape of a model emitting a social initiation and afterwards playing with the researcher using a ball (see Figure 4.43). For Paul, when this video of one set of behaviours was shown, his latency dropped to a level of about seven seconds within five sessions (see Figure 4.44). During Condition S-1,2,3, each child viewed a videotape depicting a model engaged in a sequence of three activities with the researcher. These modelled activities included playing with a ball, moving a table, and sitting on the rags (see Figure 4.45). Prior to each activity, the model had emitted a social initiation response towards the researcher. In this condition, Paul emitted a social initiation only for playing with the ball and only once (see Figure 4.46; session 24). Thus, he did not meet the criterion of emitting a social initiation response within the first 10 seconds before engaging in each activity shown in the video with the researcher in three consecutive sessions, he experienced Condition S-1,2 for an additional three sessions. This condition did not follow Condition S-1 as the name might imply. This decision had been made in an effort to assess whether a history of imitating one set of behaviours (i.e. emitting a social initiation and playing with a ball, Condition S-1) would facilitate the imitation of a sequence of three sets of behaviours (Condition S-1,2,3) without children having experienced a sequence of two sets of behaviours (Condition S-1,2). In Condition S-1,2, a child watched a video of the model emitting two social initiations and engaging in two activities with the researcher (i.e. playing with a ball and moving a table) – the first two activities of Condition S-1,2,3 (see Figure 4.47). In this condition, Paul's successful responding was sustained for four sessions, meeting the criterion

Study 5

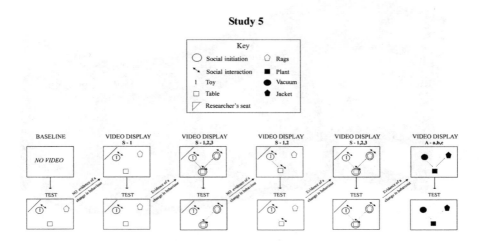

Figure 4.41: Graphical presentation of the general procedure during baseline and video modelling intervention for the children who were assessed within a multiple baseline design

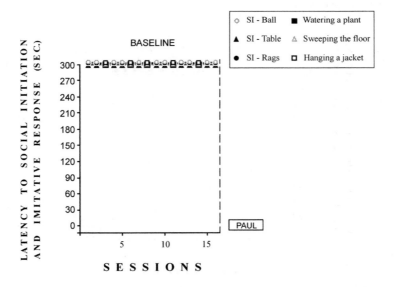

Figure 4.42: Latency to social initiation (SI) towards the researcher and to imitative responses for Paul during the baseline sessions. Reproduced from C. Nikopoulus and M. Keenan (in press) Using video modelling to teach complex social consequences to children with autism'. Journal of Autism Developmental Disorders 5 , 7. Reproduced with kind permission of Springer Science and Business Media.

Figure 4.43: An example of the first video presentation in which a peer (model) engaged in a simple social activity with the researcher using a ball. Specifically, both the model and the researcher entered the room (first picture from the left), then the model emitted a social initiation by saying 'Let's play' taking the researcher by the hand and establishing eye-contact (second picture), then he moved towards a toy (i.e. a ball third picture), and finally they both played together for a few seconds (fourth picture)

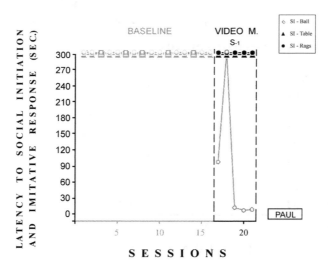

Figure 4.44: Latency to social initiation (SI) towards the researcher for Paul during the first video modelling condition showing a videotape of a model emitting a social initiation and afterwards playing with the researcher using a ball. Reproduced from C. Nikopoulus and M. Keenan (in press) Using video modelling to teach complex social consequences to children with autism'. Journal of Autism Developmental Disorders 5 , 7. *Reproduced with kind permission of Springer Science and Business Media*

Figure 4.45: An example of the video presentation in which a peer (model), after he had emitted a social initiation each time, engaged in a sequence of three simple social activities. There are two clusters of pictures and two large pictures each cluster has a bottom left right and a top bottom right. Initially, both the model and the researcher entered the room (cluster 1, bottom left), then the model emitted a social initiation (cluster 1, top left), then he moved towards a ball (cluster 1, top right), and they both played together for a few seconds (cluster 1, bottom right). Afterwards, when that play had been completed the model emitted another social initiation by now saying Let's move the table' (cluster 2, bottom left), guided the researcher towards the table (cluster 2, top left) and then they moved the table together (cluster 2, top and bottom right). Finally, the model emitted a third social initiation by now saying Let's sit down' (first large picture) and guided the researcher towards the two rags (second large picture)

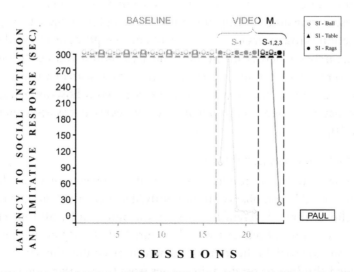

Figure 4.46: Latency to social initiation (SI) towards the researcher for Paul during the video modelling condition showing a videotape of a model engaged in a sequence of three activities with the researcher. Reproduced from C. Nikopoulus and M. Keenan (in press) Using video modelling to teach complex social consequences to children with autism'. Journal of Autism Developmental Disorders 5 , 7. Reproduced with kind permission of Springer Science and Business Media

performance to move on to the next one (i.e. S-1,2,3). There, eventually, his performance met the criterion within the minimum of three sessions (see Figure 4.48).

The three children in the multiple baseline design mainly experienced Condition S-1 and then S-1,2,3 while the order for the child in the AB design was Condition S-1,2,3 followed by S-1. If children of both designs had experienced the same sequence of behaviours, then it would have been impossible to address the following argument: Would successful imitative responding of three different behaviours (i.e. Condition S-1,2,3) have occurred if a one-behaviour imitation history had not been established (i.e. Condition S-1)? In other words, would a child with autism imitate a video clip presenting three sets of different behaviours without having any previous experience of imitating a single set of video modelled behaviours? A sufficient response to the above reasonable questions could only be provided if Conditions S-1 and S-1,2,3 replaced each other. Finally, the last condition in any video modelling sequence was Condition A-a,b,c. In that condition, each child viewed a video of a model engaging alone (A) in three different activities. These were watering a plant (a), sweeping the floor (b) and hanging a jacket (c) (see Figure 4.49).

The effectiveness of video modelling procedures to enhance these children's imitation skills were further evaluated during a generalisation assessment across peers and in two follow-up measures. It is worth noting that these assessments were exactly the same as in baseline in that there was no prior video presentation and the same room was also employed. Specifically, in the generalisation across peers (GP) assessment another peer participated instead of the researcher whereas in the one and two-month follow-up measures children were assessed in the presence of the same researcher. During all the remaining conditions (i.e. A-a,b,c, GP) and the two follow-up assessments, Paul's latency to respond remained at very low levels across assessments (see Figure 4.50).

4.2.11.2 FURTHER CONSIDERATIONS

In the present study, the results showed that a sequence of three different behaviours could be established. Importantly, it was clearly demonstrated that a video clip of three different behaviours was imitated by all four children only when a history of one or two behaviours had already been established. Furthermore, the social validation assessment showed that the ten mothers of school-aged children recognised the scenes from the intervention conditions in which the children either emitted a social initiation or used the present

Figure 4.47: An example of the video presentation in which a peer (model) engaged in a sequence of two simple social activities followed by a social initiation each time. These included playing with a ball (first cluster of pictures on the left) and moving a table (second, third and fourth pictures)

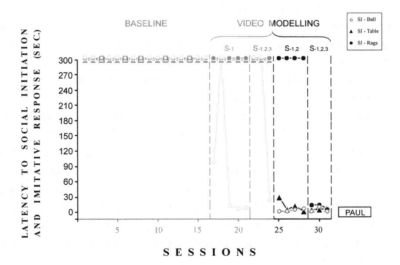

Figure 4.48: Latency to social initiation (SI) and engagement in a sequence of three activities with the researcher for Paul after having experienced a condition in which imitation of a sequence of two activities was required. Reproduced from C. Nikopoulus and M. Keenan (in press) Using video modelling to teach complex social consequences to children with autism'. Journal of Autism Developmental Disorders 5 , 7 . *Reproduced with kind permission of Springer Science and Business Media*

objects in the manner for which they were intended. These mothers further claimed that their own typically developing children would behave in a similar way as the children with autism did, under those specific circumstances. Moreover, the inter-observer agreement of the 39 per cent of all observations, which was 95 per cent (range, 88–100%) further reinforced the validity of the current results.

It also is worth emphasising the fact that, in comparison to two other children, additional practice was necessary only for Paul before imitation of the sequence of the three sets of behaviours occurred; that is, the behaviour had to be trained for a sufficient length of time. Specifically, Paul had to experience Condition S-1 three times and Condition S-1,2 once before he imitated the whole sequence of behaviours in Condition S-1,2,3. It might be the case that because he displayed some speech, mainly echolalic, his imitation and verbal or gestural development were also affected (Carpenter, Pennington and Rogers 2002). In fact, it has been suggested that abnormalities in social behaviour and play are more severe in children with autism with very limited language than in those who have some speech (Lord and Pickles 1996; Sigman and Ruskin 1999; Ungerer and Sigman 1981). This assumption was further supported by the fact that successful responding of the children who were verbal was enhanced within a few video modelling sessions, indicating that there might be a relationship between social functioning and language development in individuals with autism (Ingersoll, Schreibman and Stahmer 2001). Nonetheless, anecdotal evidence showed that both children with the restricted language skills began imitating the verbal components presented on the video (e.g. 'Let's play', 'Let's move the table' or 'Let's sit down'). Although the establishment of pragmatics in language (e.g. Paul *et al.* 2004) or temporal relatedness (e.g. Duchan 1986) was not included in the objectives of the current study, that was a major accomplishment for these children as echolalia of children with autism usually appears to serve important communicative and cognitive functions (Wetherby, Prizant and Hutchinson 1998). Indeed, these children's verbal responses along with their gestural movements functioned in promoting the social interactions between them and the researcher or peer (cf. Stevenson, Krantz and McClannahan 2000).

In conclusion, results of the current study in conjunction with those of Study 4 suggest that a video modelling intervention could be implemented in the design of a prolonged activity schedule (cf. McClannahan and Krantz 1999). This was an important accomplishment for the children as research has

Figure 4.49: An example of the video presentation in which a peer (model) engaged in a sequence of three simple activities. After he had viewed the respective video display and the TV was hidden behind a curtain (first picture from the left), he watered a plant (second picture), then swept the floor (third picture) and finally he hung a jacket

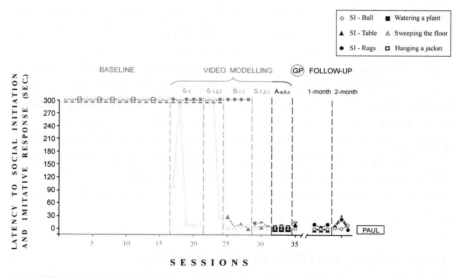

Figure 4.5 : Latency to social initiation (SI) towards the researcher and the peer (GP) and to imitative responses for Paul across generalisation and follow-up conditions. Reproduced from C. Nikopoulus and M. Keenan (in press) Using video modelling to teach complex social consequences to children with autism'. Journal of Autism   Developmental Disorders 5 , 7. *Reproduced with kind permission of Springer Science and Business Media*

suggested that children with autism face major difficulties in imitating sequential meaningful gestures even though the components of this sequence are meaningful, since it is the sequence rather than the components which is required to be imitated (Williams, Whiten and Singh 2004). Thus far, the methods developed in this study have clarified and determined either the necessary components of a video clip or the appropriate training history in children with autism that would enable video modelling procedures in any teaching environment. It would appear that the implementation of such time-efficient video modelling techniques in the treatment of children with autism holds great promise.

4.2.11.3 RECAP

Children were taken to the research room to view one of four short videos of two people engaging in a simple activity or a sequence of activities. These people were a peer with learning difficulties who acted as the model and the researcher. Specifically, the first video displayed the researcher and the model playing with a ball, the second showed them playing with a ball and moving a table, the third showed them playing with a ball, moving a table and sitting on the rags, and the fourth showed them watering a plant, sweeping the floor and hanging a jacket. Apart from baseline, there were four more conditions: Conditions S-1, S-1,2, S-1,2,3 and A-a,b,c in which the first, second, third and fourth videos were used respectively. Whenever a video was shown, the researcher engaged in the same behaviour as in the video, without providing any instructions to the child. In general, when a child succeeded in emitting one, two or three social initiation responses within the first 10 seconds each time for three consecutive sessions, he or she was transferred from Condition S-1 to either Condition S-1,2 or S-1,2,3; otherwise he or she experienced the preceding condition, just once. Condition A-a,b,c was the final phase of the research procedure, in which only three sessions were available independently of the children's responding. Finally, each session was terminated when either a child had completed the modelled activities or after a maximum of five minutes.

4.3 Maximising the effects of video modelling

The findings in each of the studies reported here have implications for general issues in the autism literature, some of each were mentioned previously. These issues include:

1.   stimulus overselectivity

2. attentional patterns

3. social deficits

4. visual superiority

5. natural contingencies of reinforcement

6. structure of play activities

7. disruptive transition behaviour.

1. Stimulus overselectivity

Stimulus overselectivity (i.e. restricted stimulus control over performance) is a phenomenon usually associated with children with autism (e.g. Lovaas and Koegel 1979; Rincover and Ducharme 1987). That is, these children usually respond to a restricted set of cues in their environment and, therefore, they may face difficulties in observational learning and generalisation of treatment gains (Handleman and Harris 1980; Rincover and Ducharme 1987). One potential solution would be specific training aiming at remediation. However, Varni and colleagues (1979) queried whether such training would facilitate the teaching of children with autism to learn through observation. Moreover, it has been suggested that any intervention should be designed on the basis of the stimulus by which the treatment provider desires to achieve control (e.g. Rincover and Koegel 1975). In the current studies, the primary objective was to determine whether a video display would acquire control over the occurrence of children's imitative responses. Adopting the suggestion that children with autism can be taught to 'overselect' relevant cues (e.g. Schreibman, Charlop and Koegel 1982), the video displays were designed in such a way that significant cues i.e. the actions of the models had been brought closer together. If our analysis is correct, this allowed the children to follow these cues and to discriminate the relationship among those events thus facilitating subsequent imitative responding (Dowrick 1991; Morgan and Salzberg 1992; Rincover and Ducharme 1987).

2. Attentional patterns

The levels of video watching behaviour for almost all children who participated in these studies were remarkably high. This could be attributed to two factors. First, it has been well documented that children with autism tend to pay selective attention directed towards viewing television (Buggey et al. 1999). Indeed, television plays a major role for people with autism (Nally, Houlton and Ralph 2000), who spend extended amounts of the day watching it (Schatzman *et al.* 2000). Second, the use of an audio component (i.e. 'Let's play', 'Let's move the table' or 'Let's sit down') in the videotapes might have served as a salient cue for the children to pay attention at the modelled behaviours. This is consistent with suggestions that the use of audio in conjunction with visual information may maximise the effects of modelling (Racicot and Wogalter 1995).

3. Social deficits

Research has documented that children with autism look longer and more often at the human figure than at neutral objects in pictures (van der Geest *et al.* 2002), whereas they may face major difficulties in orienting to social stimuli (Dawson, Matson and Cherry 1998) or looking at people in real life contexts (Swettenham *et al.* 1998). Accordingly, it seems likely that the use of videotapes promoted children's attending to the modelled behaviours as no social interactions were required that might distract them from this task (Charlop and Milstein 1989).

4. Visual superiority

In an early study conducted by Stephens and Ludy (1975), it was illustrated that film instruction was superior to both slide instruction and live demonstration in some children with learning disabilities. Among other reasons, they suggested that the superiority of film could be based on the fact that it presents the relative concepts in a systematic and relatively simple format. Here, the video clips presented in a simple social interaction and play acts by two models were designed with appropriate beginnings and endings, which apparently facilitated the children's subsequent imitative responding.

5. Natural contingencies of reinforcement

Research has suggested that children's responding can be maintained by naturally occurring contingencies of reinforcement (e.g. Gena and Kymissis 2001; Kohler and Greenwood 1986). Thus, reciprocal play may have acquired reinforcing properties (e.g. Carr and Darcy 1990; Koegel *et al.* 1998; Stahmer and Schreibman 1992), as evidenced by the fact that extinction did not occur in any of the generalisation situations (e.g. Koegel *et al.* 1998; Rincover and Koegel 1975).

6. Structure of play activities

It has been found that children with autism display more advanced skills in structured games, constructive activities (Restall and Magill-Evans 1993) or manipulative play (Stahmer 1995). It has also been suggested that structured activities with clear rules and/or goals might promote positive social interaction in children with autism (Dewey, Lord and Magill 1988). Accordingly, the toys selected in all studies were simple in format with clear rules, designed to promote structured playing. In fact, these toys were selected because all children were familiar with them and therefore guidance and instructions on how to play with the toys were not necessary for the children.

7. Disruptive transition behaviour

It has been documented that individuals with autism exhibit difficulties in situations that involve changes in the environment (American Psychiatric Association 1994), referred to as disruptive transition behaviour (Schreibman *et al.* 2000). In addition, Ferrara and Hill (1980) stated that children with autism could become seriously disorganised when they are not able to predict the sequence of events. Video modelling procedures might reduce this disruptive transition behaviour, as children were guided to the same or similar environment with that depicted in the video, and therefore they could predict the expected or required sequence of events.

4.4 Synopsis

This chapter described and evaluated video modelling procedures across five different research studies. Study 1 investigated the general notion of promoting social skills in children with autism. Results revealed that video modelling can enhance both social initiation and reciprocal interaction. Study 2 expanded on this finding and demonstrated that video modelling can be an effective procedure for establishing generalised responding of target behaviours. Data from Study 3 replicated previous findings and also demonstrated that video modelling can be a successful medium for transferring stimulus control, thus providing evidence that it can be used in any natural environment. Using more complex skills, Study 4 demonstrated that video modelling can build a sequence of different behaviours when these belong to the same response class. Based primarily on the results of Study 4, procedures in Study 5 showed that video modelling can also be effective in building a sequence of behaviours even when these belong to different response classes. In addition, results suggest that such sequences of behaviour can be imitated by children with autism when a history of a limited number of behaviours has been established.

In all of the studies, aspects of environmental contingencies were analysed to determine the effective components of video modelling, independently of the behavioural characteristics of the children and in the absence of any researcher-implemented consequences or prompts. Specifically, the procedures described here proved to be successful in children with autism who displayed limited social interactions with adults or other children, lack of interest in toys, some echolalic speech or none at all, and restricted imitation skills. Also, data revealed that all competing behaviours (e.g. stereotypic, disruptive or self-stimulatory) reduced substantially as soon as social initiation and reciprocal interaction occurred. For example, data from the baseline sessions showed that whenever the children engaged in isolated play, their behaviour was mainly characterised by rigid stereotyped actions directed towards toys and objects, such as repetitive manual manipulations and oral uses of the toys. Importantly, behaviour gains in these children generalised across stimuli, settings and peers and maintained after one, two or three-month follow-up periods.

CHAPTER 5

Discussion and Further Directions

It is a capital mistake to theorize before you have all the evidence. It biases the judgement.

Arthur Conan Doyle, A Study in Scarlet *(1888)*

5.1 Integration of findings

One of the primary developmental tasks during early childhood years is the acquisition of positive interaction skills. Thus, children need to be able to form positive relations and friendships with their peers as well as to develop their language and vocabulary repertoires (Kohler *et al.* 1990). Unfortunately, specific instructions are necessary for children with autism to develop specific social skills, because they do not usually tend to acquire skills through incidental learning (Laushey and Heflin 2000). In light of this, the dependent and independent variables in these five studies were selected for relevance to functioning in natural environments instead of artificially controlled situations (Kraijer 2000). Collectively, the results provide evidence that video modelling as a visual instructional technique is effective in promoting social initiation, reciprocal play and a sequence of different behaviours in children with autism. In all of the studies, aspects of environmental contingencies (e.g. video display components, location or number of stimuli and variability in the research settings) were analysed to determine the effective components of video modelling, independently of the behavioural characteristics of these children and in the absence of any researcher-implemented consequences or prompts. Importantly, behaviour gains in all children generalised across stimuli, settings or peers and maintained after a one, two or three-month follow-up period. In addition, the social validation assessments revealed that video modelling objectives, procedures and effects were significant and acceptable to the 'consumers' of the treatment (e.g. Wolf 1978).

The video modelling procedures described in this book expand the literature in several ways. First, the function of video modelling was isolated from other methods and implemented in as natural an environment as possible (e.g. Morgan and Salzberg 1992). Second, modelling through videos provided further evidence about the efficacy of models in comparison to language-based instruction systems (Emmen *et al.* 1985; Quill 1997). Third, the videotape format used in these studies contained all the advantages of convenience, standardisation and efficiency that may be difficult to achieve with *in-vivo* formats (Poche *et al.* 1988). Fourth, not only were short video clips shown to be effective (i.e. range, 20 to 37 seconds), but these video presentations resulted in rapid changes in behaviour that required no further prompts (in terms of video presentations) in subsequent assessments across other stimuli (e.g. Study 2). This is important since it has been well documented that children with autism become prompt dependent as intervention procedures are often based on continuous prompting techniques (Lasater and Brady 1995; Odom *et al.* 1992). Fifth, generalised outcomes occurred in all studies, and this is in keeping with the demand that research should focus on generalisation and maintenance of social behaviour (Chandler, Lubeck and Fowler 1992; Fox and McEvoy 1993). This may have occurred due to the similarities between the environments presented in the videotapes and *in vivo* (cf. Bernard-Opitz, Sriram and Nakhoda-Sapuan 2001). That is, the nature of a structured testing procedure might assist the children to exhibit successful imitative responses while distractions were minimised (McDonough *et al.* 1997). Likewise, Alcantara (1994) proposed that the use of videotape instructions may provide sufficient training for children with autism, which is as realistic as in the natural environment, mainly because of the high degree of similarity between the videotape experience and the real experience. Sixth, in contrast to Steinborn and Knapp's (1982) suggestion that video recordings should be presented in a slow motion mode, the video presentations in the current studies were at a natural speed. Finally, the use of a variety of different models throughout all the studies demonstrated that model saliency such as age or sex is not as important as previously thought (e.g. Kazdin 1974; Varni *et al.* 1979).

5.2 Further implications of findings for children with autism

The success of the procedures described in this book may have further impli-cations in other areas of deficits, such as (1) imitation, (2) play, (3) generalisa-tion, (4) disruptive behaviours, and (5) language.

1. *Imitation.* Learning through imitation (i.e. observational learning) is critical for a child's normal development, which becomes particularly true when the child starts to interact with his or her peers (Lovaas 1981). Although observational learning occurs spontaneously in typically developing children, it has to be taught to children with autism (Weiss and Harris 2001b). However, the successes reported in all of the present studies mainly relied on the ability of the children to imitate the modelled behaviours, which was apparently facilitated by the video medium. That is, children became successful imitators after being successful observational learners (Brown and Murray 2001; Garfinkle and Schwartz 2002), as they were able to attend to multiple cues (e.g. Goldstein and Brown 1989) in the videotapes and then perform them in a real environment. That was an additional important achievement of the children, as it has been stated that imitation skills may represent an altered route to social learning (Carpenter *et al.* 2002; Lovaas *et al.* 1967; Quill 2000) or to language development (e.g. Ross and Greer 2003). That is consistent with the finding that even though children with autism develop more appropriate social responses they are unlikely to be able to sustain interactions with their peers for any length of time, in the absence of imitative or more complex play behaviours (Schopler and Mesibov 1986).

2. *Play.* Play is regarded as the fabric of childhood, which as a learning process serves several important functions in development. Thus, while children engage in play activities they learn about objects and events and they discover the language for talking about these objects and events with other children or adults (Lifter *et al.* 1993; Quill 2000). Play as a naturalistic forum also offers children the opportunity to gain control over their environment and to develop interests in activities that are enjoyable to them (Moran and Whitman 1991; Restall and Magill-Evans 1993). Children with autism, however, may show impairments in spontaneous play (Libby *et al.* 1998), social play (Jordan 2003) and initiation of pretend play (Libby *et al.* 1997) as social interaction has been considered one of the principal elements in play activities (Beyer and Gammeltof

2000). Remarkably, these deficits in the social domain usually persist across time and are observed even in adulthood (Njardvik *et al.* 1999). The video modelling procedures applied to all the current studies produced significant gains in time spent in reciprocal play using a variety of toys for the children, which eventually led to a substantial increase in total time of social interaction with the researcher and peers. The importance of this finding is highlighted by the fact that play with objects is considered the most natural context for the development of social interaction and language development in children with autism (e.g. Sigman and Ruskin 1999; Tiegerman and Primavera 1981).

3.   *Generalisation.* Generalisation describes the occurrence of the same or relevant behaviour across time, settings and persons in the absence of the conditions that promoted the acquisition of the specific behaviour (Tillman 2000). A treatment is regarded as effective as long as it obtains generalised effects. That is, the greater the effects of a treatment the greater amount of generalisation occurs (e.g. Zifferblatt *et al.* 1977). The present results showed that behavioural gains acquired by the children generalised across stimuli, persons and settings and maintained across time for most of them. That is, the children were able to demonstrate successful imitative responding in the absence of video modelling, and therefore their performance, significantly, did not rely upon any treatment provider (Stahmer and Schreibman 1992). Thus, it could be speculated that after those children had experienced a short video modelling intervention they would emit a social initiation and engage in reciprocal play in any other environment wherein toys and persons would be present. These findings are consistent with those of Ihrig and Wolchik's study (1988), which revealed that modelling is an effective teaching strategy for rapidly acquiring high levels of generalisation and maintenance.

4.   *Disruptive behaviours.* Although disruptive, maladaptive or stereotypic behaviours were not the targets for training in this study, these behaviours decreased following the onset of video modelling and improvement in social and play skills. For example, data from baseline sessions showed that whenever the children engaged in isolated play their behaviour was mainly in the form of rigid stereotyped movements towards toys and objects, such as repetitive

manual manipulations and oral uses of the toys (Dewey *et al.* 1988; Tilton and Ottinger 1969). Then, after the initial introduction of video modelling procedures, there was a general tendency for children's performances to be improved more rapidly, which may be explained by a learning-to-learn or learning set phenomenon (Browder, Schoen and Lentz 1987; Harlow 1949). In general, this finding supports previous studies citing reduction of inappropriate behaviours or self-stimulation when children with autism displayed more interactive play (e.g, Ballard and Medland 1986; Eason, White and Newson 1982; Massey and Wheeler 2000; Schleien, Heyne and Berken 1988; Stahmer and Schreibman 1992; Thorp, Stahmer and Schreibman 1995).

5. *Language.* As was the case with disruptive behaviours, the procedures designed here did not focus on the development of the language skills of the children. However, anecdotal evidence showed that most children used the verbal components of the videotapes (e.g. 'Let's play', 'Let's move the table' etc.), even in an echolalic way. That was also an important behavioural achievement for them, as research has shown that the majority of verbal children with autism use echolalia, which serves important communicative and cognitive functions (e.g. Charlop 1983; Wetherby *et al.* 1998).

5.3 A step forward

Although a large number of studies have shown that children and youths with autism can improve their skills and deficits when provided with appropriate and well-planned treatment strategies, they have also had difficulties in acquiring lengthy response chains. That is, a child with autism may need continuous adult prompting to complete a sequence of already learned activities such as brushing his or her teeth, getting dressed and going to breakfast (MacDuff *et al.* 1993). In addition, it has been documented that people with autism excel in treatment modalities that are based on visual stimuli such as line drawings (e.g. Wacker and Berg 1983) or pictures (e.g. Pierce and Schreibman 1994). In fact, researchers have reported that individuals with autism may benefit more from information presented visually rather than auditorily (Schopler and Mesibov 1994; Schreibman *et al.* 2000). Indeed, a visually cued instruction should be considered an important treatment method when intervention for children with autism is being designed (Quill 1997).

Taking the above into consideration, photographic activity schedules have been designed and shown to be effective in teaching children with autism to display lengthy and complex chains of previously established functional behaviours (e.g. Bryan and Gast 2000; Krantz *et al.* 1993; MacDuff *et al.* 1993; Morrison *et al.* 2002). An activity schedule is a set of pictures or written words that, through graduated guidance, cues children with autism to engage in a sequence of activities in the absence of direct prompting by parents or teachers (McClannahan and Krantz 1999).

An additional method – and potentially a superior one – for enhancing the acquisition of lengthy response chains in children with autism could be the use of video modelling. Indeed, video modelling might be as effective as activity schedules in teaching a variety of skills in children with autism because both of the procedures make use of the visual strengths observed in children with autism requiring them to become 'picture' or 'movie readers'; both aim to enable children with autism to perform tasks and activities without direct prompting and guidance by treatment providers; both can be very detailed – breaking a task or a video clip into all of its separate parts/components – or very general and complex; both provide opportunities for initiating conversation rather than merely responding to other's instructions or queries. A video modelling intervention presents a few more advantages, however, such as:

1. It does not require any initial instructions or specific training (cf. graduated manual guidance in a form of a most-to-least physical prompting).[1]

2. It demands less prerequisite skills than activity schedules.

3. It does not require contingent reinforcement upon the successful imitations, rather an occasional delivery of a general praise or a small tangible reward would help children maintain general responding within the play context.

---

1   Graduated manual guidance involves adjusting the level of the treatment provider's physical prompting according to the child's performance. Initially, *full guidance* (maximum) may be used wherein the child is provided with the maximum of physical help in order to do or say something without an error. Over time, the amount of help decreases (i.e. *partial guidance*) as long as the child continues to perform the task in the absence of errors. Then, prompting takes the form of *shadowing* (least) which involves moving the physical contact, again depending on the child's errorless performance.

4. It promotes generalisation across stimuli, peers and settings, and therefore no continuous use of video display is needed (learning is continued even in the absence of the 'intervention medium').

Interestingly, in their study with children learning disabilities, Stephens and Ludy (1975) demonstrated that film instruction (i.e. video) was superior to slide instruction (i.e. pictures) because the film instruction (1) depicted the real actions in process, (2) presented the concepts in a systematic and simple format and (3) gained and kept the children's attention effectively. Videotape instruction can provide training that is much more similar to the natural environment because of the high degree of similarity between the videotape experience and the real experience (Alcantara 1994). Similar conclusions were drawn by Charlop-Christy and her colleagues (2000) as well as by Thelen *et al.* (1979) in their studies of a comparison of video modelling with *in-vivo* modelling using children with autism. Also, it has been suggested that video viewing is a low demand activity as well as being highly flexible and that it is naturally reinforcing to children with autism which can promote generalisation (Schreibman *et al.* 2000), and that modelling can serve as a cost-efficient and convenient teaching tool (Charlop *et al.* 1983).

Video modelling procedures could be integrated into multimedia computer programmes which have been proved to be effective in teaching a variety of skills to children with autism (e.g. Bernard-Opitz *et al.* 2001; Bosseler and Massaro 2003; Chen and Bernard-Opitz 1993; Heimann *et al.* 1995; Stromer *et al.* 1996; Vedora *et al.* 2002; Williams *et al.* 2002; Wong and Tam 2001). Interestingly, Parsons and Mitchell (2002) suggested that virtual reality-based computer programmes could be designed to augment the current teaching practices in social skills training for individuals with autistic disorders. Computer programmes can create an intrinsically interesting learning environment that appeals to children with autism, gaining their attention and motivation (Moore and Calvert 2000). Not only has it been shown that carefully constructed computer programmes can gain the attention of children with autism, motivate them and promote their learning, especially when one-to-one assistance is required (e.g. Hetzroni and Tannous 2004), but the UK National Autistic Society has pointed to a general lack of computer programmes written specifically for children with autism (Moore, McGrath and Thorpe 2000; National Autistic Society 1996). If this is the case, then there is tremendous scope for integrating video modelling procedures and multimedia programmes to be used by educators and families of children with autism. Undoubtedly, integrating computer programmes into classrooms could provide a cost-effective teaching method to supplement current educational practices (Moore and Calvert 2000). Moreover, there can be important cost-benefits if these programmes could be delivered over television networks in order to reach many homes or schools (Maurice *et al.* 2001; Webster-Stratton 1990; Winett *et al.* 1985). Such an initiative would offer an alternative route to the management of videos and television, which is an important factor that causes stress within the families of children with autism (Nally *et al.* 2000).

Finally, as any video modelling procedure can become an easy task for anyone to carry out, parents can be empowered with this intervention (e.g. Hastings and Symes 2002), providing them with ways to encourage both social initiation and responsiveness in a variety of different situations (Ruble 2001). Thus, video modelling could be conducted in the homes of children with autism not only because instructional control of parents over their children's learning is so important (Schreibman 2000) and beneficial (Feldman and Werner 2002), though, usually inconsistent (Lasater and Brady 1995), but also because laws and legislative enactments exist to help both parents and professionals in their task of providing well-designed services (Simpson 1995). Besides, research has shown that parents can provide useful information on the progress of their children with autism, facilitating even the structure of particular programmes (Charman *et al.* 2004).

5.4 Conclusion

Barriers to age appropriate communication development arise when children with autism lack skills that prevent their access to social interactions in natural environments with their age peers (Kaiser *et al.* 2001). Moreover, their lack of social skills not only impedes the reciprocal interactions of children with autism and their typically developing peers, but it may also obstruct their long-term development of social communicative behaviour and thus widen the gap between children with autism and their peers (Hwang and Hughes 2000). The more severe the difficulties in social skills, the less likely it can be for an individual with autism to form peer relationships or even friendships (Orsmond, Krauss and Seltzer 2004).

Importantly, results of the present studies suggest that complex skills such as social initiation and reciprocal play can be established in children with autism. Being able to initiate and sustain reciprocal social interaction without external help may be accomplished through the use of video modelling. Inclusion of children with autism is now being considered as the main goal in special education research and practice (Gena and Kymissis 2001; Harrower and Dunlap 2001; Koegel 200; Koegel *et al.* 2001). Specific support structures need to be designed for these children to help them engage in reciprocal peer interactions (Zercher *et al.* 2001). Video modelling is clearly a promising method.

Questionnaire for Teachers and Caregivers

Date ....

Dear ....

I would be really obliged if you could indicate/tick as appropriate on the following questions or state your comments wherever it is necessary.

Do you think that ...*(Name)*... displays any of the following behaviours?

- **presence of speech; kind of speech (please specify in the Comments section)**

Always	Often	Sometimes	Seldom	Never	Comments

- **lack of interaction with other children**

Always	Often	Sometimes	Seldom	Never	Comments

- **interaction with adults mainly in the form of compliance**

Always	Often	Sometimes	Seldom	Never	Comments

- **lack of eye-contact**

Always	Often	Sometimes	Seldom	Never	Comments

- **lack of response to people**

Always	Often	Sometimes	Seldom	Never	Comments

- **marked impairments in the use of multiple non-verbal behaviours such as eye-to-eye gaze, facial expression, body posture and gestures to regulate social interaction**

Always	Often	Sometimes	Seldom	Never	Comments

- **extremely passive behaviour**

Always	Often	Sometimes	Seldom	Never	Comments

- **extremely nervous, active behaviour**

Always	Often	Sometimes	Seldom	Never	Comments

- **behaviour that is aggressive to others**

Always	Often	Sometimes	Seldom	Never	Comments

- **failure to develop peer relationships appropriate to developmental level**

Always	Often	Sometimes	Seldom	Never	Comments

- **lack of spontaneous seeking to share enjoyment, interests or achievements with other people (e.g. by a lack of showing, bringing or pointing out objects of interest to other people)**

Always	Often	Sometimes	Seldom	Never	Comments

- **lack of social or emotional reciprocity (e.g. not actively participating in simple social play or games, preferring solitary activities or involving others in activities only as tools or 'mechanical' aids)**

Always	Often	Sometimes	Seldom	Never	Comments

- **limited concentration span**

Always	Often	Sometimes	Seldom	Never	Comments

- limited imitation repertoire (e.g. imitating gross and fine body movements, facial expressions, actions with or without objects)

Always	Often	Sometimes	Seldom	Never	Comments

- lack of interest in toys (please specify the most preferred toys/games in the Comments section)

Always	Often	Sometimes	Seldom	Never	Comments

- desire to follow set patterns of behaviour/interaction

Always	Often	Sometimes	Seldom	Never	Comments

- encompassing preoccupation with one or more stereotyped and restricted patterns of interest that is abnormal either in intensity or focus

Always	Often	Sometimes	Seldom	Never	Comments

- apparently inflexible adherence to specific, non-functional routines or rituals

Always	Often	Sometimes	Seldom	Never	Comments

- **stereotyped and repetitive motor mannerisms (e.g. hand or finger flapping or flipping, or complex whole-body movements)**

Always	Often	Sometimes	Seldom	Never	Comments

- **persistent preoccupation with parts of objects**

Always	Often	Sometimes	Seldom	Never	Comments

- **repetitive behaviour**

Always	Often	Sometimes	Seldom	Never	Comments

- **self-injurious behaviour**

Always	Often	Sometimes	Seldom	Never	Comments

Thank you very much for your co-operation

References

Adrien, J.L., Lenoir, P., Martineau, J., Perrot, A., Hameury, L., Larmande, C. and Sauvage, D. (1993) 'Blind ratings of early symptoms of autism based upon family home movies.' *Journal of the American Academy of Child and Adolescent Psychiatry 32*, 617–626.

Adrien, J.L., Perrot, A., Sauvage, D., Leddet, I., Larmande, C., Hameury, L. and Barthelemy, C. (1992) 'Early symptoms in autism from family home movies. Evaluation and comparison between 1st and 2nd year of life using I.B.S.E. Scale.' *Acta Paedopsychiatry 55*, 59–63.

Agababa, P. and Gallois, T. (1985) 'Facing one's own image: Use of video in the treatment of obsessional phenomena.' *Annales Medico-Psychologiques 143*, 287–291.

Alcantara, P.R. (1994) 'Effects of videotape instructional package on purchasing skills of children with autism.' *Exceptional Children 61*, 40–55.

Allen, R.E. (1992) *The Concise Oxford Dictionary of Current English.* Oxford: Oxford University Press.

American Academy of Pediatrics (1998) 'Auditory integration training and facilitated communication for autism.' *Pediatrics 102*, 431–433.

American Psychiatric Association (1994) *Diagnostic and Statistical Manual of Mental Disorders* (4th edn). Washington, DC: American Psychiatric Association.

Anderson, A., Moore, D.W., Godfrey, R. and Fletcher-Flinn, C.M. (2004) 'Social skills assessment of children with autism in free-play situations.' *Autism 8*, 4, 369–385.

Anderson, S.R., Avery, D.L., DiPietro, E.K., Edwards, G.L. and Christian, W.P. (1987) 'Intensive home-based early intervention with autistic children.' *Education and Treatment of Children 10*, 352–366.

Anderson, S.R. and Romanczyk, R.G. (1999) 'Early intervention for young children with autism: Continuum-based behavioral models.' *Journal of the Association for Persons with Severe Handicaps 24*, 162–173.

Apple, A.L., Billingsley, F. and Schwartz, I.S. (2005) 'Effects of video modeling alone and with self-management on compliment-giving behaviors of children with high-functioning ASD.' *Journal of Positive Behavior Interventions 7*, 1, 33–46.

Arauzo, A.C., Watson, M. and Hulgus, J. (1994) 'The clinical uses of video therapy in the treatment of childhood sexual trauma survivors.' *Journal of Child Sexual Abuse 3*, 37–57.

Autism Society of America (2004) Retrieved 12 September 2004, from www.autism-society.org/site/PageServer.

Autism Society of America (2005) Retrieved 17 February 2005, from www.autism-society.org/site/PageServer.

Autism Treatment Center of America (2004) Retrieved 28 September 2004, from www.autismtreatmentcenter.org.

Axelrod, S. and Hall, P.V. (1999) *Behavior Modification. Basic Principles* (2nd edn). Austin, TX: Pro-ed.

Bacon, A.L., Fein, D., Morris, R., Waterhouse, L. and Allen, D. (1998) 'The responses of autistic children to the distress of others.' *Journal of Autism and Developmental Disorders 28*, 129–142.

Baer, D.M. and Deguchi, H. (1985) Generalized imitation from a radical-behavioral viewpoint. In S. Reiss and R.R. Bootzin (eds) *Theoretical Issues in Behavior Therapy*. London: Academic Press, Inc.

Baer, D.M., Peterson, R.F. and Sherman, J.A. (1967) 'The development of imitation by reinforcing behavioral similarity to a model.' *Journal of the Experimental Analysis of Behavior 10*, 405–416.

Baer, D.M. and Sherman, J.A. (1964) 'Reinforcement control of generalized imitation in young children.' *Journal of Experimental Child Psychology 1*, 37–49.

Baer, D.M., Wolf, M.M. and Risley, T.R. (1968) 'Some current dimensions of applied behavior analysis.' *Journal of Applied Behavior Analysis 1*, 91–97.

Baird, G., Cass, H. and Slonims, V. (2005) 'Diagnosis of autism.' *British Medical Journal 327*, 488–493.

Baker, M.J. (2000) 'Incorporating the thematic ritualistic behaviors of children with autism into games: Increasing social play interactions with siblings.' *Journal of Positive Behavior Interventions 2*, 66–84.

Baker, M.J., Koegel, R.L. and Koegel, L.K. (1998) 'Increasing the social behavior of young children with autism using their obsessive behaviors.' *Journal of the Association for Persons with Severe Handicaps 23*, 300–308.

Baker, S. (2001) 'The Alice Project: The first UK pilot project to evaluate the Picture Exchange Communication System (PECS).' Paper presented at the First International Conference of the Association of Behavior Analysis, Venice, Italy.

Baldwin, J.D. and Baldwin, J.D. (1986) *Behavior Principles in Everyday Life*. Englewood Cliffs, NJ: Prentice-Hall.

Ballard K.D. and Crooks T.J. (1984) 'Videotape modeling for preschool children with low levels of social interaction and low peer involvement in play.' *Journal of Abnormal Child Psychology 12*, 95–109.

Ballard, K.D. and Medland, J.L. (1986) 'Collateral effects from teaching attention, imitation and toy interaction behaviors to a developmentally delayed handicapped child.' *Child and Family Behavior Therapy 7*, 47–50.

Bandura, A. (1965) 'Influence of models' reinforcement contingencies on the acquisition of imitative responses.' *Journal of Personality and Social Psychology 1*, 589–595.

Bandura, A. (1969) *Principles of Behavior Modification*. New York: Holt, Rinehart and Winston.

Bandura, A. (1971) 'Vicarious and self-reinforcing processes.' In R. Glaser (ed.) *The Nature of Reinforcement*. New York: Academic Press.

Bandura, A. (1977) *Social Learning Theory*. Englewood Cliffs, NJ: Prentice-Hall.

Bandura, A. (1986) *Social Foundations of Thought and Action. A Social Cognitive Theory*. Englewood Cliffs, NJ: Prentice-Hall.

Bandura, A. and Barab, P. (1973) 'Process governing disinhibitory effects through symbolic modeling.' *Journal of Abnormal Psychology 82*, 1–9.

Bandura, A., Ross, D. and Ross, S.A. (1961) 'Transmission of aggression through imitation of aggressive models.' *Journal of Abnormal Social Psychology 63*, 575–582.

Bandura, A., Ross, D. and Ross, S. (1963) 'Imitation of film-mediated aggressive models.' *Journal of Abnormal Social Psychology 66*, 3–11.

Bandura, A. and Walters, R.H. (1963) *Social Learning and Personality Development*. New York: Holt, Rinehart and Winston.

Baranek G.T. (1999) 'Autism during infancy: A retrospective video analysis of sensory-motor and social behaviors at 9–12 months of age.' *Journal of Autism and Developmental Disorders 29*, 213–224.

Baron-Cohen, S. (2004) 'Autism: research into causes and intervention.' *Pediatric Rehabilitation 7*, 2, 73–78.

Baum, W.M. (1994) *Understanding Behaviorism. Science, Behavior, and Culture.* New York: HarperCollins College.

Beadle-Brown, J. (2004) 'Elicited imitation in children and adults with autism: the effect of different types of actions.' *Journal of Applied Research in Intellectual Disabilities 17*, 37–48.

Bebko, J.M., Perry, A. and Bryson, S. (1996) 'Multiple method validation study of facilitated communication: II individual differences and subgroup results.' *Journal of Autism and Developmental Disorders 26*, 19–42.

Berard, G. (1993) *Hearing Equals Behavior.* New Canaan, CT: Keats.

Bernard-Opitz, V., Sriram, N. and Nakhoda-Sapuan, S. (2001) 'Enhancing social problem solving in children with autism and normal children through computer-assisted instruction.' *Journal of Autism and Developmental Disorders 31*, 377–384.

Bernard-Opitz, V., Sriram, N. and Sapuan, S. (1999) 'Enhancing vocal imitations in children with autism using the IBM SpechViewer.' *Autism: The International Journal of Research and Practice 3*, 131–147.

Best, L. and Milne, R. (1997) *Development and Evaluation Committee Report No. 66: Auditory Integration Training in Autism.* Bristol: NHS Executive R and D Directorate.

Bettison, S. (1996) 'The long-term effects of auditory training on children with autism.' *Journal of Autism and Developmental Disorders 26*, 361–374.

Beyer, J. and Gammeltof, L. (2000) *Autism and Play.* London: Jessica Kingsley Publishers.

Bidwell, M.A. and Rehfeldt, R.A. (2004) 'Using video modeling to teach a domestic skill with an embedded social skill to adults with severe mental retardation.' *Behavioral Interventions 19*, 4, 263–274.

Biederman, G.B., Stepaniuk, S., Davey, V.A., Raven, K. and Ahn, D. (1999) 'Observational learning in children with Down syndrome and developmental delays. The effect of presentation speed in videotaped modelling.' *Down Syndrome Research and Practice 6*, 1, 12–18.

Biklen, D. (1990) 'Communication unbound: Autism and praxis.' *Harvard Educational Review 60*, 291–315.

Biklen, D. (1992) 'Typing to talk: Facilitated communication.' *American Journal of Speech-Language Pathology 1*, 15–17.

Biklen, D. and Schubert, A. (1991) 'New words: The communication of students with autism.' *Remedial and Special Education 12*, 46–57.

Birnbrauer, J.S. and Leach, D.J. (1993) 'The Murdoch early intervention program after 2 years.' *Behavior Change 10*, 63–74.

Bondy, A.S. (1996) 'What parents can expect from public school programs.' In C. Maurice, G. Green and S. Luce (eds) *Behavioral Intervention for Young Children with Autism. A Manual for Parents and Professionals.* Austin, TX: Pro-ed.

Bondy, A. and Frost, L. (1994) 'The picture exchange communication system.' *Focus on Autistic Behavior 9*, 1–19.

Bondy, A. and Frost, L. (2001a) 'The picture exchange communication system.' *Behavior Modification 25*, 725–744.

Bondy, A. and Frost, L. (2001b) *A Picture's Worth. PECS and Other Visual Communication Strategies in Autism.* Bethesda State: Woodbine House.

Bosseler, A. and Massaro, D.W. (2003) 'Development and evaluation of a computer-animated tutor for vocabulary and language learning in children with autism.' *Journal of Autism and Developmental Disorders 33*, 6, 653–672.

Brady, M.P., McEvoy, M.A., Wehby, J. and Ellis, D. (1987) 'Using peers as trainers to increase an autistic child's social interactions.' *The Exceptional Child 34*, 213–219.

Brestan, E.V. and Eyberg, S.M. (1998) 'Effective psychosocial treatments of conduct-disordered children and adolescents: 29 years, 82 studies, and 5,272 kids.' *Journal of Clinical Child Psychology 27*, 180–189.

Brigham, T.A. and Sherman, J.A. (1968) 'An experimental analysis of verbal imitation in preschool children.' *Journal of Applied Behavior Analysis 1*, 151–158.

Browder, D.M., Schoen, S.F. and Lentz, F.E. (1987) 'Learning to learn through observation.' *Journal of Special Education 20*, 447–461.

Brown, G. and Middleton, H. (1998) 'Use of self-as-model to promote generalization and maintenance of the reduction of self-stimulation in a child with mental retardation.' *Education and Training in Mental Retardation and Developmental Disabilities 33*, 76–80.

Brown, J. and Murray, D. (2001) 'Strategies for enhancing play skills for children with autism spectrum disorder.' *Education and Training in Mental Retardation and Developmental Disabilities 36*, 312–317.

Brown, J. and Whiten, A. (2000) 'Imitation, theory of mind and related activities in autism.' *Autism: The International Journal of Research and Practice 4*, 185–204.

Browning, P. and White, W.A.T. (1986) 'Teaching life enhancement skills with interactive video-based curricula.' *Education and Training of the Mentally Retarded 21*, 236–244.

Bryan, L.C. and Gast, D.L. (2000) 'Teaching on-task and on-schedule behaviors to high-functioning children with autism via picture activity schedules.' *Journal of Autism and Developmental Disorders 30*, 553–567.

Buggey, T., Toombs, K., Gardener, P. and Cervetti, M. (1999) 'Training responding behaviors in students with autism: Using videotaped self-modeling.' *Journal of Positive Behavior Interventions 1*, 205–214.

Cambridge Center for Behavioral Studies (2003) 'Autism and Applied Behavior Analysis.' Retrieved 22 February 2003, from www.behavior.org.

Carpenter, M., Pennington, B.F. and Rogers, S.J. (2002) 'Interrelations among social-cognitive skills in young children with autism.' *Journal of Autism and Developmental Disorders 32*, 91–106.

Carr, E.G. and Darcy, M. (1990) 'Setting generality for peer modeling in children with autism.' *Journal of Autism and Developmental Disorders 20*, 45–59.

Catania, A.C. (1998) *Learning* (4th edn) Upper Saddle River, NJ: Prentice-Hall.

Celani, G., Battacchi, M.W. and Arcidiacono, L. (1999) 'The understanding of the emotional meaning of facial expressions in people with autism.' *Journal of Autism and Developmental Disorders 29*, 57–66.

Chance, P. (1999) *Learning and Behavior*. Pacific Grove, CA: Brooks/Cole.

Chandler, L.K., Lubeck, R.C. and Fowler, S.A. (1992) 'Generalization and maintenance of preschool children's social skills: A review and analysis.' *Journal of Applied Behavior Analysis 25*, 415–428.

Chang, B.L. and Hirsch, M. (1994) 'Videotape intervention: Producing videotapes for use in nursing practice and education.' *Journal of Continuing Education in Nursing 25*, 263–267.

Charlop, M.H. (1983) 'The effects of echolalia on acquisition and generalization of receptive labelling in autistic children.' *Journal of Applied Behavior Analyis 16*, 111–126.

Charlop, M.H. and Milstein, J.P. (1989) 'Teaching autistic children conversational speech using video modeling.' *Journal of Applied Behavior Analysis 22*, 275–285.

Charlop, M.G., Schreibman, L. and Tryon, A.S. (1983) 'Learning through observation: The effects of peer modeling on acquisition and generalisation in autistic children.' *Journal of Abnormal Child Psychology 11*, 355–366.

Charlop, M.H. and Walsh, M.E. (1986) 'Increasing autistic children's spontaneous verbalizations of affection: An assessment of time delay and peer modeling procedures.' *Journal of Applied Behavior Analysis 19*, 307–314.

Charlop-Christy, M.H., Carpenter, M., Le, L., LeBlanc, L.A. and Kellet, K. (2002) 'Using the picture exchange communication system (PECS) 'with children with autism: Assessment of PECS acquisition, speech, social-communicative behaviour, and problem behaviour.' *Journal of Applied Behavior Analysis 35*, 3, 213–231.

Charlop-Christy, M.H. and Daneshvar, S. (2003) 'Using video modeling to teach perspective taking to children with autism.' *Journal of Positive Behavior Interventions 5*, 12–21.

Charlop-Christy, M.H., Le, L. and Freeman, K.A. (2000) 'A comparison of video modeling with in vivo modeling for teaching children with autism.' *Journal of Autism and Developmental Disorders 30*, 537–552.

Charman, T. and Baron-Cohen, S. (1994) 'Another look at imitation in autism.' *Development and Psychopathology 6*, 403–413.

Charman, T., Howlin, P., Berry, B. and Prince, E. (2004) 'Measuring developmental progress of children with autism spectrum disorder on school entry using parent report.' *Autism 8*, 1, 89–100.

Chen, S.H.A. and Bernard-Opitz, V. (1993) 'Comparison of personal and computer-assisted instruction for children with autism.' *Mental Retardation 31*, 368–376.

Chez, M.G., Buchanan, C.P., Bagan, B.T., Hammer, M.S., McCarthy, K.S., Ovrutskaya, I., Nowinski, C.V. and Cohen, Z.S. (2000) 'Secretin and autism: A two-part clinical investigation.' *Journal of Autism and Developmental Disorders 30*, 87–94.

Clark, M.C. and Lester, J. (2000) 'The effect of video-based interventions on self-care.' *Western Journal of Nursing Research 22*, 8, 895–911.

Collaborative Work Group on Autistic Spectrum Disorders (1997) *Best Practices For Designing And Delivering Effective Programs For Individuals With Autistic Spectrum Disorders.* Sacramento, CA: California Departments of Education and Developmental Services.

Cone, J.D. (1997) 'Issues in functional analysis in behavioral assessment.' *Behavior Research and Therapy 3*, 259–275.

Conyers, C., Miltenberger, R.G., Peterson, B., Gubin, A., Jurgens, M., Selders, A., Dickinson, J. and Barenz, R. (2004) 'An evaluation of in vivo desensitization and video modeling to increase compliance with dental procedures in persons with mental retardation.' *Journal of Applied Behavior Analysis 37*, 2, 233–238.

Cooper, J.O. (1987a) 'Measuring and recording behavior.' In J.O. Cooper, T.E. Heron and W.L. Heward (eds) *Applied Behavior Analysis.* New York: Macmillan.

Cooper, J.O. (1987b) 'Imitation.' In J.O. Cooper, T.E. Heron and W.L. Heward (eds) *Applied Behavior Analysis.* New York: Macmillan.

Cooper, J.O. (1987c) 'Planning and directing observational procedures.' In J.O. Cooper, T.E. Heron and W.L. Heward (eds) *Applied Behavior Analysis.* New York: Macmillan.

Cooper, J.O., Heron, T.E. and Heward, W.L. (eds) (1987) *Applied Behavior Analysis.* New York: Macmillan.

Corbett, B.A. and Abdullah, M. (2005) 'Video modelling: Why does it work for children with autism?' *Journal of Early and Intensive Behavior Intervention 2*, 1, 2–8.

Coucouvanis, J. (1997) 'Behavioral intervention for children with autism.' *Journal of Child and Adolescent Psychiatric Nursing 1*, 37–46.

Coyle, C. and Cole, P. (2004) 'A videotaped self-modelling and self-monitoring treatment program to decrease off-task behaviour in children with autism.' *Journal of Intellectual and Developmental Disability 29*, 1, 3–15.

Creak, M. (1961) 'Schizophrenia syndrome in childhood: Progress report of a working party.' *Cerebral Palsy Bulletin 3*, 501–504.

Curbow, B., Fogarty, L.A., McDonnell, K., Chill.J. and Scott, L.B. (2004) 'Can a brief video intervention improve breast cancer clinical trial knowledge and beliefs?' *Social Science and Medicine 58*, 1, 193–205.

Cuvo, A.J. and Davis, P.K. (1998) 'Establishing and transferring stimulus control. Teaching people with developmental disabilities.' In J.K. Luiselli and M.J. Cameron (eds) *Antecedent Control. Innovative Approaches to Behavioral Support.* Baltimore, MA: Paul H. Brookes Publishing Co.

Damasio, A. and Maurer, R. (1978) 'A neurobiological model for childhood autism.' *Archives of Neurology 35*, 777–786.

Daoust, P.M., Williams, W.L. and Rolider, A. (1987) 'Eliminating aggression and SIB through audio/video mediated delayed consequences.' Paper presented at the meeting of the Association for Behavior Analysis, Nashville, TN.

D'Ateno, P., Mangiapanello, K. and Taylor, B.A. (2003) 'Using video modeling to teach complex play sequences to a preschooler with autism.' *Journal of Positive Behavior Interventions 5*, 5–11.

Dauphin, M., Kinney, E.M. and Stromer, R. (2004) 'Using video-enhanced activity schedules and matrix training to teach sociodramatic play to a child with autism.' *Journal of Positive Behavior Interventions 6*, 4, 238–250.

Dawson, G. and Adams, A. (1984) 'Imitation and social responsiveness in autistic children.' *Journal of Abnormal Child Psychology 12*, 209–225.

Dawson, G., Meltzoff, A.N., Osterling, J., Rinaldi, J. and Brown, E. (1998) 'Children with autism fail to orient to naturally occurring social stimuli.' *Journal of Autism and Developmental Disorders 28*, 479–485.

Dawson, G., Osterling, J., Meltzoff, A.N. and Kuhl, P. (2000) 'Case study of the development of an infant with autism from birth to two years of age.' *Journal of Applied Developmental Psychology 21*, 299–313.

Dawson, J.E., Matson, J.L. and Cherry, K.E. (1998) 'Analysis of Maladaptive behaviors in persons with autism, PDD-NOS, and mental retardation.' *Research in Developmental Disabilities 19*, 439–448.

Deguchi, H. (1984) 'Observational learning from a radical-behavioristic viewpoint.' *The Behavior Analyst 7*, 83–95.

Del Valle P.R., McEachern A.G. and Chambers H.D. (2001) 'Using social stories with autistic children.' *Journal of Poetry Therapy 14*, 187–197.

DeMyer, M.K., Hingtgen, J.N. and Jackson, R.K. (1981) 'Infantile autism reviewed: A decade of research.' *Schizophrenia Bulletin 7*, 388–451.

Department of Health (1999) *Clinical Practice Guideline: The Guideline Technical Report – Autism/Pervasive Developmental Disorders, Assessment and Intervention.* Albany, NY: Early Intervention Program, New York State Department of Health.

DeRoo, W.M. and Haralson, H.L. (1971) 'Increasing workshop production through self-visualization on videotape.' *Mental Retardation 9*, 22–25.

Dewey, D., Lord, C. and Magill, J. (1988) 'Qualitative assessment of the effect of play materials in dyadic peer interactions of children with autism.' *Canadian Journal of Psychology 42*, 242–260.

Dillenburger, K., Keenan, M., Gallagher, S. and McElhinney, M. (2002) 'Autism: Intervention and parental empowerement.' *Child Care in Practice 8*, 216–219.

Dillenburger, K., Keenan, M., Gallagher, S. and McElhinney, M. (2004) 'Applied Behaviour Analysis for children with autism: Parental programme evaluation.' *Journal of Intellectual and Developmental Disabilities 29*, 113–124.

DiSalvo, C.A. and Oswald, D.P. (2002) 'Peer-mediated interventions to increase the social interaction of children with autism: Consideration of peer expectancies.' *Focus on Autism and Other Developmental Disabilities 17*, 198–207.

Division TEACCH (2003) Home page retrieved 16 February 2003, from www.teacch.com.

Dixon, M.R., Benedict, H. and Larson, T. (2001) 'Functional analysis and treatment of inappropriate behavior.' *Journal of Applied Behavior Analysis 34*, 361–363.

Dowrick, P.W. (ed.) (1991) *Practical Guide to Using Video in the Behavioral Sciences.* New York: John Wiley.

Dowrick, P.W. (1999) 'A review of self modeling and related interventions.' *Applied and Preventive Psychology 8*, 23–39.

Dowrick, P.W. and Buggey, T. (2000) 'Creating futures through video self-modelling behavioural interventions: Social and academic development in challenging behaviours and autism.' *Journal of Intellectual Disability Research 44*, 310.

Dowrick, P.W. and Jesdale, D.C. (1991) 'Modeling.' In P.W. Dowrick (ed.) *Practical Guide to Using Video in the Behavioral Sciences.* New York: John Wiley.

Duchan, J. (1986) 'Learning to describe events.' *Topics in Language Disorders 6*, 27–36.

Dunn-Geier, J., Ho, H.H., Auersperg, E., Doyle, D., Eaves, L., Matsuba, C., Orrbine, E., Pham, B. and Whiting, S. (2000) 'Effect of secretin on children with autism: A randomized controlled trial.' *Developmental Medicine and Child Neurology 42*, 796–802.

Dunn, J. and McGuire, S. (1992) 'Sibling and peer relationships in childhood.' *Journal of Child Psychology and Psychiatry 33*, 67–105.

Durham, C. (2000) 'Evolution of services for people with autism and their families in France: Influence of the TEACCH program.' *International Journal of Mental Health 29*, 22–34.

Eason, L.J., White, M.J. and Newson, C. (1982) 'Generalized reduction of self-stimulatory behavior: An effect of teaching appropriate play to autistic children.' *Analysis and Intervention in Developmental Disabilities 2*, 157–169.

Edelson, S.M., Arin, D., Bauman, M., Lukas, S.E., Rudy, J.H., Sholar, M. and Rimland, B. (1999) 'Auditory integration training: A double-blind study of behavioral, electrophysiological, and audiometric effects in people with autism.' *Focus on Autism and other Developmental Disabilities 14*, 73–81.

Egan, P.J., Zlomke, L.C. and Bush, B.R. (1993) 'Utilizing functional assessment, behavioral consultation and videotape review of treatment to reduce aggression: A case study.' *Special Services in the Schools 7*, 27–37.

Egel, A.L., Richman, G.S. and Koegel, R.L. (1981) 'Normal peer models and autistic children's learning.' *Journal of Applied Behavior Analysis 14*, 3–12.

Eikeseth, S., Smith, T., Jahr, E. and Eldevik, S. (2002) 'Intensive behavioral treatment at school for 4- to 7-year-old children with autism.' *Behavior Modification 26*, 49–68.

Emmen, H.H., Wesseling, L.G., Bootsma, R.J., Whiting, H.T.A. and Van Wieringen, P.C.W. (1985) 'The effect of video-modelling and video-feedback on the learning of the tennis service by novices.' *Journal of Sports Sciences 3*, 127–138.

Erba, H.W. (2000) 'Early intervention programs for children with autism: conceptual frameworks for implementation.' *American Journal of Orthopsychiatry 70*, 82–94.

Esch, B.E. and Carr, J.E. (2004) 'Secretin as a treatment for autism: A review of the evidence.' *Journal of Autism and Developmental Disorders 34*, 5, 543–556.

Feldman, M.A. and Werner, S.E. (2002) 'Collateral effects of behavioural parent training on families of children with developmental disabilities and behaviour disorders.' *Behavioral Interventions 17*, 75–83.

Fenske, E.C., Zalenski, S., Krantz, P.J. and McClannahan, L.E. (1985) 'Age at intervention and treatment outcome for autistic children in a comprehensive intervention program.' *Analysis and Intervention in Developmental Disabilities 5*, 49–58.

Ferrara, C. and Hill, S.D. (1980) 'The responsiveness of autistic children to the predictability of social and nonsocial toys.' *Journal of Autism and Developmental Disorders 10*, 51–57.

Ferster, C.B. (1961) 'Positive reinforcement and behavioral deficits of autistic children.' *Child Development 32*, 437–456.

Ferster, C.B. and DeMyer, M.K. (1961) 'The development of performances in autistic children in an automatically controlled environment.' *Journal of Chronic Diseases 13*, 312–345.

Fisher, W.W., Adelinis, J.D., Thompson, R.H., Worsdell, A.S. and Zarcone, J.R. (1998) 'Functional analysis and treatment of destructive behavior maintained by termination of "Don't" (and symmetrical "Do") requests.' *Journal of Applied Behavior Analysis 31*, 339–356.

Fox, J.J. and McEvoy, M.A. (1993) 'Assessing and enhancing generalization and social validity of social-skills intervention with children and adolescents.' *Behavior Modification 17*, 339–366.

Freeman, S. and Dake, L. (1996) *Teach Me Language. A Language Manual for Children With Autism, Asperger's Syndrome and Related Developmental Disorders*. Langley, BC: SFK Books.

Fuentes, J., Barinaga, R. and Gallano, I. (2000) 'Applying TEACCH in developing autism services in Spain: The GAUTENA Project.' *International Journal of Mental Health 29*, 78–88.

Gagliano, M.E. (1988) 'A literature review on the efficacy of video in patient education.' *Journal of Medical Education 63*, 785–792.

Ganz, J.B. and Simpson, R.L. (2004) 'Effects on communicative requesting and speech development of the Picture Exchange Communicatiion System in children with characteristics of autism.' *Journal of Autism and Developmental Disorders 34*, 4, 395–409.

Garfinkle, A.N. and Schwartz, I.S. (2002) 'Peer imitation: Increasing social interactions in children with autism and other developmental disabilities in inclusive preschool classrooms.' *Topics in Early Childhood Special Education 22*, 26–38.

Garlington, W.K. and Dericco, D.A. (1977) 'The effect of modelling on drinking rate.' *Journal of Applied Behavior Analysis 10*, 207–211.

Garretson, H., Fein, D. and Waterhouse, L. (1990) 'Sustained attention in autistic children.' *Journal of Autism and Developmental Disorders 20*, 101–114.

Gena, A. and Kymissis, E. (2001) 'Assessing and setting goals for the attending and communicative behavior of three preschoolers with autism in inclusive kindergarten settings.' *Journal of Autism and Developmental Disorders 13*, 11–26.

Gewirtz, J.L. (1971) 'Conditional responding as a paradigm for observational, imitative learning and vicarious reinforcement.' In H.W. Reese (ed.) *Advances in Child Development and Behavior 6*, 273–304. New York: Academic Press.

Ghuman, J.K., Freund, L., Reiss, A., Serwint, J. and Folstein, S. (1998) 'Early detection of social interaction problems: Development of a social interaction instrument in young children.' *Journal of Developmental and Behavioral Pediatrics 19*, 411–419.

Gillberg, C.L. (1992) 'The Emanuel Miller memorial lecture 1991.' *Journal of Child Psychology and Psychiatry 33*, 813–842.

Gillberg, C., Johansson, M., Steffenburg, S. and Berlin, O. (1997) 'Auditory integration training in children with autism: Brief report of an open pilot study.' *Autism: The International Journal of Research and Practice 1*, 97–100.

Goldstein, H. and Brown, W.H. (1989) 'Observational learning of receptive and expressive language by handicapped preschool children.' *Education and Treatment of Children 12*, 5–37.

Goldstein H., Kaczmarek, L., Pennington, R. and Shafer, K. (1992) 'Peer-mediated intervention: Attending to, commenting on, and acknowledging the behavior of preschoolers with autism.' *Journal of Applied Behavior Analysis 25*, 289–305.

Goodwin, D.P. and Deering, R.J. (1993) 'The interactive video approach to preservice teacher training: An analysis of students' perceptions and attitudes.' *Teacher Education and Practice 9*, 11–19.

Grandin, T. (1996) *Thinking in Pictures and Other Reports from My Life with Autism.* New York: Vintage Books.

Grant, L. and Evans, A. (1994) *Principles of Behavior Analysis.* New York: HarperCollins College.

Gray, C.A. and Garand, J.D. (1993) 'Social stories: Improving responses of students with autism with accurate social information.' *Focus on Autistic Behavior 8*, 1–10.

Greelis, M. and Kazaoka, K. (1979) 'The therapeutic use of edited videotapes with an exceptional child.' *Academic Therapy 15*, 37–44.

Green, G. (1996) 'Evaluating claims about treatments for autism.' In C. Maurice, G. Green and S.C. Luce (eds) *Behavioral Intervention for Young Children with Autism: A Manual for Parents and Professionals.* Austin, TX: Pro-ed.

Green, G. (2001) 'Behavior analytic instruction for learners with autism: Advances in stimulus control technology.' *Focus on Autism and Other Developmental Disabilities 16*, 72–85.

Green, G. (2004) 'Autism Treatments: The Quality of the Evidence.' Paper presented at the Parent Eduation as Autism Therapists (PEAT) Conference, Belfast, Northern Ireland.

Green, G., Brennan, L.C. and Fein, D. (2002) 'Intensive behavioral treatment for a toddler at high risk for autism.' *Child Development 26*, 69–102.

Greenspan, S.I. (1992) *Infancy and Early Childhood – The Practice of Clinical Assessment and Intervention with Emotional and Developmental Challenges.* Madison, CT: International Universities Press.

Gresham, F.M. (1986) 'Conceptual issues in the assessment of social competence in children.' In P.S. Strain, M.J. Guralnick and H.M. Walker (eds) *Children's Social Behavior: Development, Assessment, and Modification.* New York: Academic Press.

Groden, J. and Cautela, J. (1988) 'Procedures to increase social interaction among adolescents with autism: A multiple baseline analysis.' *Journal of Behavior Therapy and Experimental Psychiatry 19*, 87–93.

Guralnick, M.J. (1986) 'The peer relations of young handicapped and nonhandicapped children.' In P.S. Strain, M.J. Guralnick and H.M. Walker (eds) *Children's Social Behavior.* New York: Academic Press.

Gurry, S. and Larkin, A. (1990) 'Daily Life Therapy: Its roots in the Japanese culture.' *International Journal of Special Education 5*, 359–369.

Hager, R., Bertagna, T., Prusak, K. and Hunter, I. (2004) 'The effects of multi-view video modeling and skill acquisition on learning the tennis serve.' *Medicine and Science in Sports and Exercise 36*, 5 (Supplement):S203.

Hagiwara, T. and Myles, B.S. (1999) 'A multimedia social story intervention: Teaching skills to children with autism.' *Focus on Autism and Other Developmental Disabilities 14*, 82–95.

Hall, L.J. (1997) 'Effective behavioural strategies for the defining characteristics of autism.' *Behaviour Change 14*, 139–154.

Handleman, J.S. and Harris, S.L. (1980) 'Generalization from school to home with autistic children.' *Journal of Autism and Developmental Disorders 10*, 323–333.

Happé, F. (1991) 'The autobiographical writings of three Asperger syndrome adults: Problems with interpretation and implications for theory.' In U. Frith (ed.) *Autism and Asperger Syndrome.* Cambridge: Cambridge University Press.

Happé, F. and Frith, U. (1996) 'The neuropsychology of autism.' *Brain 119*, 1377–1400.

Haring, T.G. and Breen C.G. (1992) 'A peer-mediated social network intervention to enhance the social integration of persons with moderate and severe disabilities.' *Journal of Applied Behavior Analysis 25*, 319–333.

Haring, T.G., Breen, C.G., Weiner, J., Kennedy, C.H. and Bednersh, F. (1995) 'Using videotape modeling to facilitate generalized purchasing skills.' *Journal of Behavioral Education 5*, 29–53.

Haring, T.G., Kennedy, C.H., Adams, M.J. and Pitts-Conway, V. (1987) 'Teaching generalization of purchasing skills across community settings to autistic youth using videotape modeling.' *Journal of Applied Behavior Analysis 20*, 89–96.

Haring, T.G. and Lovinger, L. (1989) 'Promoting social interaction through teaching generalized play initiation responses to preschool children with autism.' *Journal of the Association for Persons with Severe Handicaps 14*, 58–67.

Harlow, H.F. (1949) 'The formation of learning sets.' *Psychological Review 56*, 51–65.

Harris, S.L. and Handleman, J.S. (eds) (1994) *Preschool Education Programs for Children with Autism.* Austin, TX: Pro-ed.

Harris, S.L. and Weiss, M.J. (1998) *Right from the Start. Behavioral Intervention for Young Children with Autism.* Bethesda State: Woodbine House.

Harrower, J.K. and Dunlap, G. (2001) 'Including children with autism in general education classrooms. A review of effective strategies.' *Behavior Modification 25*, 762–784.

Harvey, A.G., Clark, D.M., Ehlers, A. and Rapee, R.M. (2000) 'Social anxiety and self-impression: Cognitive preparation enhances the beneficial effects of video feedback following a stressful social task.' *Behavior Research and Therapy 38*, 1183–1192.

Hastings, R.P. and Symes, M.D. (2002) 'Early intensive behavioral intervention for children with autism: Parental therapeutic self-efficacy.' *Research in Developmental Disabilities 23*, 332–341.

Hauck, M., Fein, D., Waterhouse, L. and Feinstein, C. (1995) 'Social initiations by autistic children to adults and other children.' *Journal of Autism and Developmental Disorders 25*, 579–595.

Heflin, L. and Alberto, P.A. (2001) 'ABA and instuctions of students with autism spectrum disorders: Introduction to the special series.' *Focus on Autism and Other Developmental Disabilities 16*, 66–67.

Heimann, M., Nelson, K.E., Tjus, T. and Gillberg, C. (1995) 'Increasing reading and communication-skills in children with autism through an interactive multimedia computer-program.' *Journal of Autism and Developmental Disorders 25*, 459–480.

Heimann, M., Ullstadius, E., Dahlgren, S.O. and Gillberg, C. (1992) 'Imitation in autism: A preliminary research note.' *Behavioural Neurology 5*, 219–227.

Hepting, N. and Goldstein, H. (1996) 'Requesting by preschoolers with developmental disabilities: Videotaped self-modeling and learning of new linguistic structures.' *Topics in Early Childhood Special Education 16*, 407–427.

Hetzroni, O.E. and Tannous, J. (2004) 'Effects of a computer-based intervention program on the communicative functions of children with autism.' *Journal of Autism and Developmental Disorders 34*, 2, 95–113.

Heward, W.L. (1987) 'Introduction to analysis.' In J.O. Cooper, T.E. Heron and W.L. Heward (eds) *Applied Behavior Analysis.* New York: Macmillan.

Heward, W.L. and Cooper, J.O. (1987) 'Definition and characteristics of applied behavior analysis.' In J.O. Cooper, T.E. Heron and W.L. Heward (eds) *Applied Behavior Analysis.* New York: Macmillan.

Hewitt, L.E. (1998) 'Introduction – A social interactionist view of autism and its clinical management.' *Journal of Communication Disorders 31*, 87–92.

Hobson, R.P. and Lee, A. (1998) 'Hello and goodbye: A study of social engagement in autism.' *Journal of Autism and Developmental Disorders 28*, 117–127.

Hobson, R.P. and Lee, A. (1999) 'Imitation and identification in autism.' *Journal of Child Psychology and Psychiatry 4* , 649–659.

Hodgdon, L.A. (1995) *Visual Strategies for Improving Communication.* Troy, MI: Quirk Roberts.

Holth, P. (2003) 'Generalized imitation and generalized matching to sample.' *The Behaviour Analyst 26*, 155–158.

Hosford, R.E. and Mills, M.E. (1983) 'Video in social skills training.' In P.W. Dowrick and S.J. Biggs (eds) *Using Video. Psychological and Social Applications.* New York: John Wiley.

Houlihan, D., Miltenberger, R.G., Trench, B., Larson, M., Larson, S. and Vincent, J. (1995) 'A video-tape peer/self modeling program to increase community involvement.' *Child and Family Behavior Therapy 17*, 1–11.

Houten, R.V. and Hall, R.V. (2001) *The Measurement of Behavior: Behavior Modification.* Austin, TX: Pro-ed.

Howard, J.S., Sparkman, C.R., Cohen, H.G., Green, G. and Stanislaw, H. (2005) 'A comparison of intensive behavior analytic and eclectic treatments for young children with autism.' *Research in Developmental Disabilities 26*, 4, 359–383.

Hwang, B. and Hughes, C. (2000) 'The effects of social interactive training on early social communicative skills of children with autism.' *Journal of Autism and Developmental Disorders 3* , 331–343.

Igo, M., French, R. and Kinnison, L. (1997) 'Influence of modeling and selected reinforcement on improving cooperative play skills of children with autism: Clinical Kinesiology.' *Journal of the American Kinesiotherapy Association 51*, 16–21.

Ihrig, K. and Wolchik, S.A. (1988) 'Peer versus adult models and autistic children's learning: Acquisition, generalisation and maintenance.' *Journal of Autism and Developmental Disorders 18*, 67–79.

Ingersoll, B., Schreibman, L. and Stahmer, A. (2001) 'Brief report: Differential treatment outcomes for children with autistic spectrum disorder based on level of peer social avoidance.' *Journal of Autism and Developmental Disorders 31*, 343–349.

Ingersoll, B., Schreibman, L. and Tran, Q.H. (2003) 'Effect of sensory feedback on immediate object imitation in children with autism.' *Journal of Autism and Developmental Disorders 33*, 6, 673–683.

Jensen, V.K. and Sinclair, L.V. (2002) 'Treatment of autism in young children: Behavioral intervention and applied behavior analysis.' *Infants and Young Children 14*, 42–52.

Jolly, A.C., Test, D.W. and Spooner, F. (1993) 'Using badges to increase initiations of children with severe disabilities in a play setting.' *Journal of the Association of Persons with Severe Handicaps 18*, 46–51.

Jones, M.C. (1924) 'The elimination of children's fears.' *Journal of Experimental Psychology* 7, 383–390.

Jordan, R. (2001) *Autistic Spectrum Disorders. An Introductory Handbook for Practitioners.* London: David Fulton.

Jordan, R. (2003) 'Social play and autistic spectrum disorders. A perspective on theory, implications and educational approaches.' *Autism* 7, 4, 347–360.

Jordan, R., Jones, G. and Murray, D. (1998) *Research Report. Educational Interventions for Children with Autism: A Literature Review of Recent and Current Research.* Colegate: Stationery Office.

Jordan, R. and Powell, S. (1995) *Understanding and Teaching Children with Autism.* Chichester: John Wiley.

Kaiser, A.P., Hester, P.P. and McDuffie, A.S. (2001) 'Supporting communication in young children with developmental disabilities.' *Mental Retardation and Developmental Disabilities Research Reviews* 7, 143–150.

Kamio, Y. and Toichi, M. (2000) 'Dual access to semantics in autism: Is pictorial access superior to verbal access?' *Journal of Child Psychology and Psychiatry* 41, 859–867.

Kamps, D.M., Barbetta, P.M., Leonard, B.R. and Delquadri, J. (1994) 'Classwide peer tutoring: An integration strategy to improve reading skills and promote peer interactions among students with autism and general education peers.' *Journal of Applied Behavior Analysis* 27, 49–61.

Kamps, D., Royer, J., Dugan, E., Kravits, T., Gonzalez-Lopez, A., Garcia, J., Carnazzo, K., Morrison, L. and Kane, L.G. (2002) 'Peer training to facilitate social interaction for elementary students with autism and their peers.' *Exceptional Children* 68, 173–187.

Kanner, L. (1943) 'Autistic disturbances of affective contact.' *Nervous Child* 2, 217–250.

Kanner, L. (1971) 'Follow-up study of eleven autistic children originally reported in 1943.' *Journal of Autism and Childhood Schizophrenia* 1, 119–145.

Kanner, L. (1973) *Childhood Psychosis: Initial Studies and New Insights.* Washington, DC: V.H. Winston.

Kanner, L., Rodriguez, A. and Ashenden, B. (1972) 'How far can autistic children go in matters of social adaptation?' *Journal of Autism and Childhood Schizophrenia* 2, 9–33.

Katz-Charny, J. and Goldstein, A. (1995) 'An innovative technique of video replay for reempowering an incest survivor and protecting the integrity of the family.' *Psychotherapy* 32, 688–695.

Kaufman, B.N. (1981) *A Miracle to Believe in.* New York: Ballantine Books.

Kaufman, B.N. (1994) *Son Rise. The Miracle Continues.* Tiburon, CA: H.J. Kramer.

Kaufman, B.N. and Kaufman, S. (1976) *To Love Is to Be Happy ith* . Human Horizons Series. London: Souvenir Press.

Kazdin, A.E. (1974) 'Covert modeling, model similarity, and reduction of avoidance behavior.' *Behavior Therapy* 5, 325–340.

Kazdin, A.E. (2001) *Behavior Modification in Applied Settings* (6th edn). Belmont, CA: Wadsworth/Thompson Learning.

Keller, M.F. and Carlson, P.M. (1974) 'The use of symbolic modeling to promote social skills in preschool children with low levels of social responsiveness.' *Child Development* 45, 912–919.

Kinney, E.M., Vedora, J. and Stromer, R. (2003) 'Computer-presented video models to teach generative spelling to a child with an autism spectrum disorder.' *Journal of Positive Behavior Interventions* 5, 22–29.

Kitahara, K. (1983/84) *Daily Life Therapy, Volumes 1, 2 and 3.* Tokyo: Musashino Higashi Gakuen School.

Koegel, L.K. (2000) 'Interventions to facilitate communication in autism.' *Journal of Autism and Developmental Disorders* 3 , 383–391.

Koegel.L.K., Camarata, S.M., Valdez-Menchaca, M. and Koegel, R.L. (1998) 'Setting generalization of question-asking by children with autism.' *American Journal on Mental Retardation 1 2* , 346–357.

Koegel, R.L. and Koegel, L.K. (1999) *Teaching Children ith Autism. Strategies For Initiating Positive Interactions And Improving Learning Opportunities.* Baltimore, MA: Paul H. Brookes.

Koegel, R.L., Koegel, L.K. and Carter, C.M. (1999) 'Pivotal teaching interactions for children with autism.' *School Psychology Review 28,* 576–594.

Koegel, L.K., Koegel, R.L., Frea, W.D. and Fredeen, R.M. (2001) 'Identifying early intervention target for children with autism in inclusive school settings.' *Behavior Modification 25,* 754–761.

Koegel, L.K., Koegel, R.L., Harrower, J.K. and Carter, C.M. (1999a) 'Pivotal response intervention I: Overview of approach.' *Journal of the Association for Persons with Severe Handicaps 24,* 174–185.

Koegel, L.K., Koegel, R.L., Hurley, C. and Frea, W.D. (1992) 'Improving social skills and disruptive behavior in children with autism through self-management.' *Journal of Applied Behavior Analysis 25,* 341–353.

Koegel, L.K., Koegel, R.L., Shoshan, Y. and McNerney, E. (1999b) 'Pivotal response intervention II: Preliminary long-term outcomes data.' *Journal of the Association for Persons with Severe Handicaps 24,* 186–198.

Kohler, F.W. and Greenwood, C.R. (1986) 'Toward a technology of generalization: The identification of natural contingencies of reinforcement.' *The Behavior Analyst 9,* 19–26.

Kohler, W., Strain, P.S., Hoyson, M., Davis, L., Donina, W.M. and Rapp, N. (1995) 'Using a group-oriented contingency to increase social interactions between children with autism and their peers: A preliminary analysis of corollary supportive behaviors.' *Behavior Modification 19,* 10–32.

Kohler, F.W., Strain, P.S., Maretsky, S. and DeCesare, L. (1990) 'Promoting positive and supportive interactions between preschoolers: An analysis of group-oriented contingencies.' *Journal of Early Intervention 14,* 327–341.

Kornhaber, R.C. and Schroeder, H.F. (1975) 'Importance of model similarity on extinction of avoidance behavior in children.' *Journal of Consulting and Clinical Psychology 5,* 601–607.

Kraijer, D. (2000) 'Review of adaptive behavior studies in mentally retarded persons with autism/pervasive developmental disorder.' *Journal of Autism and Developmental Disorders 3* , 39–47.

Krantz, P.J., MacDuff, M.T. and McClannahan, L.E. (1993) 'Programming participation in family activities for children with autism: Parent's use of photographic activity schedules.' *Journal of Applied Behavior Analysis 26,* 137–138.

Krantz, P.J., MacDuff, G.S., Wadstrom, O. and McClannahan, L.E. (1991) 'Using video with developmentally disabled learners.' In P.W. Dowrick (ed.) *Practical Guide to Using Video in the Behavioral Sciences.* New York: John Wiley.

Krantz, P.J. and McClannahan, L.E. (1993) 'Teaching children with autism to initiate to peers: Effects of a script-fading procedure.' *Journal of Applied Behavior Analysis 26,* 121–132.

Krantz, P.J. and McClannahan, L.E. (1998) 'Social interaction skills for children with autism: A script-fading procedure for beginning readers.' *Journal of Applied Behavior Analysis 31,* 191–202.

Kuoch, H. and Mirenda, P. (2003) 'Social story interventions for young children with autism spectrum disorders.' *Focus on Autism and Other Developmental Disabilities 18,* 4, 219–227.

Kymissis, E. and Poulson, C.L. (1990) 'The history of imitation in learning theory: The language acquisition process.' *Journal of the Experimental Analysis of Behavior 54,* 113–127.

Lanquetot, R. (1989) 'The effectiveness of peer modeling with autistic children.' *Journal of the Multihandicapped Person 2,* 25–34.

Larkin, A.S. and Gurry, S. (1998) 'Brief report: Progress reported in three children with autism using daily life therapy.' *Journal of Autism and Developmental Disorders 28*, 339–342.

Lasater, M.W. and Brady, M.P. (1995) 'Effects of video self-modeling and feedback on task fluency: A home-based intervention.' *Education and Treatment of Children 18*, 389–407.

Laushey, K.M. and Heflin, L.J. (2000) 'Enhancing social skills of kindergarten children with autism through the training of multiple peers as tutors.' *Journal of Autism and Developmental Disorders 3* , 183–193.

Le, L. and Charlop-Christy, M.H. (1999) 'PECS and Social Behavior.' Paper presented at the meeting of the California Association for Behavior Analysis, San Francisco, CA.

Leaf, R. and McEachin, J. (1999) *Behavior Management Strategies and a Curriculum for Intensive Behavioral Treatment of Autism.* New York: DRL Books.

LeBlanc, L.A., Coates, A.M., Daneshvar, S., Charlop-Christy, M.H., Morris, C. and Lancaster, B.M. (2003) 'Using video modeling and reinforcement to teach perspective-taking skills to children with autism.' *Journal of Applied Behavior Analysis 36*, 253–257.

Leslie, J.C. (2002) *Essential Behaviour Analysis.* London: Arnold.

Leslie, J.C. and O'Reilly, M.F. (1999) *Behavior Analysis. Foundations and Applications to Psychology.* Amsterdam: Harwood.

Libby, S., Powell, S., Messer, D. and Jordan, R. (1997) 'Imitation of pretend play acts by children with autism and Down syndrome.' *Journal of Autism and Developmental Disorders 27*, 365–383.

Libby, S., Powell, S., Messer, D. and Jordan, R. (1998) 'Spontaneous play in children with autism: A reappraisal.' *Journal of Autism and Developmental Disorders 28*, 487–497.

Lifter, K., Sulzerazaroff, B., Anderson, S.R. and Cowdery, G.E. (1993) 'Teaching play activities to preschool-children with disabilities – the importance of developmental considerations.' *Journal of Early Intervention 17*, 139–159.

Lord, C. (1984) 'The development of peer relations in children with autism.' In F.J. Morrison, C. Lord and D.P Keating (eds) *Advances in Applied Developmental Psychology.* New York: Academic Press.

Lord, C., Bristol, M.M. and Schopler, E. (1993) 'Early intervention for children with autism and related developmental disorders.' In E. Schopler, M.E. Van Bourgondien and M.M. Bristol (eds) *Preschool Issues in Autism.* New York: Plenum Press.

Lord, C. and Hopkins, J.M. (1986) 'The social behavior of autistic children with younger and same-age nonhandicapped peers.' *Journal of Autism and Developmental Disorders 16*, 249–262.

Lord, C. and Magill, J. (1989) 'Methodological and theoretical issues in studying peer-directed behavior and autism.' In G. Dawson (ed.) *Autism: Nature, Diagnosis, and Treatment.* New York: Guilford.

Lord, C. and Pickles, A. (1996) 'Language level and nonverbal social-communicative behaviors in autistic and language-delayed children.' *Journal of the American Academy of Child and Adolescent Psychiatry 35*, 1542–1550.

Lord.C. and Schopler, E. (1988) 'Intellectual and developmental assessment of autistic children from preschool to school age: Clinical implications of two follow-up studies.' In E. Schopler and G.B. Mesibov (eds) *Diagnosis and Assessment in Autism.* New York: Plenum Press.

Lord, C. and Schopler, E. (1989) 'The role of age at assessment, developmental level, and test in the stability of intelligence scores in young autistic children.' *Journal of Autism and Developmental Disorders 19*, 483–489.

Lovaas, O.I. (1981) *Teaching Developmentally Disabled Children: The Me Book.* Austin, TX: Pro-Ed.

Lovaas, O.I. (1987) 'Behavioral treatment and normal educational and intellectual functioning in young autistic children.' *Journal of Consulting and Clinical Psychology 55*, 3–9.

Lovaas, O.I. (1993) 'The development of a treatment-research project for developmentally disabled and autistic children.' *Journal of Applied Behavior Analysis 26*, 617–630.

Lovaas, O.I., Berberich, J.P., Perloff, B.F. and Schaffer, B. (1966) 'Acquisition of imitative speech by schizophrenic children.' *Science 151*, 705–707.

Lovaas, O.I., Freitas, L., Nelson, K. and Whalen, C. (1967) 'The establishment of imitation and its use for the development of complex behavior in schizophrenic children.' *Behavior Research and Therapy 5*, 171–182.

Lovaas, O.I. and Koegel, R.L. (1979) 'Stimulus overselectivity in autism: A review of research.' *Psychological Bulletin 86*, 1236–1254.

Lovaas, O.I., Koegel, R.L. and Schreibman, L. (1979) 'Stimulus overselectivity in autism: A review of research.' *Psychological Bulletin 86*, 1236–1254.

Lovaas, O.I., Schreibman, L., Koegel, R. and Rehm, R. (1971) 'Selective responding by autistic children to multiple sensory input.' *Journal of Abnormal Psychology 77*, 211–222.

Luiselli, J.K., Cannon, B.O'M., Ellis, J.T. and Sisson, R.W. (2000) 'Home-based behavioral interventions for young children with autism/pervasive developmental disorder: A preliminary evaluation of outcome in relation to child age and intensity of service delivery.' *Autism: The International Journal of Research and Practice 4*, 426–438.

MacDuff, G.S., Krantz, P.J. and McClannahan, L.E. (1993) 'Teaching children with autism to use photographic activity schedules: Maintenance and generalization of complex response chains.' *Journal of Applied Behavior Analysis 26*, 89–97.

MADSEC Autism Taskforce (1999) *Executive Summary*. Portland: Department of Education, State of Maine.

Maestro, S., Casella, C., Milone, A., Muratori, F. and Palacio-Espasa, F. (1999) 'Study of the onset of autism through home movies.' *Psychopathology 32*, 292–300.

Magiati, I. and Howlin, P. (2003) 'A pilot evaluation study of the picture exchange communication system (PECS) 'for children with autistic spectrum disorders.' *Autism: The International Journal of Research and Practice 7*, 3, 297–320.

Marcus, L.M., Lansing, M., Andrews, C.E. and Schopler, E. (1978) 'Improvement of teaching effectiveness in parents of autistic children.' *Journal of the American Academy of Child Psychiatry 17*, 625–639.

Martin, G. and Pear, J. (2002) *Behavior Modification. hat It Is and How To Do It* (7th edn). Upper Saddle River, NJ: Prentice-Hall.

Masia, C.L. and Chase, P.N. (1997) 'Vicarious learning revisited: A contemporary behavior analytic interpretation.' *Journal of Behavior Therapy and Experimental Psychiatry 28*, 41–51.

Massey, N.G. and Wheeler, J.J. (2000) 'Acquisition and generalization of activity schedules and their effects on task engagement in a young child with autism in an inclusive pre-school classroom.' *Education and Training in Mental Retardation and Developmental Disabilities 35*, 326–335.

Matson, J.L., Benavidez, D.A., Stabinsky-Compton, L., Paclawskyi, T. and Baglio, C. (1996) 'Behavioral treatment of autistic persons: A review of research from 1980 to the present.' *Research in Developmental Disabilities 17*, 433–465.

Maurice, C. (1993) *Let Me Hear Your Voice. A Family's Triumph Over Autism*. London: Robert Hale.

Maurice, C., Green, G. and Luce, S.C. (1996) *Behavioral Intervention For Young Children ith Autism: A Manual For Parents and Professionals*. Austin, TX: Pro-ed.

Maurice, C., Mannion, K., Letso, S. and Perry, L. (2001) 'Parent voices: Difficulty in assessing behavioural intervention for autism; working towards solutions.' *Behavioral Interventions 16*, 147–165.

McArthur, D. and Adamson, L.B. (1996) 'Joint attention in preverbal children: Autism and developmental language disorder.' *Journal of Autism and Developmental Disorders 26*, 481–496.

McClannahan, L.E. and Krantz, P.J. (1999) *Activity Schedules For Children with Autism. Teaching Independent Behavior.* Bethesda State: Woodbine House.

McDonald, M.E. and Hemmes, N.S. (2003) 'Increases in social initiation toward an adolescent with autism: Reciprocity effects.' *Research in Developmental Disabilities 24*, 453–465.

McDonough, L., Stahmer, A., Schreibman, L. and Thompson, S.J. (1997) 'Deficits, delays, and distractions: An evaluation of symbolic play and memory in children with autism.' *Development and Psychopathology 9*, 17–41.

McEachin, J.J., Smith, T. and Lovaas, O.I. (1993) 'Long-term outcome for children with autism who received early intensive behavioral treatment.' *American Journal on Mental Retardation 97*, 359–372.

McGee, G.G., Almeida, M.C., Sulzer-Azaroff, B. and Feldman, R.S. (1992) 'Promoting reciprocal interactions via peer incidental teaching.' *Journal of Applied Behavior Analysis 25*, 117–126.

McGee, G.G., Krantz, P.J. and McClannahan, L.E. (1985) 'The facilitative effects of incidental teaching on preposition use by autistic children.' *Journal of Applied Behavior Analysis 18*, 17–31.

McGrath, A.M., Bosch, S., Sullivan, C.L. and Fuqua, R.W. (2003) 'Training reciprocal social interactions between preschoolers and a child with autism.' *Journal of Positive Behavior Interventions 5*, 47–54.

Meharg, S.S. and Woltersdorf, M.A. (1990) 'Therapeutic use of videotape self-modeling: A review.' *Advances in Behaviour Research and Therapy 12*, 85–99.

Meltzoff, A.N. and Moore, M.K. (1992) 'Early imitation within a functional framework: The importance of person identity, movement, and development.' *Infant Behavior and Development 15*, 479–505.

Mesibov, G.B. (1997) 'Formal and informal measures of the effectiveness of the TEACCH program.' *Autism: The International Journal of Research and Practice 1*, 25–35.

Mesibov, G.B. (2003) 'Learning styles of students with autism.' Retrieved 12 January 2003, from www. teacch.com/edkidsls.htm.

Mesibov, G.B., Schopler, E. and Hearsey, K.A. (1994) 'Structured teaching.' In E. Schopler and G.B. Mesibov (eds) *Behavioral Issues in Autism.* Jersey: Plenum Press.

Mesibov, G.B. and Shea, V. (2003) 'The culture of autism: From theoretical understanding to educational practice.' Retrieved 12 January 2003, from www.autismuk.com/new%20web /index3sub1.htm.

Michael, J. (1993) 'Establishing operations.' *The Behavior Analyst 16*, 191–206.

Michael, J. (2000) 'Implications and refinements of the establishing operation concept.' *Journal of Applied Behavior Analysis 33*, 401–410.

Miller, N.E. and Dollard, J. (1967) *Social Learning and Imitation.* New Haven, CN: Yale University Press.

Miltenberger, R.G. (1997) *Behavior Modification. Principles and Procedures.* Pacific Grove, CA: Brooks/Cole.

Minshew, N., Goldstein, G., Muenz, L. and Payton, J. (1992) 'Neuropsychological functioning of nonmentally retarded autistic individuals.' *Journal of Clinical and Experimental Neuropsychology 14*, 749–761.

Montee, B.B., Miltenberger, R.G. and Wittrock, D. (1995) 'An experimental analysis of facilitated communication.' *Journal of Applied Behavior Analysis 28*, 189–200.

Moore, M. and Calvert, S. (2000) 'Vocabulary acquisition for children with autism: Teacher or computer instruction.' *Journal of Autism and Developmental Disorders 3* , 359–362.

Moore, D., McGrath, P. and Thorpe, J. (2000) 'Computer-aided learning for people with autism – a framework for research and development.' *Innovations in Education and Training International 37*, 218–228.

Moran, D.R. and Whitman, T.L. (1991) 'Developing generalized teaching skills in mothers of autistic children.' *Child and Family Behavior Therapy 13*, 13–37.

Morgan, R.L. and Salzberg, C.L. (1992) 'Effects of video-assisted training on employment-related skills of adults with severe mental retardation.' *Journal of Applied Behavior Analysis 25*, 365–383.

Morgan, S. (1988) 'Diagnostic assessment of autism: A review of objective scales.' *Journal of Psychoeducational Assessment 6*, 139–151.

Morris, R.J. (1985) *Behavior Modification with Exceptional Children: Principles And Practices.* Glenview, IL: Scott, Foresman.

Morrison, R.S., Sainato, D.M., Benchaaban, D. and Endo, S. (2002) 'Increasing play skills of children with autism using activity schedules and correspondence training.' *Journal of Early Intervention 25*, 58–72.

Mostert, M.P. (2001) 'Facilitated communication since 1995: A review of published studies.' *Journal of Autism and Developmental Disorders 31*, 3, 287–313.

Mudford, O.C., Cross, B.A., Breen, S., Cullen, C., Reeves, D., Gould, J. and Douglas, J. (2000) 'Auditory integration training for children with autism: No behavioral benefits detected.' *American Journal on Mental Retardation 1 5*, 118–129.

Mudford, O.C. and Cullen, C. (2005) Auditory integration training: A critical review.' In J.W. Jacobson, R.M. Foxx and J.A. Mulick (eds) *Controversial Therapies for Developmental Disabilities. Fad, Fashion, and Science in Professional Practice.* Mahwah, NJ: Lawrence Erlbaum Associates.

Mudford, O.C., Martin, N.T., Eikeseth, S. and Bibby, P. (2001) 'Parent-managed behavioral treatment for pre-school children with autism: Some characteristics of UK programs.' *Research in Developmental Disabilities 22*, 173–182.

Mundy, P. and Markus, J. (1997) 'On the nature of communication and language impairment in autism.' *Mental Retardation and Developmental Disabilities Research Reviews 3*, 343–349.

Mundy, P., Sigman, M., Ungerer, J. and Sherman, T. (1986) 'Defining the social deficits of autism: The contribution of non-verbal communication measures.' *Journal of Child Psychology and Psychiatry 27*, 657–669.

Nadel, J., Guerini, C., Peze, A. and Rivet, C. (1999) 'The evolving nature of imitation as a format of communication.' In J. Nadel and G. Butterworth (eds) *Imitation in Infancy.* Cambridge: Cambridge University Press.

Nadel, J. and Peze, A. (1993) 'What makes immediate imitation communicative in toddlers and autistic children?' In J. Nadel and L. Camaioni (eds) *New Perspectives In Early Communicative Development.* London: Routledge.

Nally, B., Houlton, B. and Ralph, S. (2000) 'Researches in brief: The management of television and video by parents of children with autism.' *Autism: The International Journal of Research and Practice 4*, 331–337.

National Autistic Society (1996) *Autism: The Invisible Children An Agenda for Action* . London: National Autistic Society.

National Autistic Society (2000) *The Autism Handbook.* London: National Autistic Society.

National Autistic Society (2005) Retrieved 05 June 05 2004, from http://www.nas.org.uk/.

National Society for Autistic Children (1978) 'National Society for Autistic Children definition of the syndrome of autism.' *Journal of Autism and Childhood Schizophrenia 8*, 162–167.

Neef, N.A., Trachtenberg, S., Loeb, J. and Sterner, K. (1991) 'Video-based training of respite care providers: An interactional analysis of presentation format.' *Journal of Applied Behavior Analysis 24*, 473–486.

Nelson R., Gibson, F. and Cutting, D.S. (1973) 'Videotaped modeling: The development of three appropriate social responses in a mildly retarded child.' *Mental Retardation 11*, 24–28.

Newman, N., Buffington, D.M., O'Grady, M.A., McDonald, M.E., Poulson, C.L. and Hemmes, N.S. (1995) 'Self-management of schedule following in three teenagers with autism.' *Behavioral Disorders 2* , 190–196.

Newman, B., Reineche, D.R. and Meinberg, D.L. (2000) 'Self-management of varied responding in three students with autism.' *Behavioral Interventions 15*, 145–151.

Neysmith-Roy, J.M. (2001) 'The Tomatis Method with severely autistic boys: Individual case studies of behavioural changes.' *South Africa Journal of Psychology 31*, 19–28.

Nikopoulos, C.K. and Keenan, M. (2003) 'Promoting social initiation in children with autism.' *Behavioral Interventions 18*, 2, 87–108.

Nikopoulos, C.K. and Keenan, M. (2004a) 'Effects of video modeling on social initiations by children with autism.' *Journal of Applied Behavior Analysis 37*, 93–96.

Nikopoulos, C.K. and Keenan, M. (2004b) 'Effects of video modelling on training and generalisation of social initiation and reciprocal play by children with autism.' *European Journal of Behaviour Analysis 5*, 1–13.

Njardvik, U., Matson, J.L. and Cherry, K.E. (1999) 'A comparison of social skills in adults with autistic disorder, pervasive developmental disorder not otherwise specified, and mental retardation.' *Journal of Autism and Developmental Disorders 29*, 287–295.

Norris, C. and Dattilo, J. (1999) 'Evaluating effects of a social story intervention on a young girl with autism.' *Focus on Autism and Other Developmental Disabilities 14*, 180–186.

O'Connor, R. (1969) 'Modification of social withdrawal through symbolic modeling.' *Journal of Applied Behavior Analysis 2*, 15–22.

O'Connor, R. (1972) 'The relative efficacy of modeling, shaping, and the combined procedures for the modification of social withdrawal.' *Journal of Abnormal Psychology 79*, 327–334.

Odom, S.L., Chandler, L.K., Ostrosky, M., McConnell, S.R. and Reaney, S. (1992) 'Fading teacher prompts from peer-initiation interventions for young children with disabilities.' *Journal of Applied Behavior Analysis 25*, 307–317.

Odom, S.L., Hoyson, M., Jamieson, B. and Strain, P.S. (1985) 'Increasing handicapped preschoolers' peer social interactions: Cross-setting and component analysis.' *Journal of Applied Behavior Analysis 18*, 3–16.

Odom, S.L., McConnell, S.R. and McEvoy, M.A. (1992) *Social Competence of Young Children with Disabilities. Issues and Strategies for Intervention.* Baltimore: Paul H. Brookes.

Odom, S.L. and Strain, P.S. (1986) 'A comparison of peer-initiation and teacher-antecedent interventions for promoting reciprocal social interaction of autistic preschoolers.' *Journal of Applied Behavior Analysis 19*, 59–71.

Oke, N.J. and Schreibman, L. (1990) 'Training social initiations to a high-functioning autistic child: Assessment of collateral behavior change and generalization in a case study.' *Journal of Autism and Developmental Disorders 2* , 479–497.

Ollendick, T.H. and King, N.J. (1998) 'Empirically supported treatments for children with phobic and anxiety disorders: Current status.' *Journal of Clinical Child Psychology 27*, 156–167.

Olley, J.G. (1986) 'The TEACCH curriculum for teaching social behavior to children with autism.' In E. Schopler and G.B. Mesibov (eds) *Social Behavior in Autism*. New York: Plenum Press.

Olley, J.G. (1999) 'Curriculum for students with autism.' *School Psychology Review 28*, 595–607.

O'Reilly, M.F. (1997) 'Assessing challenging behaviour of persons with severe mental disabilities.' In K. Dillenburger, M.F. O'Reilly and M. Keenan (eds) *Advances in Behaviour Analysis*. Dublin: University College Dublin Press.

O'Riordan, M.A. (2004) 'Superior visual search in adults with autism.' *Autism: The International Journal of Research and Practice 8*, 3, 229–248.

Orsmond, G.I., Krauss, M.W. and Seltzer, M.M. (2004) 'Peer relationships and social and recreational activities among adolescents and adults with autism.' *Journal of Autism and Developmental Disorders 34*, 3, 245–256.

Ozonoff, S. and Cathcart, K. (1998) 'Effectiveness of a home program intervention for young children with autism.' *Journal of Autism and Developmental Disorders 28*, 25–32.

Panerai, S., Ferrante, L. and Caputo, V. (1996) 'The TEACCH strategy in mentally retarded children and autism: A multidimensional assessment pilot study.' *Journal of Autism and Developmental Disorders 27*, 345–347.

Parsons, S. and Mitchell, P. (2002) 'The potential of virtual reality in social skills training for people with autistic spectrum disorders.' *Journal of Intellectual Disability Research 46*, 430–443.

Paul, R., Miles, S., Cicchetti, D., Sparrow, S., Klin, A., Volkmar, F., Coflin, M. and Booker, S. (2004) 'Adaptive behaviour in autism and pervasive developmental disorder-not otherwise specified: Microanalysis of scores on the Vineland Adaptive Behavior Scales.' *Journal of Autism and Developmental Disorders 34*, 2, 223–228.

Pear, J.J. (2001) *The Science of Learning*. Philadelphia, PA: Psychology Press.

Pelios, P., Morren, J., Tesch, D. and Axelrod, S. (1999) 'The impact of functional analysis methodology on treatment choice for self-injurious and aggressive behavior.' *Journal of Applied Behavior Analysis 32*, 185–195.

Perry, M.A. and Furukawa, M.J. (1988) 'Modeling methods.' In F.H. Kanfer and A.P. Goldstein (eds) *Helping People Change. A Textbook Of Methods* (3rd edn). New York: Pergamon Press.

Perry, R., Cohen, I. and DeCarlo, R. (1995) 'Case study: Deterioration, autism, and recovery in two siblings.' *Journal of the American Academy of Child and Adolescent Psychiatry 34*, 232–237.

Peterson, R.F. (1968) 'Some experiments on the organization of a class of imitative behaviors.' *Journal of Applied Behavior Analysis 1*, 225–235.

Peterson, R.F. and Whitehurst, G.J. (1971) 'A variable influencing the performance of generalized imitative behaviors.' *Journal of Applied Behavior Analysis 4*, 1–9.

Pierce, K., Glad, K.S. and Schreibman, L. (1997) 'Social perception in children with autism: An attentional deficit?' *Journal of Autism and Developmental Disorders 27*, 265–282.

Pierce, K. and Schreibman, L. (1994) 'Teaching daily living skills to children with autism in unsupervised settings through pictorial self-management.' *Journal of Applied Behavior Analysis 27*, 471–481.

Pierce, K. and Schreibman, L. (1995) 'Increasing complex social behaviors in children with autism: Effects of peer-implemented pivotal response training.' *Journal of Applied Behavior Analysis 28*, 285–295.

Pierce, K. and Schreibman, L. (1997) 'Multiple peer use of pivotal response training to increase social behaviors of classmates with autism: Results from trained and untrained peers.' *Journal of Applied Behavior Analysis 3* , 157–160.

Poche, C., Yoder, P. and Miltenberger, R. (1988) 'Teaching self-protection to children using television techniques.' *Journal of Applied Behavior Analysis 21*, 253–261.

Posey, D.J. and McDougle, C.J. (2000) 'The pharmacotherapy of target symptoms associated with autistic disorder and other pervasive developmental disorders.' *Harvard Review of Psychiatry 8*, 45–63.

Posey, D.J. and McDougle, C.J. (2001) 'Pharmacotherapeutic management of autism.' *Expert Opinion in Pharmacotherapy 2*, 587–600.

Posey, D.J. and McDougle, C.J. (2002) 'Risperidone: A potential treatment for autism.' *Current Opinion in Investigating Drugs 3*, 1212–1216.

Poulson, C.L. and Kymissis, E. (1988) 'Generalized imitation in infants.' *Journal of Experimental Child Psychology 46*, 3, Special Issue, 324–336.

Poulson, C.L., Kymissis, E., Reeve, K.F., Andreatos, M. and Reeve, L. (1991) 'Generalized vocal imitation in infants.' *Journal of Experimental Child Psychology 51*, 267–279.

Powers, M.D. and Handelman, J. (1984) *Behavioral Assessment of Severe Developmental Disabilities.* Rockville, MD: Aspen Systems Corporation.

Preece, D., Lovett, K., Lovett, P. and Burke, C. (2000) 'The adoption of TEACCH in Northamptonshire, UK: A unique collaboration between a voluntary organization and a local authority.' *International Journal of Mental Health 29*, 19–31.

Princeton Child Development Institute (2005) Retrieved 22 October 2005, from www.pcdi.org/index.asp.

Prizant, B.M. and Rubin, E. (1999) 'Contemporary issues in interventions for autism spectrum disorders: A commentary.' *Journal of the Association for Persons with Severe Handicaps 24*, 199–208.

Quill, K.A. (1995a) 'Visually cued instruction for children with autism and pervasive developmental disorders.' *Focus on Autistic Behavior 1* , 10–22.

Quill, K.A. (1995b) *Teaching Children with Autism. Strategies to Enhance Communication and Socialization.* New York: Delmar.

Quill, K.A. (1997) 'Instructional considerations for young children with autism: The rationale for visually cued instruction.' *Journal of Autism and Developmental Disorders 27*, 697–714.

Quill, K.A. (2000) *Do- atch-Listen-Say. Social Communication Intervention for Children with Autism* . Baltimore: Paul H. Brookes.

Quill, K., Gurry, S. and Larkin, A. (1989) 'Daily Life Therapy: A Japanese model for educating children with autism.' *Journal of Autism and Developmental Disorders 19*, 625–635.

Racicot, B.M. and Wogalter, M.S. (1995) 'Effects of a video warning sign and social modeling on behavioral compliance.' *Accident Analysis and Prevention 27*, 57–64.

Reamer, R.B., Brady, M.P. and Hawkins, J. (1998) 'The effects of video self-modeling on parents' interactions with children with developmental disabilities.' *Education and Training in Mental Retardation and Developmental Disabilities 33*, 131–143.

Receveur, C., Lenoir, P., Desombre, H., Roux, S., Barthelemy, C. and Malvy, J. (2005) 'Interaction and imitation deficits from infancy to 4 years of age in children with autism. A pilot study based on videotapes.' *Autism: The International Journal of Research and Practice 9*, 1, 69–82.

Rehfeldt, R.A., Dahman, D., Young, A., Cherry, H. and Davis, P. (2003) 'Teaching a simple meal preparation skill to adults with moderate and severe mental retardation using video modelling.' *Behavioral Interventions 18*, 209–218.

Rellini, E., Tortolani, D., Trillo, S., Carbone, S. and Montecchi, F. (2004) 'Childhood autism rating scale (CARS) and autism behavior checklist (ABC) correspondence and conflicts with DSM-IV criteria in diagnosis of autism.' *Journal of Autism and Developmental Disorders 34*, 6, 703–708.

Restall, G. and Magill-Evans, J. (1993) 'Play and preschool children with autism.' *American Journal of Occupational Therapy 48*, 113–120.

Rich, M., Lamola, S., Amory, C. and Schneider, L. (2000) 'Asthma in life context: Video Intervention/Prevention assessment (VIA).' *Pediatrics 1 5*, 469–477.

Rich, M., Lamola, S., Gordon, J. and Chalfen, R. (2000) 'Video Intervention/Prevention Assessment: A patient-centered methodology for understanding the adolescent illness experience.' *Journal of Adolescent Health 27*, 155–165.

Richardson, H. and Langley, T. (1997) 'The potential benefits of Daily Life Therapy for children with autism.' *Autism: The International Journal of Research and Practice 1*, 236–7.

Richman, S. (2001) *Raising A Child ith Autism. A Guide To Applied Behavior Analysis For Parents* . London: Jessica Kingsley Publishers.

Richer, J. (1976) 'The social-avoidance behaviour of autistic children.' *Animal Behaviour 24*, 898–906.

Rimland, B. (1999) 'B6 and Magnesium.' In *Allergy Induced Autism Resources Booklet*. AiA, 210 Pineapple Rd, Stirchley, Birmingham, B30 2TY, p.31 (Cochrane Review).

Rimland, B. and Edelson, S.M. (1994) 'The effects of auditory integration training on autism.' *American Journal of Speech-Language Pathology 5*, 16–24.

Rimland, B. and Edelson, S.M. (1995) 'Auditory integration training in autism: A pilot study.' *Journal of Autism and Developmental Disorders 25*, 61–70.

Rincover, A. and Ducharme, J.M. (1987) 'Variables influencing stimulus overselectivity and Tunnel Vision in developmentally delayed children.' *American Journal of Mental Deficiency 91*, 422–430.

Rincover, A. and Koegel.R.L. (1975) 'Setting generality and stimulus control in autistic children.' *Journal of Applied Behavior Analysis 8*, 235–246.

Risley, T. and Wolf, M.M. (1966) 'Experimental manipulation of autistic behaviors and generalization into the home.' In R. Ulrich, T. Stachnik and J. Mabry (eds) *Control of Human Behavior*. Glenview, IL: Scott, Foresman and Co.

Roeyers, H. (1995) 'A peer-mediated proximity intervention to facilitate the social interactions of children with a pervasive developmental disorder.' *British Journal of Special Education 22*, 161–164.

Roeyers, H. (1996) 'The influence of nonhandicapped peers on the social interactions of children with a pervasive developmental disorder.' *Journal of Autism and Developmental Disorders 26*, 303–320.

Roge, B. (2000) 'Meeting the needs of persons with autism: A regional network model.' *International Journal of Mental Health 29*, 35–49.

Rogers, S.J. (1999a) 'Intervention for young children with autism: From research to practice.' *Infants and Young Children 12*, 1–16.

Rogers, S.J. (1999b) 'An examination of the imitation deficit in autism.' In J. Nadel and G. Butterworth (eds) *Imitation in Infancy*. Cambridge: Cambridge University Press.

Rogers, S.J. (2000) 'Interventions that facilitate socialization in children with autism.' *Journal of Autism and Developmental Disorders 3* , 399–409.

Rogers, S.J., Hepburn, S.L., Stackhouse, T. and Wehner, E. (2003) 'Imitation performance in toddlers with autism and those with other developmental disorders.' *Journal of Child Psychology and Psychiatry 44*, 5, 763–781.

Romanczyk, R.G. (1996) 'Behavioral analysis and assessment: The cornerstone to effectiveness.' In C. Maurice, G. Green and S.C. Luce (eds) *Behavioral Intervention for Young Children with Autism: A Manual for Parents and Professionals*. Austin, TX: Pro-ed.

Romanczyk, R.G. and Matthews, A.L. (1998) 'Physiological state as antecedent: Utilization in functional analysis.' In J.K. Luiselli and M.J. Cameron (eds) *Antecedent Control Procedures for the Behavioral Support of Persons with Developmental Disabilities*. New York: Paul H. Brookes.

Rosenthal, T.L. (1977) 'Modeling therapies.' In M. Herson, R.M. Eisler and P.M. Miller (eds) *Progress in Behavior Modification Vol. 2*. New York: Academic Press.

Rosenwasser, B. and Axelrod, S. (2001) 'The contributions of Applied Behavior Analysis to the education of people with autism.' *Behavior Modification 25*, 671–677.

Rosenwasser, B. and Axelrod, S. (2002) 'More contributions of Applied Behavior Analysis to the education of people with autism.' *Behavior Modification 26*, 3–8.

Ross, A.O. (1981) *Child Behavior Therapy. Principles, Procedures, and Empirical Basis*. Chichester: John Wiley.

Ross, D.E. and Greer, R.D. (2003) 'Generalized imitation and the mind: Inducing first instances of speech in young children with autism.' *Research in Developmental Disabilities 24*, 58–74.

Rowe, C. (1999) 'Do social stories benefit children with autism in mainstream primary schools?' *British Journal of Special Education 26*, 12–14.

Ruble, L.A. (2001) 'Analysis of social interactions as goal-directed behaviors in children with autism.' *Journal of Autism and Developmental Disorders 31*, 471–482.

Runco, M.A. and Schreibman, L. (1987) 'Socially validating behavioral objectives in the treatment of autistic children.' *Journal of Autism and Developmental Disorders 17*, 141–147.

Rutter, M. (1978a) 'Diagnosis and definition of childhood autism.' *Journal of Autism and Childhood Schizophrenia 8*, 139–161.

Rutter, M. (1978b) 'Diagnosis and definition.' In M. Rutter and E. Schopler (eds) *Autism: A Reappraisal of Concepts and Treatment*. New York: Guilford.

Rutter, M., Mawhood, L. and Howlin, P. (1992) 'Language delay and social development.' In P. Fletcher and D. Hale (eds) *Specific Speech and Language Disorders in Children*. London: Whurr.

Rutter, M. and Schopler, E. (1992) 'Classification of pervasive developmental disorders: Some concepts and practical considerations.' *Journal of Autism and Developmental Disorders 22*, 459–482.

Rye, B.J. (1998) 'Impact of an AIDS prevention video on AIDS-related perceptions.' *Canadian Journal of Human Sexuality 7*, 19–30.

Saemundsen, E., Magnusson, P., Smari, J. and Sigurdardottir, S. (2003) 'Autism diagnostic interview-revised and the childhood autism rating scale: Convergence and discrepancy in diagnosing autism.' *Journal of Autism and Developmental Disorders 33*, 3, 319–328.

Salomon, G. (1984) 'Television is easy and print is tough : The differential investment and mental effort in learning as a function of perceptions and attributions.' *Journal of Educational Psychology 76*, 647–658.

Santosh, P.J. and Baird, G. (2001) 'Pharmacotherapy of target symptoms in autistic spectrum disorders.' *Indian Journal of Pediatrics 68*, 427–431.

Sarafino, E.P. (2001) *Behavior Modification: Principles of Behavior Change* (2nd edn). Mountain View, CA: Mayfield.

Sarokoff, R.A., Taylor, B.A. and Poulson, C.L. (2001) 'Teaching children with autism to engage in conversational exchanges: Script fading with embedded textual stimuli.' *Journal of Applied Behavior Analysis 34*, 81–84.

Schatzman, S., Rinaldi, L., Berntsen, K., Celiberti, D. and Muia, L. (2000) 'The relationship between television watching and parent perceptions of observational learning and maladaptive behaviors in children with autism: A parent survey.' Paper presented at the Applied Behavior Analysis Convention, New Orleans.

Schleien, S.J., Heyne, L.A. and Berken, S.B. (1988) 'Integrating physical education to teach appropriate play skills to learners with autism: A pilot study.' *Adapted Physical Activity uarterly 5* , 185–192.

Schopler, E. (1994) 'A statewide program for the Treatment and Education of Autistic and related Communications handicapped Children (TEACCH).' *Child and Adolescent Psychiatric Clinics of North Carolina 3*, 91–103.

Schopler, E. (1997) 'Implementation of TEACCH philosophy.' In D. Cohen and F. Volkmar (eds) *Handbook of Autism and Developmental Disorders*. New York: John Wiley.

Schopler, E., Brehm, S., Kinsbourne, M. and Reichler, R.J. (1971) 'Effect of treatment structure on development in autistic children.' *Archives of General Psychiatry 24*, 415–421.

Schopler, E. and Mesibov, G.B. (1986) *Social Behavior in Autism*. New York: Plenum Press.

Schopler, E. and Mesibov, G.B. (1994) *Behavioral Issues in Autism*. New York: Plenum Press.

Schopler, E. and Mesibov, G.B. (2000) 'International priorities for developing autism services via the teacch model – 1 – guest editor's introduction – cross-cultural priorities in developing autism service.' *International Journal of Mental Health 29*, 3–21.

Schopler, E., Mesibov, G. and Baker, A. (1982) 'Evaluation of treatment for autistic children and their parents.' *Journal of the American Academy of Child Psychiatry 21*, 262–267.

Schopler, E., Mesibov, G.B. and Hearsey, K. (1995) 'Structured teaching in the TEACCH system.' In E. Schopler and G.B. Mesibov (eds) *Learning and Cognition in Autism*. New York: Plenum Press.

Schopler, E., Mesibov, G.B. and Kunce, L.J. (1998) *Asperger Syndrome or High-functioning* New York: Plenum Press.

Schopler, E. and Reichler, R. (1971) 'Parents as cotherapists in the treatment of psychotic children.' *Journal of Autism and Childhood Schizophrenia 1*, 87–102.

Schopler, E., Reichler, R. and Renner, B.R. (2002) *The Childhood Autism Rating Scale (CARS) for Diagnostic Screening and Classification of Autism* (9th edn). New York: Irvington.

Schopler, E., Short, A. and Mesibov, G. (1989) 'Relation of behavioral treatment to normal functioning : Comment on Lovaas.' *Journal of Consulting and Clinical Psychology 57*, 162–164.

Schreibman, L. (1988) *Autism*. Newbury Park, CA: Sage.

Schreibman, L. (1994) 'General principles of behavior management.' In E. Schopler and G.B. Mesibov (eds) *Behavioral Issues in Autism*. New York: Plenum Press.

Schreibman, L. (2000) 'Intensive behavioral/psychoeducational treatments for autism: research needs and future directions.' *Journal of Autism and Developmental Disorders 3* , 373–378.

Schreibman, L., Charlop, M.H. and Koegel, R.L. (1982) 'Teaching autistic children to use extra-stimulus prompts.' *Journal of Experimental Child Psychology 33*, 475–491.

Schreibman, L. and Lovaas, O.I. (1973) 'Overselective response to social stimuli by autistic children.' *Journal of Abnormal Child Psychology 1*, 152–168.

Schreibman, L., Whalen, C. and Stahmer, A.C. (2000) 'The use of video priming to reduce disruptive transition behavior in children with autism.' *Journal of Positive Behavior Interventions 2*, 3–11.

Shabani, D.B., Katz, R.C., Wilder, D.A., Beauchamp, K., Taylor, C.R. and Fischer, K.J. (2002) 'Increasing social initiations in children with autism: Effects of a tactile prompt.' *Journal of Applied Behavior Analysis 35*, 79–83.

Sheinkopf, S.J. and Siegel, B. (1998) 'Home-based behavioural treatment of young children with autism.' *Journal of Autism and Developmental Disorders 28*, 15–23.

Sherer, M., Pierce, K.L., Paredes, S., Kisacky, K.L., Ingersoll, B. and Schreibman, L. (2001) 'Enhancing conversational skills in children with autism via video technology. Which is better, Self or Other as a model?' *Behavior Modification 25*, 140–158.

Shipley-Benamou, R., Lutzker, J.R. and Taubman, M. (2002) 'Teaching daily living skills to children with autism through instructional video modeling.' *Journal of Positive Behavior Interventions 4*, 165–175.

Short, A.B. (1984) 'Short-term treatment outcome using parents as co-therapists for their own autistic children.' *Journal of Child Psychology and Psychiatry 25*, 443–458.

Sigafoos, J., Roberts-Pennell, D. and Graves, D. (1999) 'Longitudinal assessment of play and adaptive behavior in young children with developmental disabilities.' *Research in Developmental Disabilities 2* , 147–162.

Sigman, M. and Ruskin, E. (1999) 'Continuity and change in the social competence of children with autism, Down syndrome, and developmental delays.' *Monographs of the Society of Research in Child Development 64*, 1, serial no. 256.

Simpson, R.L. (1995) 'Individualized education programs for students with autism: Including parents in the process.' *Focus on Autistic Behavior 1* , 11–15.

Simpson, R.L. (2001) 'ABA and students with autism spectrum disorders: Issues and considerations for effective practice.' *Focus on Autism and Other Developmental Disabilities 16*, 68–71.

Simpson, A., Langone, J. and Ayres, K.M. (2004) 'Embedded video and computer based instruction to improve social skills for students with autism.' *Education and Training in Developmental Disabilities 39*, 3, 240–252.

Sines, D. (1996) *A Study to Evaluate the TEACCH Project in the South Eastern Education and Library Board of Northern Ireland 1995 96* . Belfast: Parents and Professionals and Autism.

Sinha, Y., Silove, N., Wheeler, D. and Williams, K. (2004) 'Auditory integration training and other sound therapies for autism spectrum disorders.' *Cochrane Database of Systematic Reviews 1*, 1–15.

Skinner, B.F. (1953) *Science and Human Behavior.* New York: Macmillan.

Skinner, B.F. (1957) *Verbal Behavior.* New York: Appleton-Century-Crofts.

Skinner, B.F. (1969) *Contingencies of Reinforcement: A Theoretical Analysis.* New York: Appleton-Century-Crofts.

Skinner, B.F. (1974) *About Behaviorism.* New York: Vintage Books.

Skinner, B.F. (1978) *Reflections on Behaviorism and Society.* Englewood Cliffs, NJ: Prentice-Hall, Inc.

Smith, C. (2001) 'Using social stories to enhance behaviour in children with autistic spectrum difficulties.' *Educational Psychology in Practice 17*, 337–345.

Smith, T., Eikeseth, S., Levestrand, M. and Lovaas, O.I. (1997) 'Intensive behavioral treatment for preschoolers with severe mental retardation and pervasive developmental disorder.' *American Journal of Mental Retardation 1 2* , 238–249.

Smith, T., Groen, A.D. and Wynn, J.W. (2000) 'Randomized trial of intensive early intervention for children with pervasive developmental disorder.' *American Journal of Mental Retardation 1 5* , 269–285.

Sommer, B. and Sommer, R. (1997) *A Practical Guide to Behavioral Research* (4th edn). New York: Oxford University Press.

Sowers, J.A., Verdi, M., Bourbeau, P. and Sheehan, M. (1985) 'Teaching job independence and flexibility to mentally retarded students through the use of self-control package.' *Journal of Applied Behavior Analysis 18*, 81–85.

Stahmer, A.C. (1995) 'Teaching symbolic play skills to children with autism using pivotal response training.' *Journal of Autism and Developmental Disorders 25*, 123–141.

Stahmer, A.C. and Schreibman, L. (1992) 'Teaching children with autism appropriate play in unsupervised environments using a self-management treatment package.' *Journal of Applied Behavior Analysis 25*, 447–459.

Stehli, A. (1991) *The Sound of a Miracle: A Child's Triumph over Autism.* New York: Doubleday.

St. James, P.J. and Tager-Flusberg, H. (1994) 'An observational study of humor in autism and Down syndrome.' *Journal of Autism and Developmental Disorders 24*, 603–617.

Steinborn, M. and Knapp, T.J. (1982) 'Teaching an autistic child pedestrian skills.' *Journal of Behavior Therapy and Experimental Psychiatry 13*, 347–351.

Steinke, E.E. (2001) 'Use of videotaped interventions.' *estern Journal of Nursing Research 23* , 6, 627–643.

Stella, J., Mundy, P. and Tuchman, R. (1999) 'Social and nonsocial factors in the Childhood Autism Rating Scale.' *Journal of Autism and Developmental Disorders 29*, 307–317.

Stephens, W.E. and Ludy, I.E. (1975) 'Action-concept learning in retarded children using photographic slides, motion picture sequences and live demonstrations.' *American Journal of Mental Deficiency 8* , 277–280.

Stevenson, C.L., Krantz, P.J. and McClannahan, L.E. (2000) 'Social interaction skills for children with autism: A script-fading procedure for nonreaders.' *Behavioral Interventions 15*, 1–20.

Stone, W.L. and Lemanek, K.L. (1990) 'Parental report of social behaviors in autistic preschoolers.' *Journal of Autism and Developmental Disorders 2* , 513–522.

Stone, W.L., Ousley, O.Y. and Littleford, C.D. (1997) 'Motor imitation in young children with autism: What's the object?' *Journal of Abnormal Child Psychology 25*, 475–485.

Strain, P.S. (1983) 'Generalization of autistic children's social behavior change: Effects of developmentally integrated and segregated settings.' *Analysis and Intervention in Developmental Disabilities 3*, 23–34.

Strain, P.S. (1985) 'Social and nonsocial determinants of acceptability in handicapped preschool children.' *Topics in Early Childhood Special Education 4*, 47–58.

Strain P.S., Kerr M.M. and Ragland E.U. (1979) 'Effects of peer-mediated social initiations and prompting/reinforcement procedures on the social behavior of autistic children.' *Journal of Autism and Developmental Disorders 9*, 41–54.

Strain, P.S., Kohler, F.W., Storey, K. and Danko, C.D. (1994) 'Teaching preschoolers with autism to self-monitor their social interactions: an analysis of results in home and school settings.' *Journal of Emotional and Behavioral Disorders 2*, 78–88.

Strain, P. and Shores, R. (1977) 'Social interaction development among behaviorally handicapped preschool children: Research and educational implications.' *Psychology on the Schools 14*, 493–502.

Striefel, S. (1974) *Behavior Modification: Teaching A Child To Imitate.* Austin, TX: Pro-ed.

Stromer, R., Mackay, H.A., Howell, S.R., McVay, A.A. and Flusser, D. (1996) 'Teaching computer-based spelling to individuals with developmental and hearing disabilities: Transfer of stimulus control to writing tasks.' *Journal of Applied Behavior Analyis 29*, 25–42.

Sturmey, P. (2003) 'Video technology and persons with autism and other developmental disabilities: An emerging technology for PBS.' *Journal of Positive Behavior Interventions 5*, 3–4.

Swaggart, B., Gagnon, E., Bock, S.J., Earles, T.L., Quinn, C., Myles, B.S. and Simpson, R.L. (1995) 'Using social stories to teach social and behavioral skills to children with autism.' *Focus on Autistic Behavior 1* , 1–16.

Sweeten, T.L., Posey, D.J., Shekhar, A. and McDougle, C.J. (2002) 'The amygdala and related structures in the pathophysiology of autism.' *Pharmacology, Biochemistry and Behavior 71*, 449–455.

Swettenham, J., Baron-Cohen, S., Charman, T., Cox, A., Bairg, G., Drew, A., Rees, L. and Wheelwright, S. (1998) 'The frequency and distribution of spontaneous attention shifts between social and nonsocial stimuli in autistic, typically developing and nonautistic developmentally delayed infants.' *Journal of Child Psychology and Psychiatry 39*, 747–753.

Taber, T.A., Seltzer, A., Heflin, L.J. and Alberto, P.A. (1999) 'Use of self-operated auditory prompts to decrease off-task behavior for a student with autism and moderate mental retardation.' *Focus on Autism and Other Developmental Disabilities 14*, 159–166.

Taylor, B.A. and Levin, L. (1998) 'Teaching a student with autism to make verbal initiations: Effects of a tactile prompt.' *Journal of Applied Behavior Analysis 31*, 651–654.

Taylor, B.A., Levin, L. and Jasper, S. (1999) 'Increasing play-related statements in children with autism toward their siblings: Effects of video modeling.' *Journal of Developmental and Physical Disabilities 11*, 253–264.

Thelen, M.H., Fry, R.A., Fehrenbach, P.A. and Frautschi, N.M. (1979) 'Therapeutic videotape and film modeling: A review.' *Psychological Bulletin 86*, 701–720.

Thorp, D.M., Stahmer, A.C. and Schreibman, L. (1995) 'Effects of sociodramatic play training on children with autism.' *Journal of Autism and Developmental Disorders 25*, 265–282.

Tiegerman, E. and Primavera, L.H. (1981) 'Object manipulation: An interactional strategy with autistic children.' *Journal of Autism and Developmental Disorders 11*, 427–438.

Tillman, T.C. (2000) 'Generalization programming and behavioral consultation.' *The Behavior Analyst 1*, 30–34.

Tilton, J.R. and Ottinger, D.R. (1969) 'Comparison of the toy play behavior of autistic, retarded, and normal children.' *Psychological Reports 25*, 967–975.

Tincani, M. (2004) 'Comparing the picture exchange communication system and sign language training for children with autism.' *Focus on Autism and Other Developmental Disabilities 19*, 3, 152–163.

Tissot, C. and Evans, R. (2003) 'Visual teaching strategies for children with autism.' *Early Child Development and Care 173*, 4, 425–433.

Trevarthen, C., Aitken, K., Papoudi, D. and Robarts, J. (1998) *Children with Autism. Diagnosis and Interventions to Meet Their Needs.* London: Jessica Kingsley Publishers.

Tryon, A.S. and Keane, S.P. (1986) 'Promoting imitative play through generalized observational learning in autisticlike children.' *Journal of Abnormal Child Psychology 14*, 537–549.

Ungerer, J.A. and Sigman, M. (1981) 'Symbolic play and language comprehension in autistic children.' *Journal of the American Academy of Child Psychiatry 2* , 318–337.

US Department of Health and Human Services (1999) *Mental Health: A Report of the Surgeon General.* Rockville, MD: US Department of Health and Human Services, Substance Abuse and Mental Health Services Administration, Center for Mental Health Services, National Institutions of Health, National Institute of Mental Health.

Vandereycken, W., Probst, M. and van Bellinghen, M. (1992) 'Body-oriented therapy for anorexia nervosa patients.' *Journal of Adolescent Health 13*, 403–405.

Van der Geest, J.N., Kemner C., Camfferman G., Verbaten M.N. and van Engeland, H. (2002) 'Looking at images with human figures: Comparison between autistic and normal.' *Journal of Autism and Developmental Disorders 32*, 69–75.

Varni, J.W., Lovaas, O.I., Koegel, R.L. and Everett, N.L. (1979) 'An analysis of observational learning in autistic and normal children.' *Journal of Abnormal Child Psychology 7*, 31–43.

Vedora, J., Varisco, A., Kinney, E.M. and Stromer, R. (2002) 'Computer-mediated activity schedules for children with autism spectrum disorders. Teaching number and money skills.' Paper presented at Applied Behavior Analysis Annual Convention, Toronto.

Venn, M.L., Wolery, M., Werts, M.G., Morris, A., DeCesare, L.D. and Cuffs, M.S. (1993) 'Embedding instruction in art activities to teach preschoolers with disabilities to imitate their peers.' *Early Childhood Research uarterly 8* , 227–294.

Volkmar, F.R., Carter, A., Sparrow, S.S. and Cicchetti, D.V. (1993) 'Quantifying social development in autism.' *Journal of the American Academy of Child and Adolescent Psychiatry 32*, 627–632.

Volkmar, F.R., Lord, C., Bailey, A., Schultz, R.T. and Klin, A. (2004) 'Autism and pervasive developmental disorders.' *Journal of Child Psychology and Psychiatry 45*, 1, 135–170.

Volkmar, F.R. and Pauls, D. (2003) 'Autism.' *Lancet 362*, 1133–1141.

Wacker, D.P. and Berg, W.K. (1983) 'Effects of picture prompts on the acquisition of complex vocational tasks by mentally retarded adolescents.' *Journal of Applied Behavior Analysis 16*, 417–433.

Walther, M. and Beare, P. (1991) 'The effect of videtape feedback on the on-task behavior of a student with emotional/behavioral disorders.' *Education and Treatment of Children 14*, 53–60.

Weatherly, J.N., Miller, K. and McDonald, T.W. (1999) 'Social influence as stimulus control.' *Behavior and Social Issues 9*, 25–45.

Webster-Stratton, C. (1990) 'Enhancing the effectiveness of self-administered videotape parent training for families with conduct-problem children.' *Journal of Abnormal Child Psychology 18*, 479–492.

Weiss, M.J. (1999) 'Differential rates of skill acquisition and outcomes of early intensive behavioral intervention for autism.' *Behavioral Interventions 14*, 3–22.

Weiss, M.J. and Harris, S.L. (2001a) 'Teaching social skills to people with autism.' *Behavior Modification 25*, 785–802.

Weiss, M.J. and Harris, S.L. (2001b) *Reaching Out, Joining In. Teaching Social Skills to Young Children with Autism*. Bethesda State: Woodbine House.

Wert, B.Y. and Neisworth, J.T. (2003) 'Effects of video self-modeling on spontaneous requesting in children with autism.' *Journal of Positive Behavior Interventions 5*, 30–34.

Werts, M.G., Caldwell, N.K. and Wolery, M. (1996) 'Peer modeling of response chains: Observational learning by students with disabilities.' *Journal of Applied Behavior Analysis 29*, 53–66.

Wetherby, A.M., Prizant, B.M. and Hutchinson, T.A. (1998) 'Communicative, social/affective, and symbolic profiles of young children with autism and pervasive developmental disorders.' *American Journal of Speech-Language Pathology 7*, 79–91.

Wetherby, A.M., Woods, J., Allen, L., Cleary, J., Dickinson, H. and Lord, C. (2004) 'Early indicators of autism spectrum disorders in the second year of life.' *Journal of Autism and Developmental Disorders 34*, 5, 473–493.

Willemsen-Swinkles, S.H.N., Buitelaar, J.K., Weijen, G.G. and van Engeland, H. (1998) 'Timing of social gaze behavior in children with pervasive developmental disorder.' *Journal of Autism and Developmental Disorders 28*, 199–210.

Williams, C., Wright, B., Callaghan, G. and Coughlan, B. (2002) 'Do children with autism learn to read more readily by computer assisted instruction or traditional book methods?: A pilot study.' *Autism: The International Journal of Research and Practice 6*, 71–91.

Williams, J.H.G., Whiten, A. and Singh, T. (2004) 'A systematic review of action imitation in autistic spectrum disorder.' *Journal of Autism and Developmental Disorders 34*, 3, 285–299.

Williams, K.R. and Wishart, J.G. (2003) 'The Son-Rise program intervention for autism: an investigation into family experiences.' *Journal of Intellectual Disability Research 47*, 4/5, 291–299.

Winett, R.A., Hatcher, J.W., Fort, T.R., Leckliter, I.N., Love, S.Q., Riley, A.W. and Fishback, J.F. (1982) 'The effects of videotape modelling and daily feedback on residential electricity conservation, home temperature and humidity, perceived comfort, and clothing worn: Winter and summer.' *Journal of Applied Behavior Analysis 15*, 381–402.

Winett, R.A., Leckliter, I.N., Chinn, D.E., Stahl, B. and Love, S.Q. (1985) 'Effects of television modeling on residential energy conservation.' *Journal of Applied Behavior Analysis 18*, 33–44.

Wolf, M.M. (1978) 'Social validity: The case for subjective measurement or how applied behavior analysis is finding its heart.' *Journal of Applied Behavior Analysis 11*, 203–214.

Wolf, M.M., Risley, T.R., Johnston, M., Harris, F. and Allen, E. (1967) 'Application of operant conditioning procedures to the behavior problems of an autistic child: A follow-up and extension.' *Behaviour Research and Therapy 5*, 103–111.

Wolf, M.M., Risley, T.R. and Mees, H. (1964) 'Application of operant conditioning procedures to the behavioural problems of an autistic child.' *Behaviour Research and Therapy 1*, 305–312.

Wolfberg, P.J. and Schuler, A.L. (1993) 'Integrated play groups: A model for promoting the social and cognitive dimensions of play in children with autism.' *Journal of Autism and Developmental Disorders 23*, 467–489.

Wong, S.K. and Tam, S.F. (2001) 'Effectiveness of a multimedia programme and therapist instructed training for children with autism.' *International Journal of Rehabilitation Research 24*, 269–278.

World Health Organization (1992) *International Statistical Classification of Diseases and Related Health Problems* (10th rev. edn). Geneva: World Health Organization.

Yeung-Courchesne, R. and Courchesne, E. (1997) 'From impasse to insight in autism research: From behavioral symptoms to biological explanations.' *Development and Psychopathology 9*, 389–419.

Young, J.M., Krantz, P.J., McClannahan, L.E. and Poulson, C. (1994) 'Generalized imitation and response-class formation in children with autism.' *Journal of Applied Behavior Analysis 27*, 685–697.

Zanolli, K., Daggett, J. and Adams T. (1996) 'Teaching preschool age autistic children to make spontaneous initiations to peers using priming.' *Journal of Autism and Developmental Disorders 26*, 407–422.

Zelenko, M. and Benham, A. (2000) 'Videotaping as a therapeutic tool in psychodynamic infant-parent therapy.' *Infant Mental Health Journal 21*, 192–203.

Zercher, C., Hunt, P., Schuler, A. and Webster, J. (2001) 'Increasing joint attention, play and language through peer supported play.' *International Journal of Research and Practice 5*, 374–398.

Zifferblatt, S.M., Burton, S.D., Horner, R. and White, T. (1977) 'Establishing generalization effects among autistic children.' *Journal of Autism and Childhood Schizophrenia 7*, 337–347.

Zollweg, W., Palm, D. and Vance, V. (1997) 'The efficacy of auditory integration training: A double blind study.' *American Journal of Audiology 6*, 39–47.

Subject Index

Author Index